The
NATURETRAIL
OMNIBUS

Written by
Malcolm Hart, Sue Tarsky, Ingrid Selberg, Su Swallow and
Ruth Thomson

Consultant Editors
Peter Holden, Sally Heathcote, Jean Mellanby, Esmond Harris,
Staff of the Zoology and Botany Departments of the Natural
History Museum, London, Anthony Wootton, Alfred Leutscher,
Chris Humphries, Alwyne Wheeler

Designed by
Sally Burrough and Nick Eddison

Edited by
Sue Jacquemier, Ingrid Selberg and Rosamund Kidman-Cox

Illustrated by
Dave Ashby, John Barber, David Baxter, Joyce Bee, Stephen Bennett,
Roland Berry, Hilary Burn, Liz Butler, Terry Callcut, Patrick Cox,
Don Forrest, John Francis, Victoria Gordon, Tim Hayward, Bob Hersey,
Chris Howell-Jones, Christine Howes, Colin King, Deborah King,
Richard Lewington, Ken Lilly, Andy Martin, Malcolm McGregor,
Richard Millington, Annabel Milne and Peter Stebbing,
Patricia Mynott, David Nash, Barbara Nicholson, Charles Pearson,
Gillian Platt, Phillip Richardson, Jim Robins, Valerie Sangster,
Gwen Simpson, George Thompson, Joan Thompson, Joyce Tuhill,
Peter Warner, David Watson, Phil Weare, Adrian Williams,
Roy Wiltshire, John Yates.

Printed in Belgium by
Henri Proost, Turnhout

The NATURETRAIL OMNIBUS
Contents

Mistle Thrush

Part 1 written by
Malcolm Hart

Consultant Editor
Peter Holden, National
Organizer of the Young
Ornithologists' Club

Nuthatch

Siskin

2

Part 1 BIRDS

This section tells you where to look for common European birds and how best to study them. It shows you some clues to look for, how birds live in different kinds of places, and how to collect information. Before you go out birdwatching, read the instructions and hints given in the first part of the section about what to take and what to wear. Remember to move very quietly so as not to disturb the birds, and never touch nests or eggs.

If you want to identify a bird, look first at the illustrations on pages 28–33, or look on the pages that deal with the kind of place where you saw the bird.

Once you can recognize common birds, you might like to study some of them in more detail. To help you to see them more often, try building a nesting box like the one shown on page 12, or make a bird garden (see page 10). These need not be expensive and you will be able to see plenty of birds that come to visit even when the weather is too bad to go out birdwatching.

Some of the birds in this book, and many others that can be seen, are now becoming rarer. This is mainly because their habitats are being destroyed —they often live only in very special kinds of places, like heaths or wetlands. They are also threatened by hunters and by pesticides, which kill off their food.

Stonechat

Bearded Reedlings

How to be a Birdwatcher

The most important thing for any birdwatcher to have is a notebook. It is difficult to keep all the facts in your head and if you try you will probably forget some important points.

Try to keep any notes you make clear and readable. The picture shows how to set your notebook out. Try to draw the birds you see. Even a bad drawing is better than nothing.

When you get home, look up the bird you have seen in this book.

A birdwatcher has to take notes quickly. Use a spiralbound notebook like the one here. It has a stiff back to help you write easily. File your notes away in date order when you get home. When you are out, keep your book in a plastic bag to keep it dry.

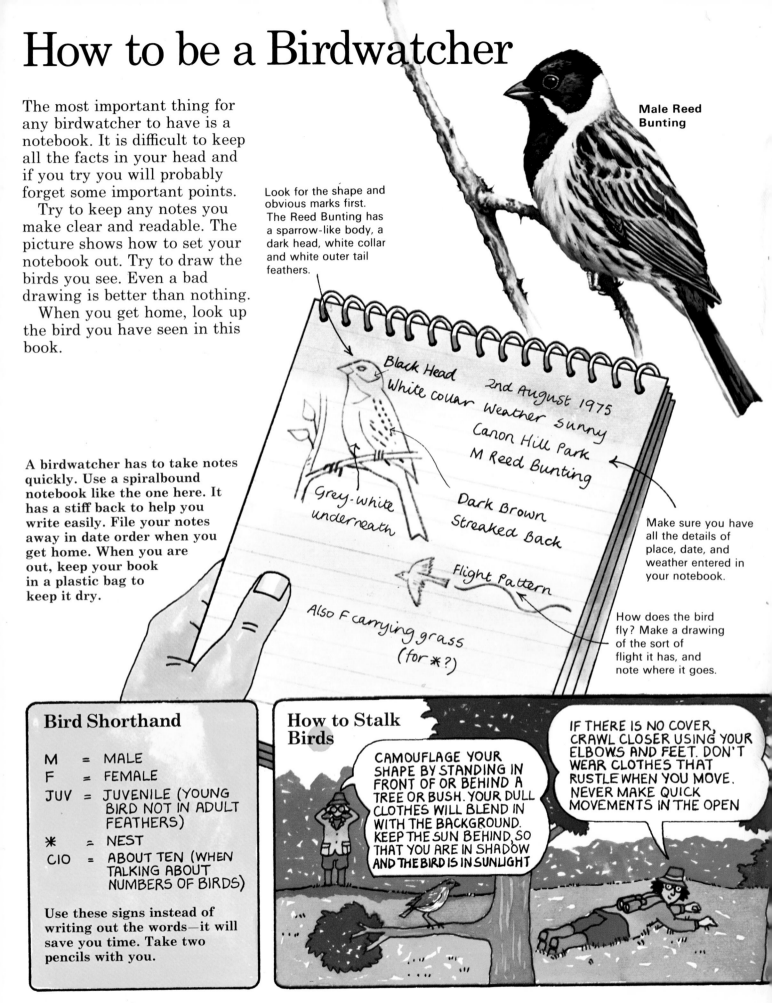

Male Reed Bunting

Look for the shape and obvious marks first. The Reed Bunting has a sparrow-like body, a dark head, white collar and white outer tail feathers.

Black Head
White collar
2nd August 1975
Weather sunny
Canon Hill Park
M Reed Bunting
Grey-white underneath
Dark Brown Streaked Back
Flight Pattern
Also F carrying grass (for ✱?)

Make sure you have all the details of place, date, and weather entered in your notebook.

How does the bird fly? Make a drawing of the sort of flight it has, and note where it goes.

Bird Shorthand

M   = MALE
F   = FEMALE
JUV = JUVENILE (YOUNG BIRD NOT IN ADULT FEATHERS)
✱   = NEST
C10 = ABOUT TEN (WHEN TALKING ABOUT NUMBERS OF BIRDS)

Use these signs instead of writing out the words—it will save you time. Take two pencils with you.

How to Stalk Birds

CAMOUFLAGE YOUR SHAPE BY STANDING IN FRONT OF OR BEHIND A TREE OR BUSH. YOUR DULL CLOTHES WILL BLEND IN WITH THE BACKGROUND. KEEP THE SUN BEHIND, SO THAT YOU ARE IN SHADOW AND THE BIRD IS IN SUNLIGHT

IF THERE IS NO COVER, CRAWL CLOSER USING YOUR ELBOWS AND FEET. DON'T WEAR CLOTHES THAT RUSTLE WHEN YOU MOVE. NEVER MAKE QUICK MOVEMENTS IN THE OPEN

What to Wear

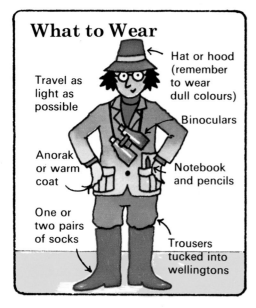

Hat or hood (remember to wear dull colours)

Travel as light as possible

Binoculars

Anorak or warm coat

Notebook and pencils

One or two pairs of socks

Trousers tucked into wellingtons

Buying Binoculars

The best size to get is 7×50 or 8×30

Choose the lightest pair you can find

Binoculars are not essential for the beginner, but if you want some, go to a shop with someone who knows about binoculars, and try several pairs to see how they feel.

HOWEVER LIGHT YOUR BINOCULARS ARE, THEY WILL START TO FEEL HEAVY AFTER A WHILE. TO TAKE THE WEIGHT OFF YOUR NECK, TIE SOME STRING ONTO THE STRAP AS SHOWN

Binocular strap

String tied to strap and belt

Belt

Quick Field Sketches

1 Two circles for head and body

2 Add beak, neck, tail, legs

3 Add feather detail

The best way to take notes on the birds you see is to draw quick sketches of them. Begin by drawing two circles—one for the body and one for the head. Notice the size and position of the head and body before you start. Then add the tail, beak and legs. Fill in the details of the feathers if you have time. Practise drawing the birds you can see from your window first.

IF YOU GO TO THE SAME PLACE OFTEN, PUT UP A LITTLE SCREEN OF BRANCHES THEN YOU CAN MOVE ABOUT WITHOUT FRIGHTENING THE BIRDS

TRY TO APPROACH DOWNWIND OF THE BIRD— THAT IS, WITH THE WIND BLOWING IN YOUR FACE. THEN SOUND WILL NOT CARRY SO EASILY TO THE BIRD

WIND

RUSTLE

CLOMP

WRONG! THIS BIRDWATCHER WILL NOT GET FAR. HE IS LOADED DOWN WITH HEAVY EQUIPMENT AND CANNOT MOVE EASILY AND QUIETLY. THE BIRDS CAN SEE HIS HUMAN SHAPE SILHOUETTED AGAINST THE SKY SO THEY FLY OFF

What to Look for

These pages tell you what to look for when you want to identify a bird. When you see a bird for the first time, there are several questions you should ask. What size is it? Compare it with a bird you know like a Sparrow or a Blackbird.

Has it any obvious marks like the Reed Bunting's black head and white outer tail feathers? How does it fly and feed? How does it behave? Where is it? What colour is it? Some differences in colour can be confusing: there are some examples opposite.

Rounded wings

A female Sparrowhawk chasing a male Reed Bunting. The labels give examples of the kind of things to note down when you see a bird.

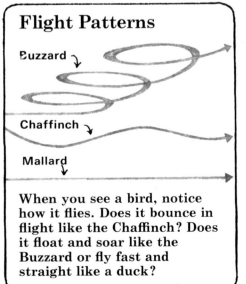

Black head

White collar

Hooked beak

White outer tail feathers

Long tail feathers

Yellow legs

Flight Patterns

Buzzard

Chaffinch

Mallard

When you see a bird, notice how it flies. Does it bounce in flight like the Chaffinch? Does it float and soar like the Buzzard or fly fast and straight like a duck?

Shapes in Flight

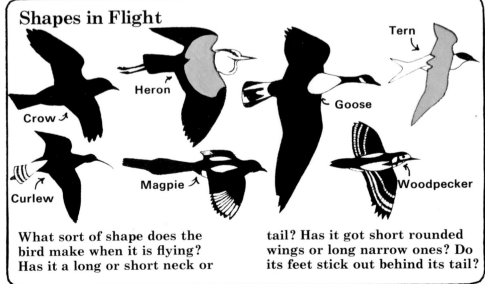

Tern

Heron

Crow

Goose

Curlew

Magpie

Woodpecker

What sort of shape does the bird make when it is flying? Has it a long or short neck or tail? Has it got short rounded wings or long narrow ones? Do its feet stick out behind its tail?

Sex Differences

Male

Female

Blackbirds

The males of some birds, like the Blackbird, have different coloured feathers and beaks from the females.

Colour Changes

Summer

Winter

Black-Headed Gulls

Some birds, like the Black-Headed Gull, have a different plumage in winter from the one they have in summer.

Age Differences

Adult

Juvenile (Young)

Robins

In some birds, like the Robin, the young look very different from their parents.

Looking at Beaks

Curlew

Carrion Crow

Greenfinch

Heron

ONE WAY TO IDENTIFY A BIRD IS FROM ITS SONG. GO OUT WITH SOMEONE WHO KNOWS BIRD SONG WELL, OR BORROW RECORDS OF BIRD SONG FROM YOUR LOCAL LIBRARY

Beaks can give you clues to what a bird eats. The Crow's beak is a general-purpose tool. The Greenfinch's beak is more suited to eating seeds. The Curlew uses its long beak for probing for food in mud and the Heron uses its beak for catching fish.

Watch What Birds are Doing

Grey Wagtail

Treecreeper

Turnstone

The Wagtail often patrols in mud or short grass. It wags its tail up and down. Sometimes it makes a dash after an insect.

The treecreeper creeps around tree trunks, picking out insects from the bark with its thin, curved bill.

The turnstone walks along the beach turning over seaweed and stones, looking for small creatures to eat.

Clues and Tracks

Sometimes you can tell which birds have been in an area by the clues that they leave behind. After some practice these are easy to recognize. Their feathers and the remains of meals are the ones you will see most often.

You may not be able to identify the feathers you find straight away. But later you may find a dead bird or see a bird in a zoo or museum that has feathers like the ones you have collected. Remember that most birds have feathers of many different colours and sizes.

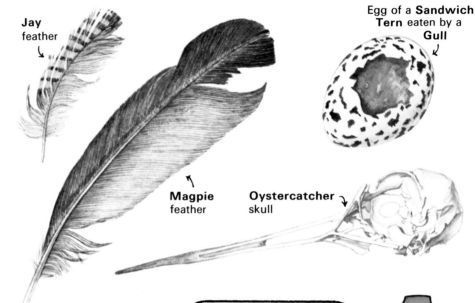

Jay feather

Magpie feather

Oystercatcher skull

Egg of a **Sandwich Tern** eaten by a **Gull**

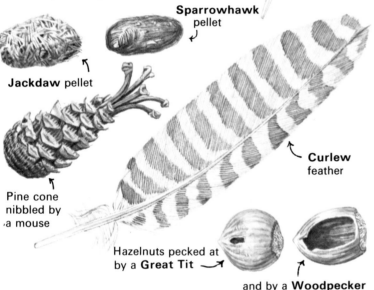

Sparrowhawk pellet

Jackdaw pellet

Pine cone nibbled by a mouse

Curlew feather

Hazelnuts pecked at by a **Great Tit**

and by a **Woodpecker**

ALWAYS MAKE SURE YOU HAVE SOMEWHERE TO KEEP THE THINGS THAT YOU COLLECT. LABEL EVERYTHING CAREFULLY AND IN DETAIL ~ THE MORE INFORMATION THE BETTER. ALWAYS WASH YOUR HANDS AFTER TOUCHING THINGS YOU HAVE COLLECTED

If you find the remains of nuts and pinecones, be careful how you identify the creatures that have been eating them, as these things are the food of squirrels and mice, as well as of birds.

Collecting Feathers and Wings

Cuts

Sticky tape

Quill

Date

Where found

Bird

Type of feather

Pin

Pin

Pin

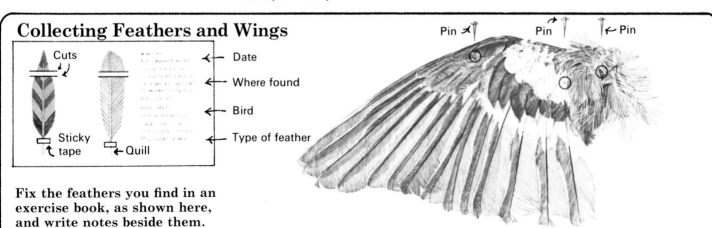

Fix the feathers you find in an exercise book, as shown here, and write notes beside them. Make two cuts 6 mm. apart in the page. Thread the feather through and stick the quill down with tape.

Wings cut from dead birds can be dried and kept. Pin the wing out on a piece of stiff board. It

should dry in a few days and can then be placed in an envelope with a label and some mothballs.

Pinecones

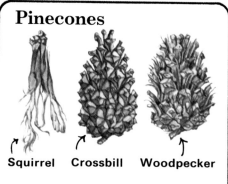

Squirrel   Crossbill   Woodpecker

Here are three examples of pinecones that have been attacked by birds or animals. They break open the cones in different ways to search for seeds.

Nuts

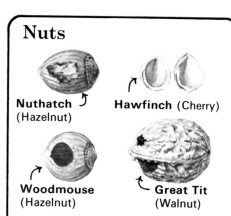

Nuthatch (Hazelnut)

Hawfinch (Cherry)

Woodmouse (Hazelnut)

Great Tit (Walnut)

Animals all have their own ways of opening nuts. Mice chew neat little holes while birds leave jagged holes or split the nuts in half.

The Thrush's Anvil

Snail shell

Anvil

Broken shells

Song Thrushes use stones to break open snail shells. Look for the thrush's "anvil"—it will be surrounded by the remains of the bird's meal.

Owl Pellets

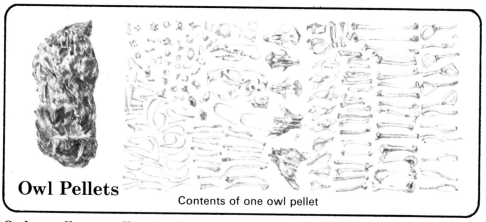

Contents of one owl pellet

Other Pellets

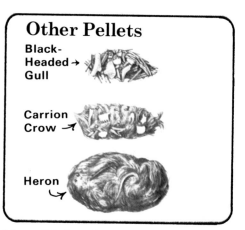

Black-Headed Gull →

Carrion Crow →

Heron →

Owls swallow small animals and birds whole, and then cough up the fur, feathers and bones as a pellet. You can find these beneath trees or posts where the owl rests. Pull a pellet apart and sort out the bones. The easiest to identify are the skulls of animals which the owl has eaten.

Many birds other than owls produce pellets. But it is harder to identify what is in them as most other birds do not eat large enough animals.

1 Footprint Casts

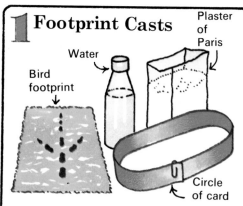

Plaster of Paris

Water

Bird footprint

Circle of card

To make plaster casts you will need water, plaster of Paris, a beaker and a strip of card bent into a circle, and held by a paperclip.

2

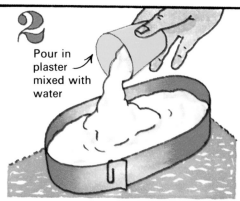

Pour in plaster mixed with water

Put the card around the footprint. Mix the plaster, pour it into the circle and let it harden. Wrap the cast in tissues and take it home.

3

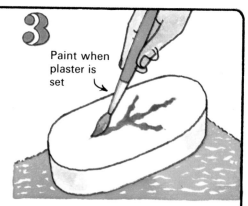

Paint when plaster is set

Wash off any dirt. Leave the cast for a few days and then carefully remove it from the card. Paint the footprint and then varnish it.

9

Making a Bird Garden

This picture shows many of the birds that visit gardens or window-sills for food. Different kinds of food attract different birds. Put out bones, suet, cheese, oats, peanuts, sunflower seeds, currants and bits of bacon rind. Scatter food in the open for birds that prefer to eat on the ground, and build a bird bath.

Key to Birds

1 Greenfinch
2 House Sparrow
3 Blue Tit
4 Great Tit
5 Robin
6 Coal Tit
7 Starling
8 Chaffinch
9 Blackbird
10 Mistle Thrush
11 Goldfinch
12 Song Thrush
13 Dunnock
14 Bullfinch

REMEMBER:- DON'T ATTRACT BIRDS TO A SPOT WHERE YOU KNOW CATS ARE LURKING. DON'T STOP FEEDING BIRDS SUDDENLY IN WINTER—THEY RELY ON YOUR FOOD SUPPLY AND MAY STARVE IF THEY CANNOT FIND FOOD ELSEWHERE

Feeding Chart

	CHEESE	BACON	NUTS
BLUE TIT	✓	✓✓✓	✓✓✓✓
ROBIN			
STARLING			
BLACKBIRD			

Make a chart of the kinds of food you see different birds eating. Which birds like nuts best? Tick the boxes each time you see the bird eat something.

Plants That Birds Like to Eat

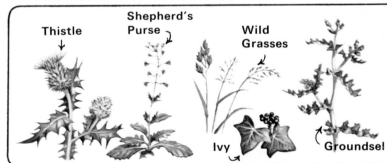

Thistle

Shepherd's Purse

Wild Grasses

Ivy

Groundsel

All these plants are good bird food. If you have a garden try to let a little patch grow wild. Weeds like Thistles, Groundsel and Shepherd's Purse have seeds that birds like to eat. Trees and bushes like Hawthorn, Cotoneaster, Rowan and Elder have lots of good berries in the autumn. Some birds like over-ripe apples and sultanas. Dig

Putting out Food

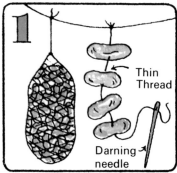

Supermarkets often sell vegetables in nets. Fill one of these with unsalted peanuts, or thread peanuts on a string, and hang them up.

To make a feeding bell with a yoghurt pot, fill the pot with a mixture of breadcrumbs, currants, cooked (not raw) potato and oatmeal. Pour on

some melted fat and wait until it hardens before you hang the feeder up. Tits and Finches will be able to cling on and feed.

Make a Bird Table

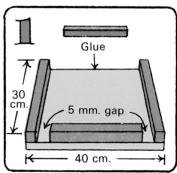

You will need a piece of outdoor quality plywood about 40 cm. × 30 cm., and four strips of dowel, each about 30 cm. long. Glue the dowel to the plywood.

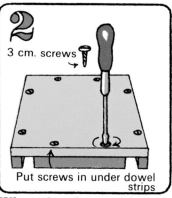

When the glue has dried, turn the table over and put in two screws on every side as shown. Protect your table with a wood preservative and screw it to a box or tub.

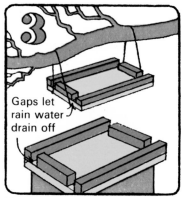

To make a hanging table, put four screw-eyes into the sides and hang it from a branch. Clean the table regularly with disinfectant.

Make a Bird Bath

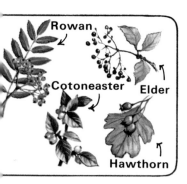

over a patch of earth to make it easier for Blackbirds and Thrushes to find worms and insects.

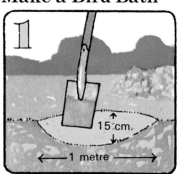

Choose a place not too close to the feeding area. Dig a hole with sloping sides about 15 cm. deep and one metre wide. Dig from the middle outwards.

Line the hole with a piece of strong polythene (a dustbin liner will do). Weight the plastic down with stones and sprinkle gravel or sand over the lining.

Put a few stones and a short branch in the middle of the bath to make a perch. Fill the bath with water. Keep it full (and ice-free in winter).

Making a Nesting Box

You can encourage birds to come to your garden in spring by building them a nesting box. If the entrance hole is small a Blue Tit is the bird most likely to nest in the box. If it is larger you may find a House Sparrow using it. Other birds, like Great Tits, Starlings, Tree Sparrows, Nuthatches and even Wrens sometimes use nesting boxes. You can look inside your box but try not to disturb the birds. You can always watch them from indoors.

TO MAKE YOUR NESTING BOX YOU WILL NEED SOME PLYWOOD THAT IS 12 MM THICK. EITHER GET THE WOOD CUT TO SIZE AT THE SHOP OR ASK AN ADULT TO SAW IT FOR YOU

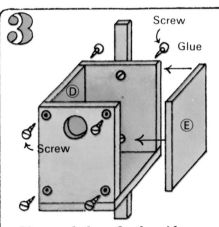

Side E removed to show how box is made

How to Cut the Wood

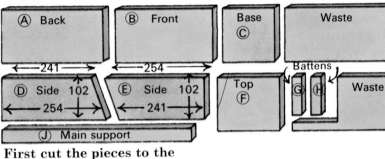

First cut the pieces to the following sizes:

A 254 mm. × 127 mm.   G 102 mm. × 25 mm.
B 241 mm. × 127 mm.   H 102 mm. × 25 mm.
C 127 mm. × 127 mm.   J 510 mm. × 25 mm.
D 241 mm. × 102 mm.
E 254 mm. × 102 mm.   Overall length: 915 mm.
F 152 mm. × 127 mm.   Overall width: 254 mm.

Drill the entrance hole with a hand drill about 50 mm. from the top of the front section. The hole should be 25 mm. wide.

50 mm.

25 mm.

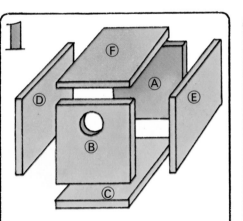

1 First arrange all the pieces to make sure that they fit together properly. Then drill holes for all the screws.

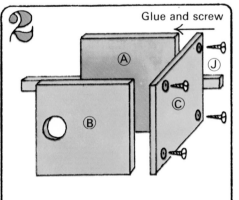

2 Fix the main support onto the back with two screws. Glue and screw the bottom onto the back and then the front.

Glue and screw

3 Glue and then fit the side pieces into place. Screw them on if they fit properly.

Screw

Glue

Where to Put the Box

Your completed box should be fixed to a tree or to an ivy-covered wall. The entrance hole should not face south or west as the heat from direct sunlight might kill the young birds. Fix it about two metres above the ground (away from cats). Empty out the old nest every winter, disinfect the box and give it a new coat of wood preservative before replacing it.

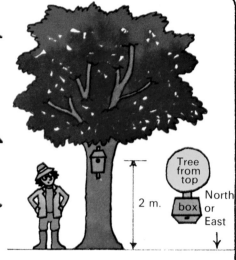

Tree from top

2 m.

box

North or East

Keeping a Record

Try to make a note of what happens in your nesting box. You may even see some birds visiting the box in winter. They use boxes to sleep in. The notes below tell you the sort of thing to record.

1 Date of first visit.
2 Number of birds visiting.
3 Date bird first enters box.
4 Dates birds bring nest material.
5 Type of nest material.
6 Date birds first bring food.
7 Type of food.
8 Date young leave nest.

Other Types of Box

Special nesting boxes can be bought for House Martins. You can fix them under the edge of the roof.

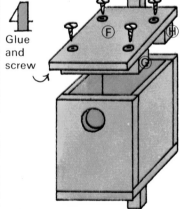

4 Glue and screw

(F) (H) (G)

Screw the two short battens onto the top piece. Make sure the removable lid fits tightly.

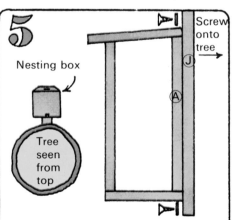

5 Nesting box

Screw onto tree

(A) (J)

Tree seen from top

Paint the outside of the box with wood preservative and let it dry. Screw or nail it on to a tree (see above).

Side removed to show how box is made

165 mm.

An open-fronted box can be made for other birds. It is like the nesting box shown opposite but the front panel is only 165 mm. high.

The Nesting Season

The nesting season is a time of great activity for all birds. First they have to find a place where they can build their nests and feed. This area then becomes their territory. When they have found a mate they have to build a nest, lay eggs and rear their young. With all this going on, it is not difficult to find out when and where a bird is building its nest or feeding its young. A bird carrying something in its beak is the most common sign. On these pages are some clues to help you.

Food Chart
Make a food chart to record which birds you see carrying

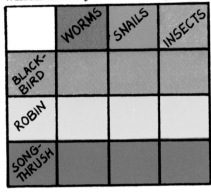

	WORMS	SNAILS	INSECTS
BLACK-BIRD			
ROBIN			
SONG-THRUSH			

food to their young, and the type of food.

REMEMBER – IT IS AGAINST THE LAW TO DISTURB BREEDING BIRDS OR THEIR NESTS AND EGGS. BUT IF YOU ARE CAREFUL YOU CAN WATCH FROM A DISTANCE WITHOUT UPSETTING THEM AT ALL

The Song Thrush builds its nest in a bush. There are usually four or five eggs. Both parents feed the young birds with worms and snails.

The adult bird arrives at the nest with food. It pushes the food into the mouth of one of the young birds, removes any droppings from the nest and flies off to collect more food.

When a parent bird approaches the nest, the young birds beg for food with wide, open mouths.

Spotting Nesting Birds

Rook

Nightingale

Stonechat

Droppings

In the spring you will often see birds carrying nest material in their beaks. Rooks break off large twigs from trees for their nests.

Look out and listen for a bird singing in the same place every day during spring and summer. It is probably a sign that it is breeding.

You may see adult birds carrying droppings away from the nest in their beaks. They do this to keep the nest clean.

Nest Materials

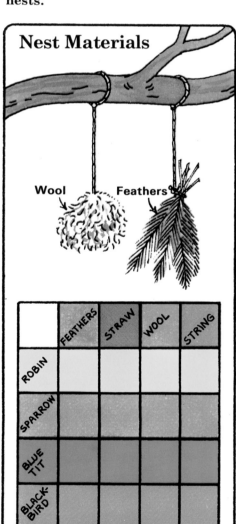

Wool   Feathers

	FEATHERS	STRAW	WOOL	STRING
ROBIN				
SPARROW				
BLUE TIT				
BLACK-BIRD				

Hang up bits of wool, feathers, straw and string from a tree. Make a note of what different materials birds collect to use for their nests.

Where Birds Nest

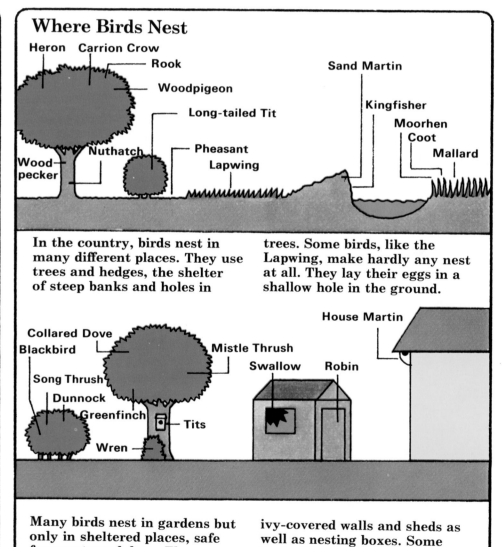

Heron   Carrion Crow
Rook
Woodpigeon
Long-tailed Tit
Sand Martin
Kingfisher
Moorhen
Coot
Mallard
Wood-pecker   Nuthatch   Pheasant   Lapwing

In the country, birds nest in many different places. They use trees and hedges, the shelter of steep banks and holes in trees. Some birds, like the Lapwing, make hardly any nest at all. They lay their eggs in a shallow hole in the ground.

Collared Dove
Blackbird   Mistle Thrush
Song Thrush   Swallow   Robin
Dunnock
Greenfinch
Tits
Wren
House Martin

Many birds nest in gardens but only in sheltered places, safe from cats and dogs. They use thick bushes, trees, ivy-covered walls and sheds as well as nesting boxes. Some birds, like the House Martin, even build under the roof.

Ponds and Inland Waterways

Ducks are the birds you are most likely to see on a pond. They have quite long necks, webbed feet and wide, flat bills. They are all good swimmers. Most of them feed on the water weeds and plant life in the pond. There are three kinds of duck—the diving ducks, like the Tufted Duck, the dabblers, like the Mallard, that often up-end for their food and the rarer fish-eating ducks called Sawbills. Look out for other water birds like Swans, Geese, Moorhens and Coots.

Mallards are probably the commonest birds on the pond. The females (ducks) are much less colourful than the males. The correct word for a male duck is "drake".

Young Mallards

Male Mallard

Female Mallard

It uses its long, flat bill to sift the water for food.

Both male and female ducks have a blue flash on each wing called a speculum.

How Water Birds Feed

Swallow catching insects over the water

Pintail up-ending

Kingfisher diving for fish

Tufted Duck diving

Wigeon grazing on land

Moorhen feeding in reeds by the water

Heron fishing on the edge of the pond

Mallard dabbling on the surface

Mute Swan fishing with head and neck under water

Watch how the birds feed on your local pond. Which birds up-end the most? Which dive most often?

Why do you think some birds feed differently from others?

Taking-Off and Landing

Goldeneye

Most water birds are heavy, and have to work hard to get airborne. Many of them run over the surface, flapping their wings until they get up enough speed to take off. To land, they fly low over the water, with their feet sticking out to act as a brake.

Swimming

Shoveler

Coot

Moorhen

Webbed feet are the best feet for swimming. The web opens to push hard against the water, like a frogman's flipper. When the foot comes back, the web closes so that the foot does not drag through the water. Coots spend a lot of time on land. They have partly webbed feet. Moorhens have hardly any webbing. They jerk their heads backwards and forwards when swimming.

Moulting

Female Mallard

Male Mallard

Ducks moult in late summer. The drake loses his colourful feathers and for a time looks rather like the female. New feathers have grown by early winter.

Chicks

Mallard

Young Mallards

New chicks are taken to the water by their mother. The chicks fall in and can swim straight away.

Gull

Mallard

When danger threatens Mallard chicks, the duck stretches out her neck and quacks loudly. The chicks dive to escape.

Great Crested Grebe

Great Crested Grebes are fish-eating water birds. The male and female both look after the young and carry their chicks on their backs.

Woodlands and Forests

All types of woods are good places for birds but you will see the bird most easily in places that are not too dark. Woods with open spaces or pools have more plants and insects for the birds to feed on.

The **Chiffchaff** (11 cm) is smaller than a Sparrow and is a summer migrant from Africa. It is often found in deciduous woods and in young pine plantations.

The **Goldcrest** (9 cm) is the smallest European bird. It is often found in coniferous or mixed woods.

The **Black Woodpecker** (46 cm) is the largest European Woodpecker. It is not found in Britain but breeds in other parts of Europe, mainly in coniferous forests.

CONIFEROUS FORESTS

The **Coal Tit** (11.5 cm) is only a little larger than a Goldcrest. It nests in coniferous forests.

BROADLEAVED WOODS

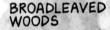

The **Green Woodpecker** (32 cm) is the same size as a domestic pigeon. It is frequently seen on the ground, feeding on ants, and is usually found in deciduous woods.

The **Nightingale** (16.5 cm) can often be heard singing in woods and forests but is rarely seen. It builds its nest among trees and bushes close to the ground.

The **Chaffinch** (15 cm) is a common bird, often found in broad-leaved woodlands and coniferous woods. In winter it prefers open land.

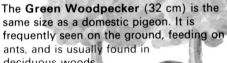

The **Woodcock** (34 cm) is found in deciduous woods where its plumage blends in perfectly with the dead leaves on the ground.

The **Lesser Spotted Woodpecker** (14.5 cm) is the smallest European Woodpecker. It is found in deciduous woods.

The **Nuthatch** (14 cm) feeds on nuts from hazel, beech and oak trees.

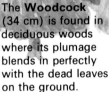

Woods with broad-leaved trees such as oak and beech contain many more birds than old pine forests or other coniferous forests. Young pine plantations and mixed woods which have many different kinds of trees in them, also have lots of birds.

The sizes given are beak-to-tail measurements.

18

IF IT IS WINDY, WATCH OUT FOR FALLING BRANCHES IN THE WOODS. TRY NOT TO STAND OR SIT NEAR TREES WHICH HAVE NESTS IN THEM. YOU MIGHT FRIGHTEN AWAY THE PARENT BIRDS

Food of Woodland Birds

In autumn **Jays** collect the acorns from oak trees. They bury many of them and dig them up when they are short of food.

The **Tawny Owl** feeds on small animals like mice. It has very good eyesight and hearing and can catch its food even on the darkest nights.

Many birds, like the **Garden Warbler,** feed on caterpillars which are very common in woods.

The **Pied Flycatcher** catches insects by swooping down on them in a short flight from a lookout branch.

Holes in Trees

Mud plastered by Nuthatch

Hole used by a Nuthutch

Hole made by a Woodpecker

Woodpecker holes

4 cm. Lesser Spotted

4.5 cm. Greater Spotted

6.5 cm. Green

10 cm. Black

The different kinds of Woodpecker all make nesting holes in trees. These are sometimes used by other birds like the Nuthatch, or animals like bats and dormice.

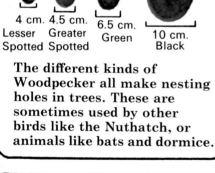

Hawfinch

Crossbill

Special Beaks

Some birds like the Hawfinch and the Crossbill have special beaks for eating seeds.

Woodlands at Night

Many different kinds of owl live in woods. They range in size from the Pygmy Owl which is only 16.5 cm. high, to the Eagle Owl, which can be as large as 71 cm.

These four owls are all drawn to the same scale

These three owls are all drawn to the same scale

Pygmy Owl

Scops Owl

Little Owl

Little Owl

Long-eared Owl

Tawny Owl

Eagle Owl

Nightjar

The Nightjar sleeps during the day, so is rarely seen. Its song can be heard after dark in summer.

Towns and Cities

You do not have to live in the country to be a birdwatcher. In the middle of towns you may only find Pigeons, Starlings and House Sparrows but where there are gardens and parks you will see many other kinds of birds. Some of these birds are quite used to people and can be very tame. This means that you will probably be able to get quite close to them and see them very clearly. The illustrations show some of the more common birds you might see in towns and cities.

The **Kestrel** is a town as well as a country bird. But the town Kestrel usually feeds on Sparrows instead of mice and beetles, and nests on high buildings instead of in trees.

1 Cliff Birds that Live in Towns

Black Redstart

Black Redstarts once nested on sea-cliffs and rocks. Now you are more likely to find them in towns. They build their nests on buildings.

The **Long-tailed Tit** is a hedge bird that can often be seen in parks and gardens. In autumn and winter family groups of about a dozen gather together.

The **Black-headed Gull** is one of the commonest town gulls. You will often see large numbers of them near reservoirs and gravel pits.

You will sometimes hear the warbling song of the **Skylark** as it flies high above parks and wasteland. In winter you may see flocks around gravel pits and sewage works.

You will hardly ever see a **Swift** on the ground. It feeds and even sleeps as it is flying. At dusk you may see flocks of Swifts circling high above the roof-tops.

Cities are surprisingly good places to look for birds. All birds need food and places to nest and sleep. Most gardens (3) and parks (2) have some trees and bushes where birds can nest and sleep without being disturbed by people. Many birds find perching places on buildings (5). Gulls fly out to sleep at gravel pits (1) or reservoirs (4) at night. Everywhere people spill or leave food on which birds can live. On the edge of cities birds find lots of food at sewage works (4), rubbish dumps(1). Railway

2

Rock Dove

Pigeons

The Pigeon is a relation of the Rock Dove, which nests on sea-cliffs. But the town Pigeon is now much more common than the Rock Dove and is often very tame. It feeds on bread and any other scraps it finds in parks or in the streets.

Starling

Starlings are one of the commonest city birds and are usually found in huge, noisy flocks. In summer many of them move to the country.

House Martins build their mud nests under the roofs of many town houses.

Carrion Crows are quite common in parks and gardens.

Magpies are large black and white birds and are common in parks and gardens. They use twigs to build their nests in trees and tall hedges.

Swallows look rather like House Martins but have longer tail feathers. You can often see them catching flies over rivers, gravel pits and sewage works.

sidings and canals (6) where food is unloaded and often spilt are also good places for birds to find food, and have fewer people to disturb them. Many birds eat the seeds of weeds growing on waste ground and building sites. In winter, when there is little food in the countryside, many birds fly to the cities. There people put out food for them in parks and gardens.

Sea Coasts

The coast is always a good place for birds. In summer many birds fly to Europe from Africa and the Antarctic. They come to the shore to breed. In winter, small wading birds like the Knot come from the north to feed and wait for spring. Most of the cliff-nesting birds spend the winter far out at sea. Unfortunately, every year many birds lose their eggs and babies because people tread on the nests or stop the parent birds from feeding their young by frightening them away.

Waders' Beaks

Birds can find a lot of food on the beach. The shape of a wading bird's beak depends on the sort of food it eats. You can try to find out what the birds are eating by digging up the sand and looking for the food in it.

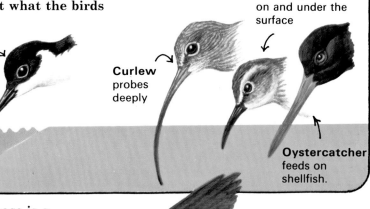

Avocet sifts for food

Curlew probes deeply

Dunlin picks food on and under the surface

Oystercatcher feeds on shellfish.

The Brent Goose is a rare winter visitor from Greenland or northern Russia where it breeds. It feeds on a plant called eelgrass which grows only on mudflats. It is the smallest wild goose.

Brent Goose

Shelduck

Shelduck

The Shelduck is one of the commonest large birds you will see on a salt marsh. It sometimes builds its nest in an old rabbit burrow.

Knot (summer plumage)

In winter large flocks of Knot fly south from their northern breeding grounds. They feed on sandy or muddy shores.

Common Tern

The Tern breeds on salt marshes, shingle or sandy shores. It builds its nest in a hollow in the ground.

Salt Marsh

Sandy Shore

Shingle Beach

Fish-Eaters' Beaks

Fish-eating birds do not all have the same kind of beak. The shape of the beak depends on the size and type of fish that the bird eats.

Common Tern

Razorbill

← Gannet

Nesting Places

In winter cliffs are almost deserted but during the breeding season they are like large bird cities. The whole cliff is used for nesting. Each type of bird has its favourite spot for nesting.

Puffins dig nesting burrows in the soil on the cliff-top. They use their huge, brightly coloured bills for digging and push away the soil with their webbed feet.

Puffin

Gannet

The cliff-top is also the Gannet's favourite nesting place. Gannets nest in large numbers and build their untidy nests only about one metre apart from each other.

The Fulmar is a large silver-grey bird that spends most of its time out at sea. It looks rather like a gull but holds its wings straighter and stiffer when it is flying. It nests on rock ledges and sometimes on window ledges.

Razorbill

The Razorbill lays its one egg in cracks in the cliff or under rocks.
The nest is sometimes a few pieces of seaweed but there is usually no proper nest at all.

Guillemot

Like the Razorbill, the Guillemot makes no nest. It lays a single pear-shaped egg on a rock ledge. The shape of the egg helps to stop it rolling off. Guillemots nest in large numbers, crowded very close together.

Fulmar

The Cormorant's feathers are not waterproof, so when it leaves the water it often stands on a rock or post holding out its wings to dry. It builds a large untidy nest of seaweed and sticks in which it lays three or four eggs.

WATCH THE BIRDS AND TRY TO SEE WHAT THEY EAT. HOW DO THEY USE THEIR BEAKS WHEN FEEDING? HAVE THEY ANY SPECIAL WAY OF GETTING THEIR FOOD?

The Shag and the Cormorant are quite difficult to tell apart. The Shag is the smaller of the two and does not have the Cormorant's white face. In the breeding season it grows a little curly crest.

Cormorant

Shag

Cliffs

23

Mountains and Moorlands

Many of the birds that live on mountains and moorlands are well known because they are game-birds like the Grouse, or large and powerful birds of prey like the Buzzard or Golden Eagle. But you will see fewer birds here than by the coast or in woods because there is less food for them to eat. The smaller birds eat bilberries, the young shoots of heather and the seeds from mosses and grasses. The larger birds of prey feed mainly on small birds and animals.

The **Golden Eagle** is the largest bird that is found on moors and mountains. It is very rare in most parts of Europe.

The **Buzzard** is one of the commonest of the large birds of prey. It is similar to the Golden Eagle but is smaller and stubbier.

The **Short-eared Owl** nests on the ground. It often hunts in the daytime and feeds on small animals like voles and lemmings.

The **Raven** is the largest of the Crow family. It is even larger than the Buzzard. It flies slowly but powerfully and sometimes tumbles through the air.

The **Meadow Pipit** is the commonest small bird that you will see on moorland. It feeds on insects.

Willow Grouse

These two birds look different but are in fact very closely related. **The Red Grouse** is only found in Britain and the **Willow Grouse** only in Europe. The Willow Grouse is shown here in its partial winter plumage.

Red Grouse

Short-tailed Vole

EVERY YEAR PEOPLE GET LOST ON MOUNTAINS OR MOORS. MAKE SURE IT IS NOT YOU. NEVER GO ON YOUR OWN AND ALWAYS TELL SOMEONE WHERE YOU ARE GOING. KEEP TO PATHS AND WEAR WARM CLOTHES. MOUNTAINS CAN BE COLD EVEN IN SUMMER

An Underwater Fisher

The Dipper lives by fast-flowing mountain streams. It feeds on insects that it catches under the water.

Dipper

Shrikes

Shrikes (or Butcher Birds) have a habit of pinning their spare food such as bees, beetles and even small birds, onto branches or barbed wire. When food is scarce they may go back to collect it. The Redbacked Shrike is a rather rare summer visitor. The Great Grey Shrike breeds in Northern Europe and flies south in the winter.

Redbacked Shrike

Beetle

Great Grey Shrike

Changing Colour with the Seasons

Ptarmigan in summer

Ptarmigan in winter

The Ptarmigan can hide from its enemies because it always looks the same colour as the countryside. In summer its coat is mainly brown but in winter it turns pure white. It lives in the mountains of northern Europe.

The **Golden Plover** usually breeds on moors and hills. It lays its four eggs in a nest on the ground.

The **Wheatear** builds its nest in holes in walls and in old rabbit burrows.

The **Ring Ouzel** is a relative of the Blackbird and lives in remote mountain valleys.

The **Black Grouse** lives on the borders of moorland. The male (Blackcock) has a lyre-shaped tail.

Lemming (not found in Britain)

Migrating Birds

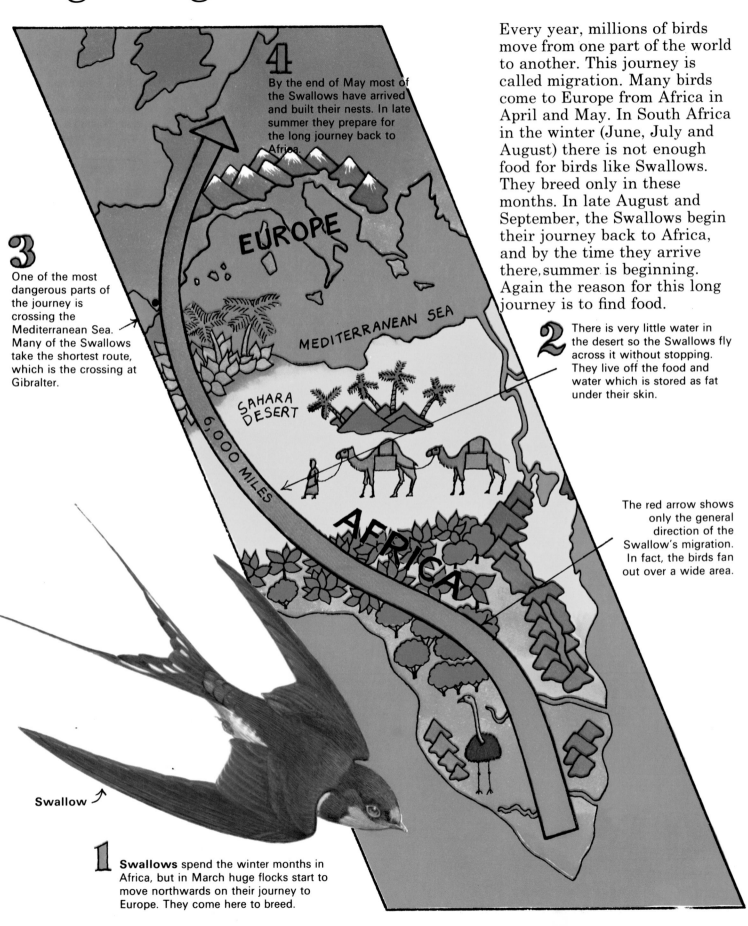

Every year, millions of birds move from one part of the world to another. This journey is called migration. Many birds come to Europe from Africa in April and May. In South Africa in the winter (June, July and August) there is not enough food for birds like Swallows. They breed only in these months. In late August and September, the Swallows begin their journey back to Africa, and by the time they arrive there, summer is beginning. Again the reason for this long journey is to find food.

4 By the end of May most of the Swallows have arrived and built their nests. In late summer they prepare for the long journey back to Africa.

3 One of the most dangerous parts of the journey is crossing the Mediterranean Sea. Many of the Swallows take the shortest route, which is the crossing at Gibralter.

EUROPE

MEDITERRANEAN SEA

2 There is very little water in the desert so the Swallows fly across it without stopping. They live off the food and water which is stored as fat under their skin.

SAHARA DESERT

6,000 MILES

AFRICA

The red arrow shows only the general direction of the Swallow's migration. In fact, the birds fan out over a wide area.

Swallow ↗

1 **Swallows** spend the winter months in Africa, but in March huge flocks start to move northwards on their journey to Europe. They come here to breed.

Redwing

White Stork

In some areas of Europe, flocks of large birds like the White Stork can be seen waiting by the coast. When the weather is good enough, they cross the sea and continue their migration.

The Redwing is a member of the Thrush family. In winter it flies south through Europe travelling mainly at night in large flocks.

TRY TO KEEP A NOTE OF THE FIRST AND LAST DATES ON WHICH YOU SEE MIGRANT BIRDS. KEEP A RECORD OF THE WEATHER IN YOUR AREA DURING SPRING AND AUTUMN AND SEE IF THIS AFFECTS THE DATES ON WHICH BIRDS ARRIVE OR LEAVE

Summer Visitors

Blackcap

Willow Warbler

These warblers are two of the commonest small birds that visit Europe in the summer. They come from Africa but in some winters a few Blackcaps stay in Europe.

Hoopoe

The Hoopoe, with its floppy flight, does not seem capable of flying far, but every autumn it flies to Africa and returns in spring.

Starling

Arctic Tern

Some birds fly even longer distances than the Swallow. One of these is the Arctic Tern. It flies from the Arctic, where it breeds, all the way to the southern tip of South America or South Africa. During the journey it stays mostly out at sea.

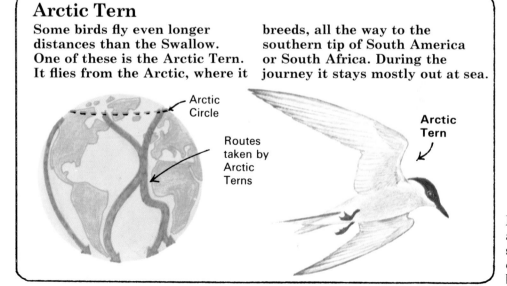

Arctic Circle

Routes taken by Arctic Terns

Arctic Tern

Many Starlings fly south in winter and are attracted to bright lights, such as lighthouses, at night. Many of them are killed by flying into buildings where they see lights.

27

Common Birds to Spot

Sparrow-sized Birds

The notes under each bird give its size from beak to tail. Each panel contains birds of a similar size. The coloured dots beside each bird tell you where to look for it and the red arrows show the points to look for.

- ● Water
- ● Woods
- ● Towns and Gardens
- ● Fields

The birds inside this panel are all drawn to the same scale.

Wren. 9.5 cm. Smallest bird you will see in gardens. Holds its tail cocked over its back.

Goldcrest. 9 cm. Smallest European bird. Feeds on insects and spiders.

Blue Tit. 11.5 cm. Only tit with blue head and wings. One of the most common garden birds.

Treecreeper. 12.5 cm. This mouse-like bird climbs trees.

Nuthatch. 14 cm. Has a long straight bill used for cracking open nuts.

Long-tailed Tit. 14 cm. Tail very long. Often seen in small flocks.

Great Tit. 14 cm. Has a black band down its belly.

Coal Tit. 11.5 cm. Has a white stripe on its neck.

Sand Martin. 12 cm. Has brown back and collar. Nests in holes in banks.

House Martin. 12.5 cm. Has a white rump and a shorter tail than the Swallow. Often nests in large groups.

Swallow. 19 cm. Has long tail feathers and a dark throat. Feeds on insects.

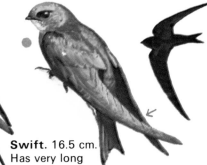

Swift. 16.5 cm. Has very long curved wings.

Blackbird-sized Birds

The birds inside this panel are all drawn to the same scale.

Adult

Juvenile

Male

Female

Starling. 21.5 cm. On the ground has an upright way of walking. Often seen in large flocks.

Blackbird. 25 cm. The male is all black with an orange beak. The female is brown with a brown beak.

Song Thrush. 23 cm. Both sexes look the same, with a brown back and spotted breast. Often feeds on snails.

Mistle Thrush. 27 cm. A greyer bird than the Song Thrush and the spots on the breast are larger and closer together.

Remember—if you cannot see a picture of the bird you want to identify on these pages, turn to the page earlier in the book which deals with the kind of place where you saw the bird.

Robin. 14 cm. Can be very tame. Has an orange breast.

Bullfinch. 14.5–16 cm. Has a black cap, white rump and short black bill.

Greenfinch. 14.5 cm. Has yellow wing bars and a greenish rump.

Goldfinch. 12 cm. Has a red face and a black and white head.

Dunnock. 14.5 cm. Feeds on the ground and moves slowly with a kind of creeping walk.

House Sparrow. 14.5 cm. A very common bird. The male has a grey and brown head and black throat.

Tree Sparrow. 14 cm. Has a brown head and a black spot on its white cheeks. Likes to nest in old trees.

Chaffinch. 15 cm. Has white wing bars and white outer tail feathers.

Kingfisher. 16.5 cm. Catches small fish for food.

The **Pied Wagtail** (18 cm.) lives in Britain, the **White** (18 cm.) in Europe.

Skylark. 18 cm. Has white outer tail feathers.

Yellowhammer. 16.5 cm. The male has a yellow head.

Linnet. 13.5 cm. The male has a red forehead and chest.

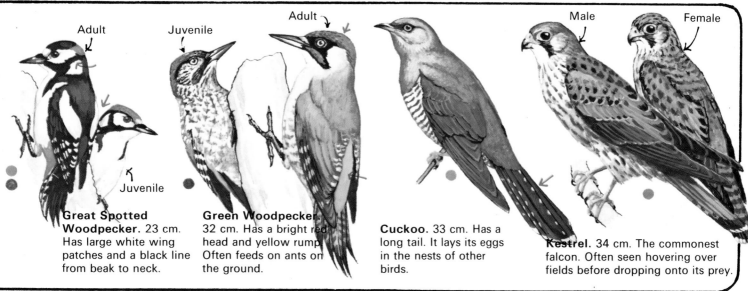

Great Spotted Woodpecker. 23 cm. Has large white wing patches and a black line from beak to neck.

Green Woodpecker. 32 cm. Has a bright red head and yellow rump. Often feeds on ants on the ground.

Cuckoo. 33 cm. Has a long tail. It lays its eggs in the nests of other birds.

Kestrel. 34 cm. The commonest falcon. Often seen hovering over fields before dropping onto its prey.

Remember—if you cannot see a picture of the bird you want to identify on these pages, turn to the page earlier in the book which deals with the kind of place where you saw the bird.

Crow-sized Birds

The birds inside this panel are all drawn to the same scale.

Collared Dove. 32 cm. Has a black half collar at the back of the neck.

Woodpigeon. 41 cm. Has a white patch on each side of the neck.

Buzzard. 51–56 cm. Has broad wings and tail. Plumage varies from pale to dark.

Barn Owl. 34 cm. A large white-looking owl. It hunts in twilight or at night. The remains of food can be found as pellets.

Lapwing. 30 cm. Has a thin crest and broad, black and white wings which show up when it is flying.

Breeding plumage (summer)

Herring Gull. 56–66 cm. Commonest gull on the coast. Has a large yellow beak with a red spot near the tip and grey wings.

Non-breeding plumage (winter)

Black-headed Gull. 35–38 cm. In winter, instead of a dark head, it has only a dark mark behind the eyes.

Mallard-sized Birds

The birds inside this panel are all drawn to the same scale.

Breeding plumage (summer)

Non-breeding plumage (winter)

Coot. 38 cm. Larger than a Moorhen. Is all black with a white beak and forehead. Likes large, open stretches of water.

Moorhen. 33 cm. Its beak is red and the underside of its tail white. Swims with a jerky movement.

Great Crested Grebe. 48 cm. The largest grebe. In summer, has brownish frills round the neck. In winter, blackish ear tufts.

Female

←Female

Male

Male

Female

Tufted Duck. 43 cm. The most common diving duck. The male has a long drooping crest, the female is browner with a much smaller crest. Forms large flocks on lakes and reservoirs.

Mallard. 58 cm. The male has a green head, white collar and purple-brown breast. Both birds have a blue patch and white bars on their wings, which show up best in flight.

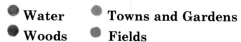

● Water   ● Towns and Gardens
● Woods   ● Fields

Hooded

Carrion

Jackdaw. 33 cm. Has a grey head and is smaller than the all-black crows.

Magpie. 46 cm. A large bird with a long tail and black and white plumage.

The northern form of the **Carrion Crow** has black and grey feathers. It is called the **Hooded Crow** (47 cm.)

Rook. 46 cm. Has a thinner beak than the crow, with a bare white face.

Male

Female

Curlew. 51–58 cm. Largest wader. Has a long downward curved beak, a brown body, and long legs.

Pheasant. Male 66–89 cm. Female 53–63 cm. A large game-bird. The male is brightly coloured, the female browner with a shorter tail.

Larger Birds

These birds are not drawn to the same scale.

Whooper Swan

Juvenile Mute Swan

Female Mute Swan

Male Mute Swan

Bewick's Swan

Grey Heron. 90 cm. A large grey bird often seen standing at the water's edge. The nest is usually built in a tree.

Cormorant. 90 cm. Has a white chin and cheeks. Often seen sitting on rocks with its wings half-open.

Mute Swan. 152 cm. Has an orange bill with a black knob at the base. Swims with its neck curved.

Bewick's and Whooper Swan. 122 and 152 cm. Bewick's has a shorter bill with a smaller yellow patch. Both hold their necks stiffly when swimming.

Birds in Flight

Here are some illustrations
to help you identify
birds in flight. The sizes
given are beak-to-tail
measurements.

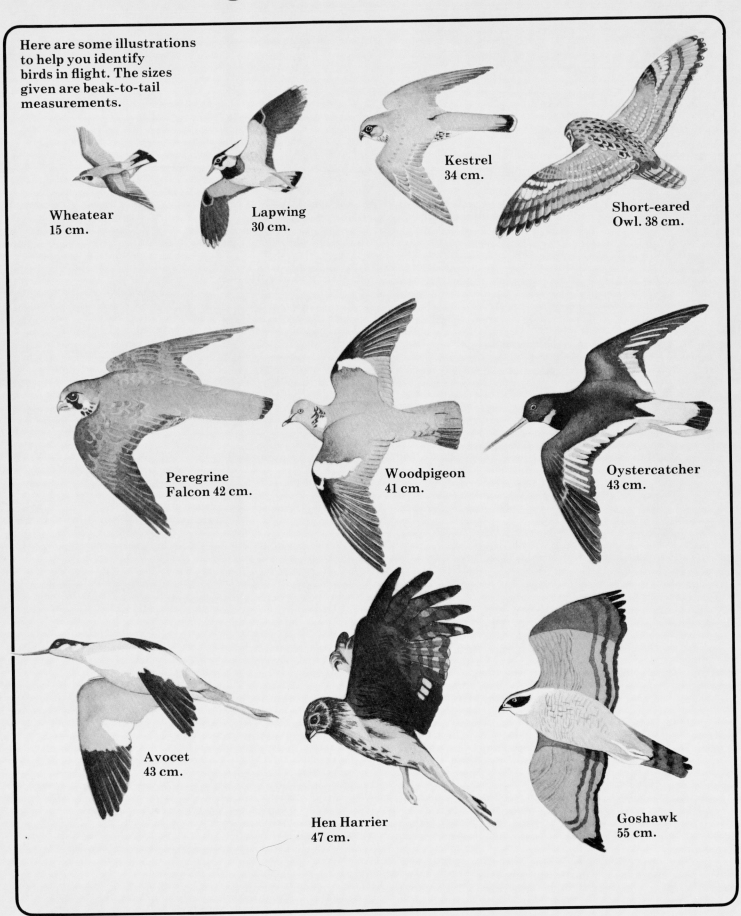

Wheatear
15 cm.

Lapwing
30 cm.

Kestrel
34 cm.

Short-eared
Owl. 38 cm.

Peregrine
Falcon 42 cm.

Woodpigeon
41 cm.

Oystercatcher
43 cm.

Avocet
43 cm.

Hen Harrier
47 cm.

Goshawk
55 cm.

Buzzard
54 cm.

Osprey
54 cm.

Black Kite
56 cm.

Herring Gull
60 cm.

Mallard
58 cm.

White-tailed
Eagle 69–91 cm.

Greylag Goose
76–89 cm.

White Stork
102 cm.

Pheasant
66–89 cm.

Mute Swan
152 cm.

Silver Birch

Part 2 written by
Ingrid Selberg

Consultant Editor
E. H. M. Harris,
Director of the Royal
Forestry Society

Norway Maple

Red Horse Chestnut

Apples

Part 2 TREES

Trees are around you everywhere: in gardens and parks, along city streets and in the countryside. Trees are one of the easiest living things to see.

This section is about common trees and how to study them. It shows you the different parts of a tree—the leaves, buds, flowers, fruits, bark and wood—and it explains how they work. It also shows you how each of these parts can help you to identify the tree. It tells the whole life story of a tree, from when it sprouts from a seed to when it dies from disease or is cut down for timber.

The best way to learn about how a tree grows is by growing one yourself. Page 50 shows you how to do this in easy-to-follow, step-by-step pictures.

If you want to identify a tree, look first at the illustrations on pages 60–65, or look on the pages which deal with the part of the tree that you are looking at. Remember that there are many clues to help you to identify a tree, not just its leaves, so try to use more than one.

Once you can recognize some common trees, try to find some rarer ones. A good place to look is in parks and in botanical gardens.

Making a tree survey, as described on pages 58–59, is great fun to do with a friend and it is a good way to test your skills as a tree detective.

If you take specimens from a tree, to put in a collection or to study at home, make sure you ask the permission of the owner.

Always use pruning shears to cut off twigs, never break them off. And, if you must climb trees, be very careful not to damage the trees or to hurt yourself.

Sitka Spruce

How to Identify Trees

When you want to identify a tree, the first things to look at are its leaves. But there are some trees whose leaves are very similar—for example, a Lombardy Poplar leaf could be confused with a Birch leaf. So always use at least one other feature, such as the flowers or bark, to help you identify a tree. (See pictures below.)

Trees can be divided into three groups: broadleaved, coniferous, and palm trees (see right). Try to decide to which group your tree belongs.

There is something to help you identify trees in every season. In spring and summer, look at the leaves and flowers. In autumn, many trees bear fruits which are good clues for identification. Winter is the best time to study buds, twigs, bark and tree shapes.

You do not need to go into a forest to find trees. Look at the many different kinds that grow in gardens, roads and in parks. Sometimes you can find rare trees in gardens.

Broadleaved Trees

Oak (summer)
Beech (spring)
Lime (winter)
Beech leaf and flower
Japanese Maple (autumn)

Most broadleaved trees have wide, flat leaves which they **drop in winter**. Some broadleaved trees, however, such as Holly, Laurel, Holm Oak and Box, are evergreen and keep their leaves in winter.

Broadleaved trees have seeds that are enclosed in fruits. The timber of broadleaved trees is called hardwood, because it is usually harder than the wood of most conifers, or softwood trees.

Tree or Shrub?

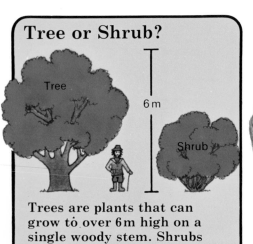

Tree
Shrub
6 m

Trees are plants that can grow to over 6 m high on a single woody stem. Shrubs are generally smaller, and have several stems. See page 59 for how to measure trees.

What to Look for

Leaves

Yew (Conifer)
Oak (Broadleaf)
Beech (Broadleaf)

The leaves will give you the biggest clue to the identity of the tree, but look at other parts of the tree as well. There is a guide to leaves on page 40.

Shape and Bark

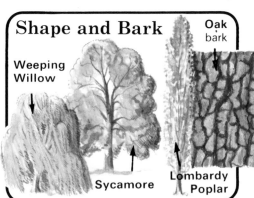

Oak bark
Weeping Willow
Sycamore
Lombardy Poplar

The overall shape of the tree, and of its top, or crown, are also good clues. Some trees can be recognized just by looking at their bark. See pages 44-5.

Conifers

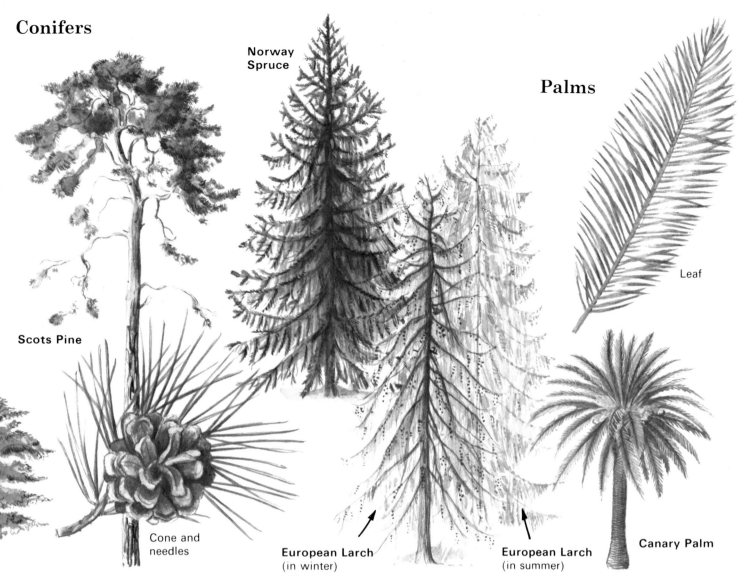

Norway Spruce

Scots Pine

Cone and needles

European Larch (in winter)

European Larch (in summer)

Palms

Leaf

Canary Palm

Most conifers have narrow, needle-like or scaly leaves, and are evergreen. The Larch is one conifer that is not evergreen. Conifer fruits are usually woody cones, but some conifers, like the Yew, have berry-like fruits. The overall shape of conifers is more regular than that of most broadleaved trees.

Palms have trunks without branches that look like giant stalks. The leaves grow at the top of the tree. Unlike other trees, the Palm grows taller, without getting thicker.

Winter Buds

Beech

Sycamore

Oak

In winter, when there are no leaves to look at, you can still identify some trees from their buds, bark and shape. See page 43 for a guide to bud shapes.

Flowers

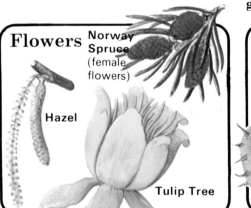

Norway Spruce (female flowers)

Hazel

Tulip Tree

In certain seasons trees have flowers which can help you to recognize the tree. But some trees do not flower every year. See pages 46-7.

Fruits and Seeds

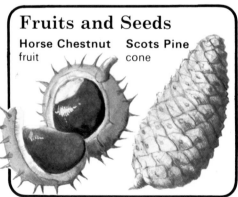

Horse Chestnut fruit

Scots Pine cone

All trees have fruits bearing seeds which may grow into new trees. This Horse Chestnut 'conker' and pine cone are both fruits. See pages 48-9.

How a Tree Grows

This is the life story of a Sycamore, but all trees grow in a similar way. Although there are many different kinds of trees, they all sprout from seeds, grow larger, flower, form fruits and shed seeds.

There are many stages of a tree's life story that you can study. You can watch it sprout from a seed and then chart its growth. You can count the girdle scars on a young tree to find out how old it is.

Older trees all have flowers and fruits at some time in most years, although they may be hard to see on some trees. They are not all as large as the Horse Chestnut's flowers or the fruit of the Apple tree. Not all fruits ripen in autumn. Some appear in early summer and even in spring.

An important part of a tree that you do not see is the roots. If you find an overturned tree, look at the roots and try to measure them. Look also at logs and tree stumps for the layers of wood and bark. They can tell you the age of the tree and its rate of growth.

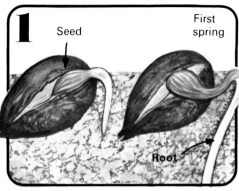

1 Seed — First spring — Root

The tree starts growing in spring from a seed which has been lying in the soil all winter. Now, with the help of the food stored inside it, the seed sends down a root into the soil to suck up water and minerals.

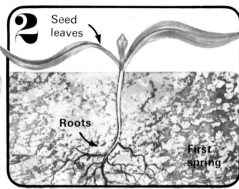

2 Seed leaves — Roots — First spring

Then the seed sends up a shoot which pokes above the ground and into the light. Two fleshy seed leaves open up with a small bud between them. These leaves are not the same shape as the tree's ordinary leaves will be.

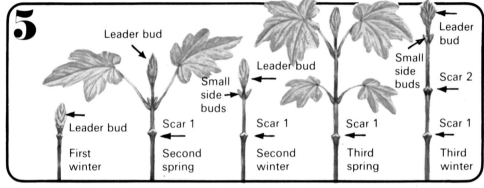

5 Leader bud — Leader bud — Small side buds — Scar 1 — Leader bud — Small side buds — Scar 2 — Leader bud — Scar 1 — First winter — Second spring — Second winter — Third spring — Scar 1 — Third winter

The following spring, the bud opens and a new shoot grows, with leaves at the tip. In autumn, they drop off. The next year, the same thing happens, and each year when the leaves fall off, they leave a girdle scar on the stem. Buds on the sides of the stem also grow shoots in the summer. But they do not grow as fast as the leader shoot at the top of the tree. Each year the tree grows taller, and the roots grow deeper.

8 Pollen on the flowers

When the tree is about twelve years old, it grows flowers on its branches in the spring. Bees, searching for nectar, visit the flowers and some of the pollen from the flowers sticks on to their hairy bodies.

9 Fruits

When the bees visit other Sycamore flowers, some of the pollen on their bodies rubs off on to the female parts of the flowers. When the male (pollen) and female parts are joined, the flowers are fertilized and become fruits.

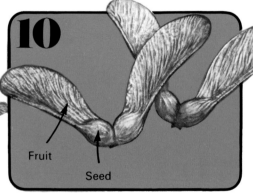

10 Fruit — Seed

Later that year, the fruits fall off the tree, spinning like tiny helicopters, carrying the seeds away from the parent tree. The wings rot on the ground, and the seeds are ready to grow the following spring.

3 Leaves

Seed leaves

First summer

The seed leaves have stored food in them to help the tree grow. Soon the bud opens, and the first pair of ordinary leaves appears. The seed leaves then drop off. The roots grow longer.

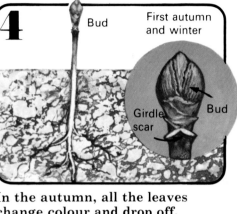

4 Bud

First autumn and winter

Girdle scar

Bud

In the autumn, all the leaves change colour and drop off, leaving a "girdle scar" around the stem where they were attached, and a bud at the end of the shoot. The bud does not grow during the winter.

Holly leaf

Many broadleaved trees are deciduous, which means that they lose their leaves in autumn. They do this because their leaves cannot work properly in cold weather, and there is not enough sunlight in winter for the leaves to make food for the tree.

Most conifers are called evergreens because they keep their leaves throughout the winter. Their needles are tougher than most broadleaves, and they can keep making food even in the dark of winter.

A few broadleaved trees, such as Holly, are also evergreen. Like conifer needles, their leaves have a waxy coating which helps them survive the winter.

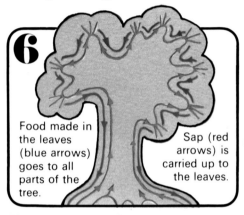

6

Food made in the leaves (blue arrows) goes to all parts of the tree.

Sap (red arrows) is carried up to the leaves.

The tree makes food for itself in its leaves, which contain a green chemical called chlorophyll. In sunlight, the chlorophyll can change air, water and minerals brought up from the soil into food for the tree.

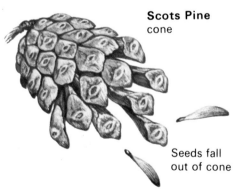

Scots Pine cone

Seeds fall out of cone

Some trees, like the Scots Pine, have fruits called cones, which stay on the tree, but open up to let the seeds fall out by themselves. When the cones are old and dried up, they usually fall off the tree too.

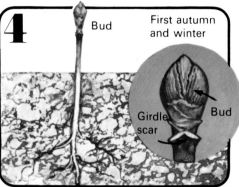

7

4
5
6
2
3
1

1

Bark is the outer layer which protects the tree from sun, rain and fungi which might attack it.

2

Tubes. Just inside the bark are tubes which carry food down from the leaves to all parts of the tree including the roots.

3

Cambium. This layer is so thin that you can hardly see it. Its job is to make a new layer of sapwood each year. This makes the trunk thicker and stronger.

4

Sapwood. This layer also has tiny tubes in it which carry the sap (water and minerals) to all parts of the tree from the roots. Each year a new "ring" of this wood is made by the cambium.

5

Heartwood. This is old sapwood which is dead and has become very hard. It makes the tree strong and rigid.

6

Rays. In a cross-section of a log you can see pale lines. These are called rays and they carry food sideways.

Each year the tree bears more branches. The stem thickens to hold them up, and the roots grow deeper and wider. The stem adds a new layer of wood. This picture shows you the inside of the stem, or trunk, and its different parts.

Leaves

The first thing that most people notice about a tree is its leaves. A big Oak tree has more than 250,000 leaves and a conifer may have many millions of needles.

The leaves fan out to the sunlight, and with the green chlorophyll inside them, they make food for the tree. They take in gases from the air and give out water vapour through tiny holes. Once the food is made, it is carried through veins to other parts of the leaf. The veins also strengthen the leaf like a skeleton.

The leaf stem brings water from the twig and also helps the leaf to move into the light. It is tough so that the leaf does not break off in strong winds.

Although the leaves of conifers and broadleaved trees look different, they both do the same work. Most conifer leaves can survive the winter, but broadleaves fall off in the autumn. Conifers also lose their leaves, but not all at once. A pine needle stays on a tree for about three to five years.

TRACKING DOWN YOUR MYSTERY LEAF

1. DECIDE IF THE LEAF IS FROM A CONIFER OR A BROADLEAVED TREE.
2. LOOK AT ITS SHAPE AND ITS EDGE.
3. NOTICE THE WAY THE LEAVES ARE ARRANGED ON THE TWIG.
4. LOOK AT THE COLOUR AND LEAF SURFACE.

Conifer Leaves

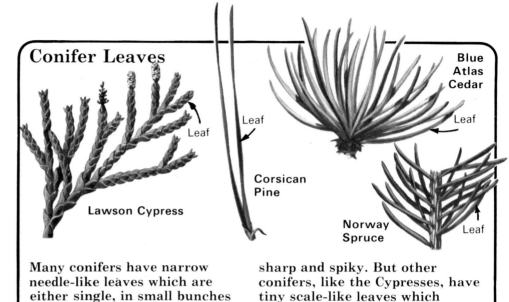

Lawson Cypress · Leaf

Corsican Pine · Leaf

Blue Atlas Cedar · Leaf

Norway Spruce · Leaf

Many conifers have narrow needle-like leaves which are either single, in small bunches or in clusters. They can be very sharp and spiky. But other conifers, like the Cypresses, have tiny scale-like leaves which overlap one another.

Broadleaves

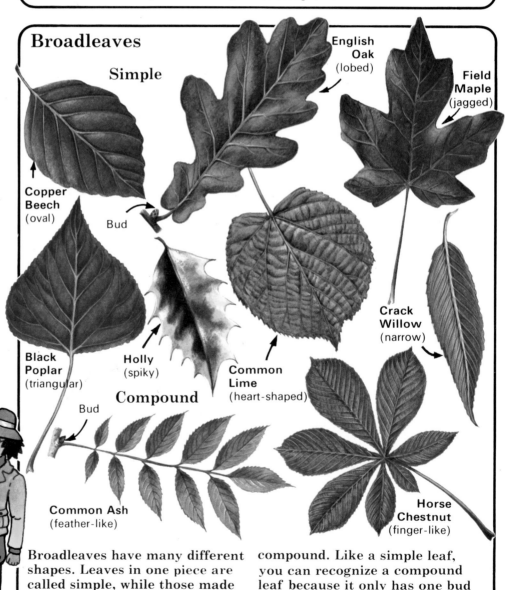

Simple

Copper Beech (oval)

Bud

Black Poplar (triangular)

English Oak (lobed)

Field Maple (jagged)

Holly (spiky)

Common Lime (heart-shaped)

Crack Willow (narrow)

Compound

Bud

Common Ash (feather-like)

Horse Chestnut (finger-like)

Broadleaves have many different shapes. Leaves in one piece are called simple, while those made up of many leaflets are called compound. Like a simple leaf, you can recognize a compound leaf because it only has one bud at the base of its stem.

These leaves are not drawn to the same scale.

Twigs

Opposite

Dawn Redwood

Alternate

Silver Birch

Larch

Horse Chestnut

Leaves are arranged on twigs in various ways. They can be opposite each other in pairs, or they can be single and alternate from one side of the twig to the other.

Colour

Beech

Maidenhair Tree

Rowan

Red Oak

Pear

Leaves are green because of the chlorophyll inside them. In autumn, the chlorophyll in broadleaves decays. They change colour before they fall.

Leaf Close-up

White Poplar

Underside

Magnified veins

If you look closely at a leaf you can see its network of veins. The leaf's upper surface is tough and often glossy to stop the sun from drying out the leaf. The underside is often hairy.

Leaf Scrapbook

Leaf skeleton

Keep a notebook of the leaves you find. Place each leaf between two sheets of paper. Then put them between books with a heavy object

on top. Leave them for a week. When the leaves are flat and dry, mount them in a notebook with tiny pieces of sellotape. Label the leaves and write down where and

when you found them. You may also find leaf skeletons, from which the dried leaf has crumbled away, leaving only the strong stem and veins.

Leaf Tiles

Press the leaf on to the "clay" with a rolling pin.

The finished tile can be painted or varnished.

Make your clay by mixing together:
2 cups flour (not self-raising)
1 cup salt
1 cup water

2 tablespoons cooking oil
Shape your "clay" into a ball. Roll it out with a rolling pin until it is about 2 cm thick. Press your leaf, vein side down, on to the clay so

that it leaves a mark. Remove the leaf and bake in the oven at Gas Mark $\frac{1}{2}$ (250°F) for about two hours.

Winter Buds

Most broadleaved trees have no leaves in winter, but you can still identify them by their winter buds.

A winter bud contains the beginnings of next year's shoot, leaves and flowers. The thick, overlapping bud scales protect the shoot from the cold and from attack by insects. In places where winter is the dry season, the bud scales keep the new shoot from drying out. If the undeveloped leaf does not have bud scales, it may be covered with furry hairs to protect it.

In spring, when it gets warmer, the new shoot swells and breaks open the hard protective scales. Each year's shoot comes from a bud and ends by forming a new bud at the end of the growing season.

There are many buds on a twig. The leading bud, which is usually at the tip, contains the shoot which will grow most. The shoot becomes a twig and eventually a branch. The other buds hold leaves and flowers. They are also reserves in case the leading bud is damaged.

Inside a bud there are tiny leaves and flowers, all folded up. If you cut a bud in half and look at it through a lens, you can see the different parts.

This is a three-year-old Horse Chestnut twig. You can tell its age by counting the girdle scars. It has large brown buds in opposite pairs. The bud scales are sticky.

Outer scales of bud

Flower

Leaf

This side bud will not grow into a twig unless the leading bud is damaged.

The leading bud contains next year's shoot.

A leaf scar left by last year's leaf

This side twig is two years old.

These buds will become leaves.

Last year's leading bud was here. Notice the girdle scar.

One year's growth.

Leading bud

Last year's buds were here.

An undeveloped twig.

A two-year-old Spruce twig.

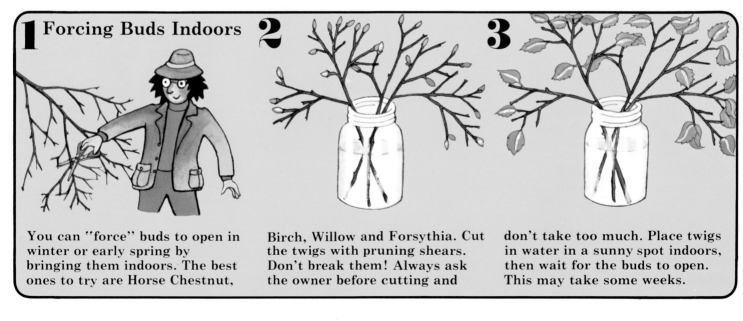

1 Forcing Buds Indoors

You can "force" buds to open in winter or early spring by bringing them indoors. The best ones to try are Horse Chestnut,

2

Birch, Willow and Forsythia. Cut the twigs with pruning shears. Don't break them! Always ask the owner before cutting and

3

don't take too much. Place twigs in water in a sunny spot indoors, then wait for the buds to open. This may take some weeks.

Winter Bud Identification Chart

What to Look for

If you try to identify trees by their winter buds, you will see that they vary a great deal. Here is a list of things to look for:

1. How are the buds positioned on the twig? Like leaves, buds can be in opposite pairs or single and alternate.
2. What colour are the buds and the twig?
3. What shape is the twig? Are the buds pointed or rounded?
4. Is the bud covered with hairs or scales? If there are scales, how many? Is the bud sticky?

Ash—Smooth, grey twig. Large, black buds opposite.

Sycamore— Large, green, opposite buds with dark-edged scales.

Beech—Slender twig. Alternate, spiky, brown buds sticking out.

Willow—Slender twig. Alternate buds close to twig.

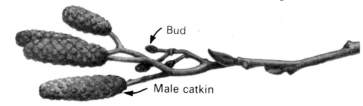

Alder—Alternate, stalked, purple buds often with male catkins.

White Poplar—Twig and alternate buds covered with white down.

Sweet Chestnut—Knobbly twig. Large, reddish, alternate buds.

Plane—Alternate, cone-shaped buds. Ring scar around bud.

Whitebeam—Downy, green, alternate buds.

False Acacia—Grey twig. Thorns next to tiny, alternate buds.

Elm—Zigzag twig. Alternate, blackish-red buds.

Lime—Zigzag twig. Alternate, reddish buds with two scales.

Walnut—Thick, hollow twig. Big, black, velvety, alternate buds.

Turkey Oak—Clusters of alternate, whiskered buds.

Wild Cherry—Large, glossy, red buds grouped at tip of twig.

Magnolia—Huge, furry, green-grey buds.

These twigs are drawn life size.

Shape

Look at all these different tree shapes. Each type of tree has its own typical shape which depends on the arrangement of its branches. Winter is the best time of year to see the shapes of broadleaved trees because their branches are not hidden by leaves.

Practise making quick shape sketches when you are outside.

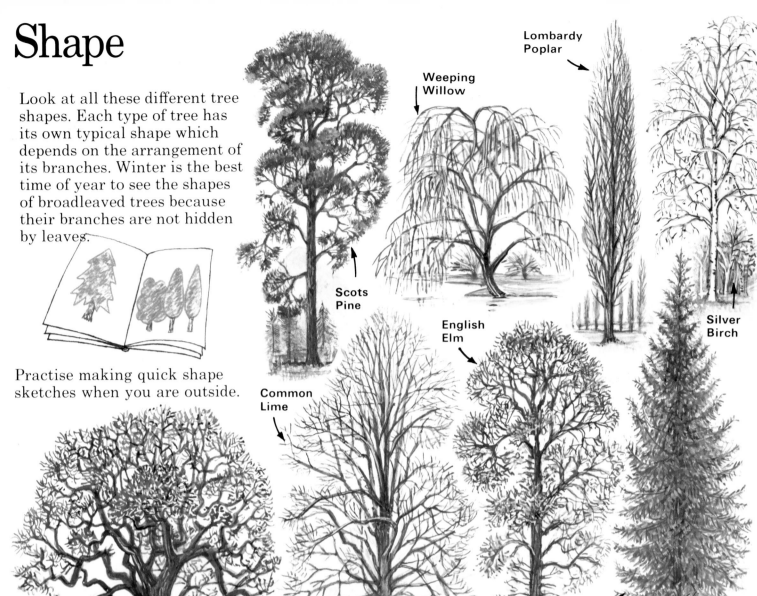

Weeping Willow

Lombardy Poplar

Scots Pine

English Elm

Silver Birch

Common Lime

English Oak

Norway Spruce

How Trees are Shaped

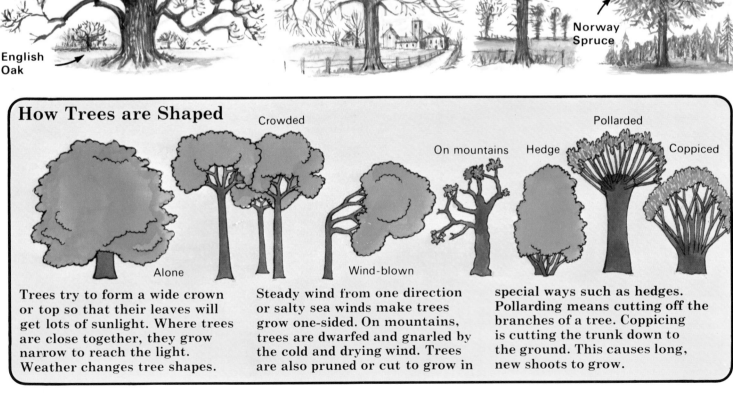

Crowded

Alone

On mountains

Hedge

Pollarded

Coppiced

Wind-blown

Trees try to form a wide crown or top so that their leaves will get lots of sunlight. Where trees are close together, they grow narrow to reach the light. Weather changes tree shapes.

Steady wind from one direction or salty sea winds make trees grow one-sided. On mountains, trees are dwarfed and gnarled by the cold and drying wind. Trees are also pruned or cut to grow in

special ways such as hedges. Pollarding means cutting off the branches of a tree. Coppicing is cutting the trunk down to the ground. This causes long, new shoots to grow.

Bark

The outside of the tree trunk is covered in a hard, tough layer of bark. It protects the inside of the tree from drying out and from damage by insects or animals. It also insulates the tree from extremes of heat and cold. Under the bark there are tubes carrying food (sap) which can be damaged if the bark is stripped off. If this happens, the tree may die.

When the tree is young the bark is thin and smooth, but with age it thickens and forms different patterns. You can identify trees by their bark.

Birch bark peels off in ribbon-like strips.

English Oak bark has deep ridges and cracks.

How Bark Patterns Form

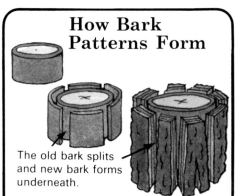

The old bark splits and new bark forms underneath.

Bark is dead and cannot grow or stretch. As wood inside the bark grows outwards, the bark splits, peels or cracks in a way that is special to each type of tree.

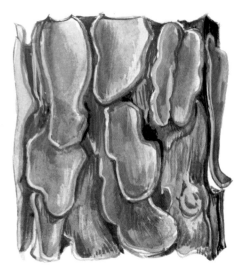

Scots Pine bark flakes off in large pieces.

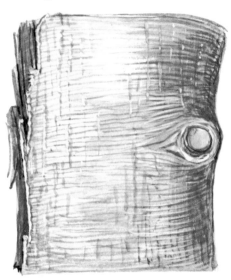

Beech has smooth thin bark, which flakes off in tiny pieces.

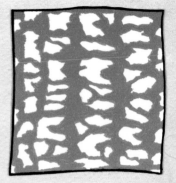

To make bark rubbings you need strong thin paper, sellotape and wax crayons or heel-ball. Tape the paper to the tree. Rub firmly with the crayon but do not tear the paper. Watch the bark pattern appear.

You can also rub the paper with candle wax. At home, paint over the rubbing. The bark pattern will stay white.

Cork

The bark on the Cork Oak is so thick that it can be removed without damaging the tree. Cork is used in many ways to keep in moisture and to resist heat.

Flowers

All trees produce flowers in order to make seeds that can grow into new trees. The flowers vary from tree to tree in size, shape and colour. Some are so small that you may not have noticed them.

Flowers have male parts called stamens and female parts called ovaries. The stamen produces pollen, while the ovary contains ovules. When pollen from the stamen reaches the ovules in the ovary, the flower is fertilized. Fertilized flowers grow into fruits (see pages 48-9), which contain seeds.

Flowers with both ovaries and stamens in the same flower, like the Cherry, are called perfect. On other trees the ovaries and the stamens are in separate flowers. Clusters of all-female flowers grow together and so do all-male flowers. The clusters can be cone-shaped or long and dangling (these are called catkins). A few trees, such as Yew, Holly and Willow, have their male and female flowers on entirely separate trees.

Parts of a Flower

Petal

The top of the ovary is called the stigma.

Ovary with ovules

Stamen with pollen

Stalk

Sepal

This is a cross-section of a Cherry blossom, which is a typical perfect flower. It has male and female parts.

European Larch

Male flowers

Female flowers

Pollen

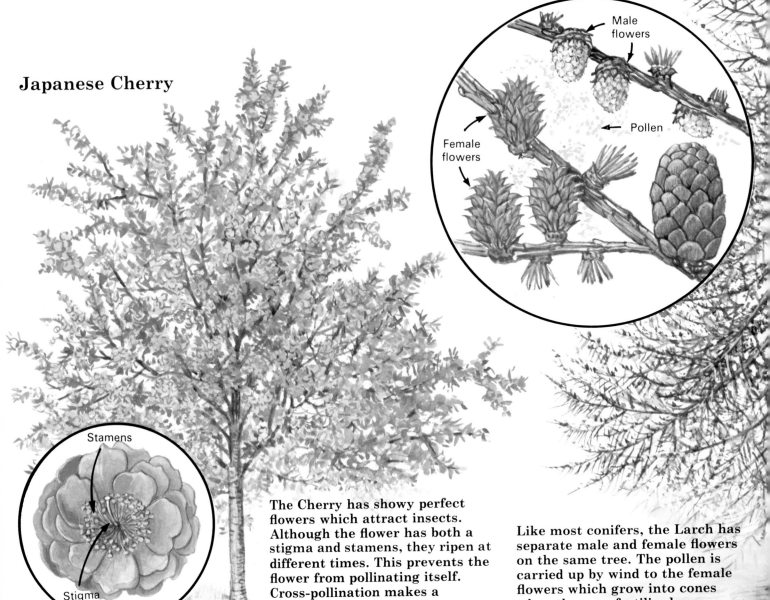

Japanese Cherry

Stamens

Stigma

The Cherry has showy perfect flowers which attract insects. Although the flower has both a stigma and stamens, they ripen at different times. This prevents the flower from pollinating itself. Cross-pollination makes a healthier seed.

Like most conifers, the Larch has separate male and female flowers on the same tree. The pollen is carried up by wind to the female flowers which grow into cones when they are fertilized.

Pollination

Crab Apple

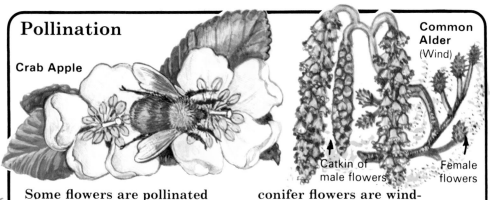

Common Alder (Wind)

Catkin of male flowers

Female flowers

Some flowers are pollinated by insects. Insects, feeding on flowers, accidentally pick up pollen on their bodies, and it rubs off on the next flower they visit. This is called cross-pollination. Most catkins and conifer flowers are wind-pollinated. They are small and dull because they do not need to attract insects. The wind blows pollen off the long stamens and the sticky stigmas catch the pollen.

Fertilization

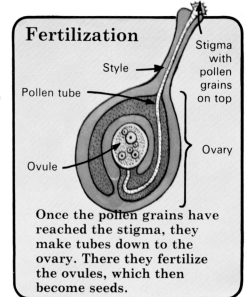

Stigma with pollen grains on top

Style

Pollen tube

Ovary

Ovule

Once the pollen grains have reached the stigma, they make tubes down to the ovary. There they fertilize the ovules, which then become seeds.

Crack Willow

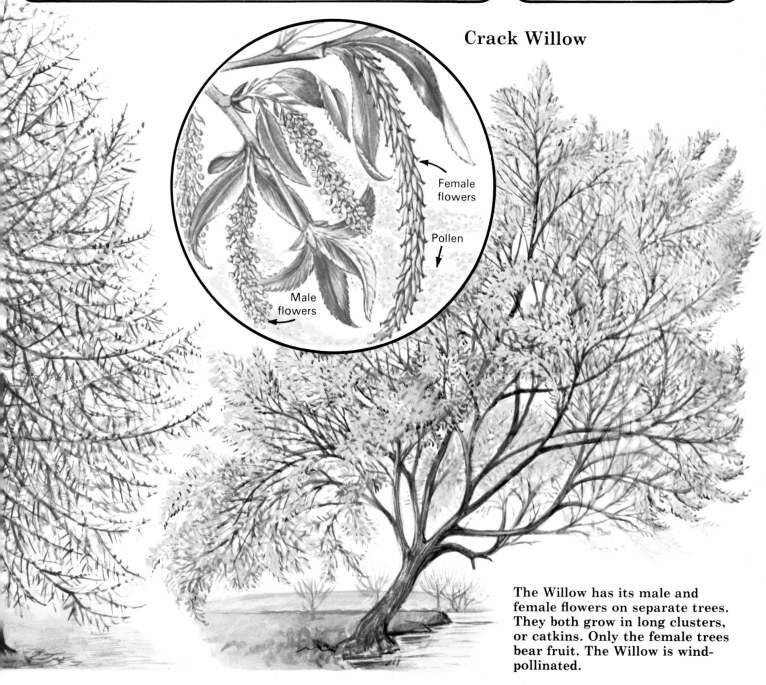

Female flowers

Pollen

Male flowers

The Willow has its male and female flowers on separate trees. They both grow in long clusters, or catkins. Only the female trees bear fruit. The Willow is wind-pollinated.

Fruits and Seeds

Fruits containing seeds grow from fertilized flowers. An Apple and the prickly conker case of the Horse Chestnut are both fruits. Although they look different, they do the same job. They protect the seeds they carry and help them to spread to a place where they can grow.

Conifers bear fruits whose seeds are uncovered, but which are usually held in a scaly cone. Broadleaved trees have fruits which completely surround their seeds. They take the form of nuts, berries, soft fruits, and many other kinds.

Many fruits and cones are damaged by insects and disease, are eaten by birds and animals, or fall off the trees before they can ripen. The seeds inside the remaining fruits ripen in the autumn. They need to get far away from the parent tree, or it will take all the food and light.

Seeds are spread by birds, animals, wind and water. Very few seeds ever get to a place where they can reach full growth. About one in a million acorns becomes an Oak tree.

How a Cone Ripens

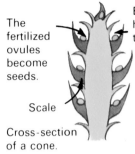

The fertilized ovules become seeds.

Each scale holds two seeds.

Scale

Cross-section of a cone.

Cones develop from the female flowers. After pollination, the scales harden and close. The stalk often bends, so the cone hangs down. The cone turns from green to brown. When the seeds are ripe and the weather is warm and dry, the scales open. The seeds flutter out on papery wings. Most cones stay on the tree for a year. Others take two years to ripen, and some remain long after the seeds have been dropped.

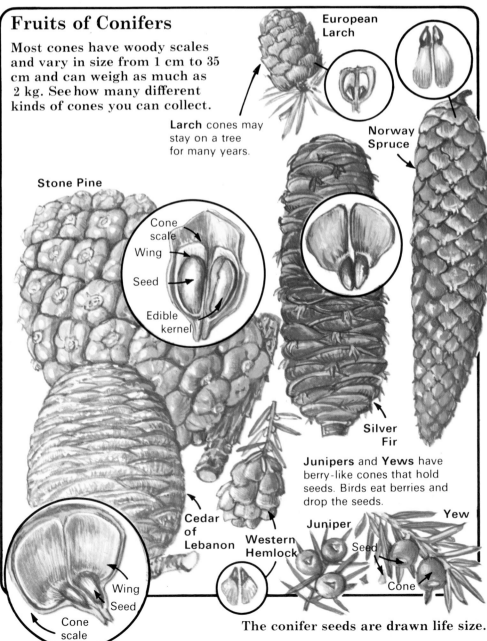

Female flowers in spring

Male flowers in spring

Seeds
Douglas Fir

Young cone in summer

Last year's cone which is now empty

Fruits of Conifers

Most cones have woody scales and vary in size from 1 cm to 35 cm and can weigh as much as 2 kg. See how many different kinds of cones you can collect.

Larch cones may stay on a tree for many years.

European Larch

Norway Spruce

Stone Pine

Cone scale
Wing
Seed
Edible kernel

Silver Fir

Junipers and **Yews** have berry-like cones that hold seeds. Birds eat berries and drop the seeds.

Cedar of Lebanon

Western Hemlock

Juniper

Seed

Yew

Cone

Wing
Seed
Cone scale

The conifer seeds are drawn life size.

Scots Pine

Cones open in warm, dry weather to release their seeds. If it is wet, the scales close. Find a cone and make it open by placing it near a heater. Then put it in a damp place, and it will close.

How a Peach Ripens

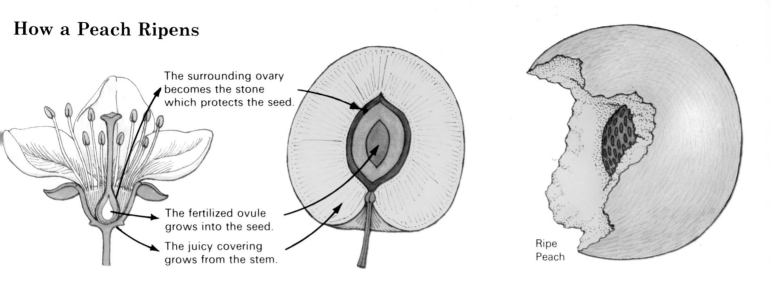

The surrounding ovary becomes the stone which protects the seed.

The fertilized ovule grows into the seed.

The juicy covering grows from the stem.

Ripe Peach

The pictures above show how the different parts of a flower grow into the different parts of a fruit. The flower is a Peach blossom.

Water from the stem and sunshine make the fleshy part of the fruit swell. As the fruit ripens, it turns golden pink and softens. The

bright colour and sweet smell attract hungry animals or people who eat the juicy outer layer and throw away the stone.

Fruits of Broadleaved Trees

Broadleaved trees produce many different kinds of fruits. Some are nuts with hard outer shells, some are soft fruits, some are pods, and some have wings or hairs.

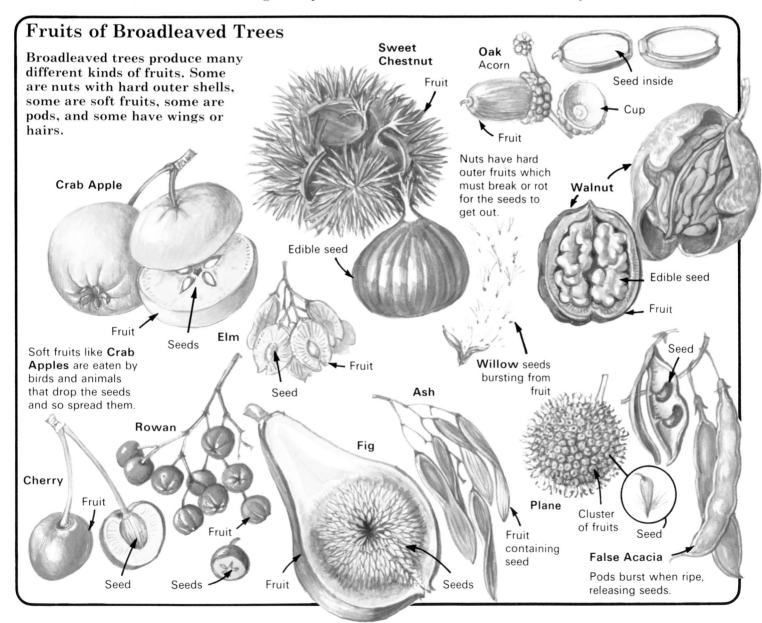

Sweet Chestnut

Fruit

Oak
Acorn

Seed inside

Cup

Fruit

Nuts have hard outer fruits which must break or rot for the seeds to get out.

Walnut

Edible seed

Crab Apple

Edible seed

Fruit

Fruit

Seeds

Elm

Fruit

Soft fruits like **Crab Apples** are eaten by birds and animals that drop the seeds and so spread them.

Seed

Willow seeds bursting from fruit

Ash

Seed

Rowan

Fig

Plane

Cluster of fruits

Seed

Cherry

Fruit

Fruit containing seed

Seed

Fruit

False Acacia

Pods burst when ripe, releasing seeds.

Seed

Seeds

Fruit

Seeds

The cones and fruits are drawn two thirds life size.

Grow Your Own Seedling

Try growing your own tree from a seed. Pick ripe seeds from trees or collect them from the ground if you know that they are fresh. The time a seed takes to sprout varies, but an acorn takes about two months. Some seeds, like those from conifers, may need to lie in the ground for over a year. Once your seedling has sprouted, keep a diary of its growth with drawings or photographs.

What You Need

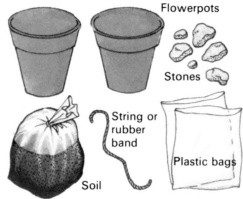

Flowerpots

Stones

Soil

String or rubber band

Plastic bags

What to Plant

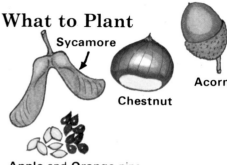

Sycamore

Chestnut

Acorn

Apple and Orange pips

Here are some seeds which are easy to grow. Acorns are usually successful, but try anything!

1 Soak acorns or other hard nuts in warm water overnight. Peel off the hard outer shells if you can, but do not try to cut the shells off acorns.

2 Put a handful of stones in the bottom of your pot. This is to help the water to drain properly. Place a saucer under the pot.

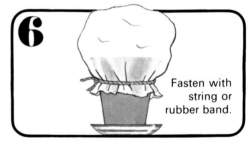

3 Put some soil, or compost, on top of the stones until the pot is about two thirds full. Water the soil until it is moist but not soggy.

4 Place the acorns or other seeds on top of the soil. They need lots of room to grow, so only put one acorn in each pot.

5 Cover the acorns or other seeds with a layer of soil about as thick as the seeds.

6 Place a plastic bag over the pot and fasten it. This will keep the seed moist without watering. Put the pot in a sunny place and wait.

Fasten with string or rubber band.

7 As soon as you see the seedling appear, remove the plastic bag. Water the seedling once or twice a week. The soil should be moist, but not wet.

8 Put your seedling outside in the summer if you can. In autumn, it will be ready to be planted in the ground (or you can leave it in its pot).

9 Dig a hole a bit larger than the pot. Gently scoop out the seedling and the soil around it from the pot. Plant it in the hole, pat down the soil on top, and water it.

Forestry

Trees have been growing on Earth for about 350 million years. The land was once covered by natural forests, but they have been cut down for timber and cleared for land. New forests are planted to replace the trees that are cut down.

Because conifers grow faster than broadleaved trees and produce straight timber, they are preferred for wood production.

Seedbeds

The seeds are sown in seedbeds. When the seedlings are 15-20 cm high, they are planted in rows in another bed where they have more room. They are weeded regularly.

Planting Out

When the seedlings are about 50 cm high, they are planted out in the forest ground, which has been cleared and ploughed. There are about 2,500 trees per hectare.

This picture and the two above show the story of a Douglas Fir plantation, and what the foresters do to care for the trees.

Fire towers on hills help to spot fire — the forest's worst enemy. Fires can be started by a carelessly dropped match or an unguarded campfire.

Trees can be sprayed with herbicides or treated with fertilizers from the air.

When the trees are felled, they are taken away to sawmills to be cut up.

Every few years the poorer trees are cut out to give more light and room to the stronger ones. These thinnings are used for poles or are made into paper pulp.

Dead and lower branches are cut off trees. This lessens the risk of fire and stops knots from forming in the wood.

Trees are felled when they are full-grown (about 70 years for conifers and 150 years for Oaks). About one in every ten trees reaches its full growth.

Annual Rings

Inside the bark is the wood which is made up of many layers (see page 39). Each year the cambium makes a ring of wood on its inner side and grows outwards. This layer is called an annual ring. The early wood made in spring is pale and has wide tubes to carry sap. Late wood, which is formed in summer, is darker and stronger. In wet years, the layers of wood are broad and the annual rings are far apart, but in dry years they are narrow. They are also narrow if the trees are not thinned.

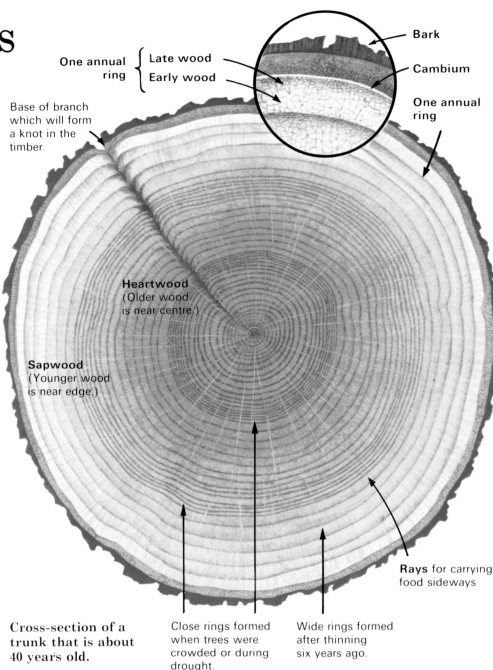

One annual ring { Late wood / Early wood

Bark

Cambium

One annual ring

Base of branch which will form a knot in the timber.

Heartwood
(Older wood is near centre.)

Sapwood
(Younger wood is near edge.)

Rays for carrying food sideways

Close rings formed when trees were crowded or during drought.

Wide rings formed after thinning six years ago.

Cross-section of a trunk that is about 40 years old.

Palms

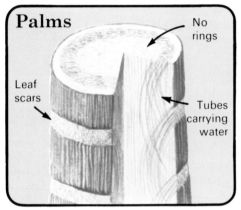

No rings

Leaf scars

Tubes carrying water

Palm trees do not have annual rings because they have no cambium to grow new wood. Their trunks are like giant stalks which do not grow thicker.

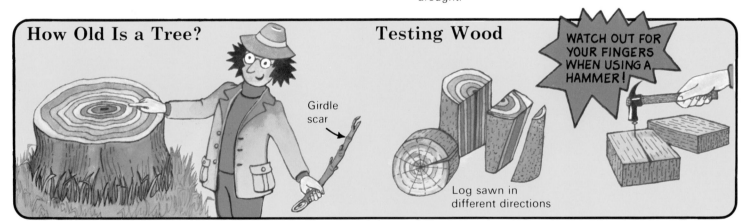

How Old Is a Tree?

Girdle scar

Testing Wood

WATCH OUT FOR YOUR FINGERS WHEN USING A HAMMER!

Log sawn in different directions

You can find out the age of a tree by counting the annual rings in a cross-section of its trunk. It is easiest to count the dark rings of late wood. Twigs also have annual layers. Cut off a twig on the slant and count its rings. Then count the girdle scars on the outside. Do they agree?

Saw a small log in different ways and look at the patterns the wood makes. Test the strength of different woods by hammering nails into them.

Wood

The wood inside different types of trees varies in colour and pattern just as their outside appearances vary. Different kinds of wood are especially suited for certain uses. Wood from conifers, called softwood, is mainly used for building and paper pulp, while broadleaved trees, called hardwoods, are used to make furniture.

At the sawmill, the person operating the saw decides the best way to cut each log. A log can be made into many different sizes of planks as well as into paper pulp.

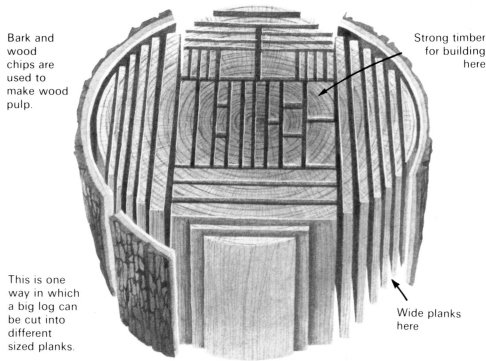

Bark and wood chips are used to make wood pulp.

This is one way in which a big log can be cut into different sized planks.

Strong timber for building here

Wide planks here

Grain

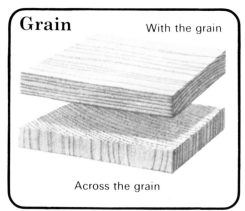

With the grain

Across the grain

When a plank is cut from a log, the annual rings make vertical lines which may be wavy or straight. This pattern is called the grain. **Wood cut with the grain is stronger.**

Knots

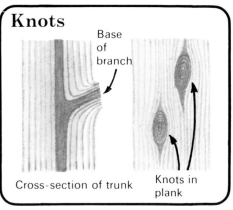

Base of branch

Cross-section of trunk

Knots in plank

In a plank you may see dark spots called knots. These were where the base of a branch was buried in the trunk of the tree. This distorts the grain, leaving a knot.

Seasoning

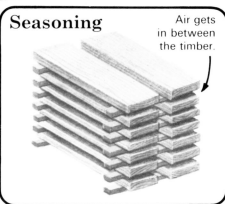

Air gets in between the timber.

Fresh wood contains water which is why green logs spit in the fire. As wood dries, it shrinks and often cracks or warps. Planks must be dried out, or seasoned, before they can be used.

Processed Wood

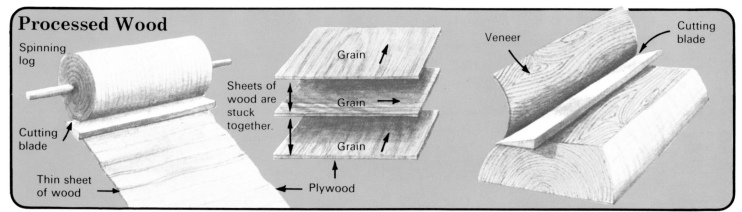

Spinning log

Cutting blade

Thin sheet of wood

Sheets of wood are stuck together.

Grain

Grain

Grain

Plywood

Veneer

Cutting blade

Much of the wood that you see around you has been 'processed'. Plywood is thin layers of wood which are glued together with the grain lying in different directions. It is stronger than ordinary wood and does not warp. The thin sheet of wood is peeled off the log like a Swiss roll. Veneer is a thin sheet of wood with a beautiful grain which is used on the surface of plain furniture. Chipboard (not shown) is made of small chips and shavings mixed with glue.

Pests and Fungi

Trees are attacked by insects and fungus diseases. Insects use trees for food, shelter and as places to breed. They can cause serious damage to trees, but they rarely kill them.

Fungi are a group of non-flowering plants which include mushrooms. Because fungi cannot make their own food, they may feed off other living things and sometimes kill them. Fungi spread by releasing microscopic seeds, called spores, into the air. If these spores get into the tree and spread, they will rot it.

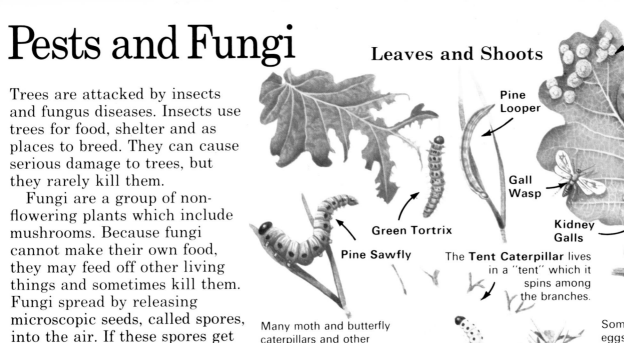

Leaves and Shoots

Spangle Galls

Cherry Galls

Pine Looper

Gall Wasp

Kidney Galls

Green Tortrix

Pine Sawfly

The **Tent Caterpillar** lives in a "tent" which it spins among the branches.

Oak Apple Galls

Many moth and butterfly caterpillars and other larvae eat leaves. Often each species only feeds on a certain type of tree.

Some insects lay their eggs in leaves or shoots. The tree forms swellings, called galls, around the eggs. The larvae feed inside the galls.

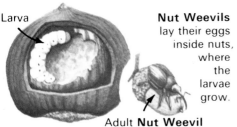

Larva

Nut Weevils lay their eggs inside nuts, where the larvae grow.

Adult **Nut Weevil**

Leaf Miner

Leaf Roller

Aphid

Leaf Miners eat tunnels through leaves. **Leaf Rollers** fold leaves over themselves for protection.

"Pineapple" Gall

An **Aphid** made this "pineapple" gall by piercing a shoot to suck out the sap.

Bark and Wood

Conifer Heart Rot is caused by this bracket fungus. It attacks conifers and rots the inside of trees until they die.

White Pine Blister Rust is a fungus which causes swellings on pine trunks or branches.

Look for **Scale** insects on bark. If you pull one off, you may see the grub which sucks sap from the tree.

Elm Bark Beetles make tunnels under Elm bark. They spread the fungus which causes Dutch Elm Disease.

Honey Fungus attacks the roots of many trees. In autumn, the toadstools appear at the base of infected ones.

The **Pine Weevil** strips the bark off newly planted conifers.

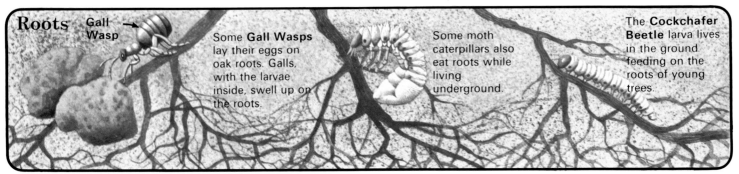

Roots

Gall Wasp

Some **Gall Wasps** lay their eggs on oak roots. Galls, with the larvae inside, swell up on the roots.

Some moth caterpillars also eat roots while living underground.

The **Cockchafer Beetle** larva lives in the ground feeding on the roots of young trees.

54

Keeping an Oak Gall

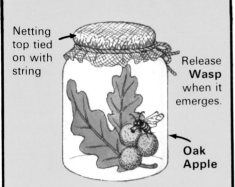

Netting top tied on with string

Release **Wasp** when it emerges.

Oak Apple

In summer, collect Oak Apples and other galls which do not have holes in them. Keep them in a jar with netting on top. The wasps living inside the galls should emerge in a month.

Making Spore Prints

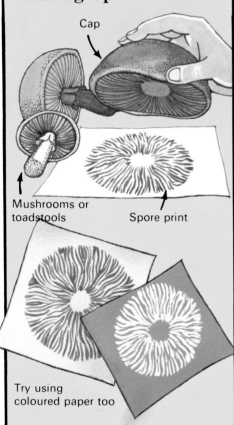

Cap

Mushrooms or toadstools

Spore print

Try using coloured paper too

Make spore prints from mushrooms. Cut off the stalk and place the cap on some paper. Leave it overnight. It will release its spores on the paper, leaving a print. Always wash your hands after handling fungus.

Injuries

Bark stripped by a **Deer's** antlers

Tree struck by lightning

Bark gnawed by a **Field Vole**

Sometimes trees are damaged by animals. Deer strip the bark off trees when they scrape the "velvet" off their antlers. Squirrels, voles and rabbits eat young bark. If lightning strikes a tree, the trunk often cracks. This happens because the sap gets so hot that it becomes steam. It expands and then explodes, shattering the tree.

How a Tree Heals Itself

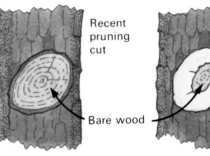

Recent pruning cut

Three years later

Six years later

Bare wood

New bark covering wound

If a branch is pruned off a tree properly, the wound usually heals. A new rim of bark grows from the cambium around the cut. This finished seal will keep out fungus and disease. It takes years for a wound to heal. But if a wound completely surrounds the trunk, the tree will die because its food supply is cut off.

How Trees Die

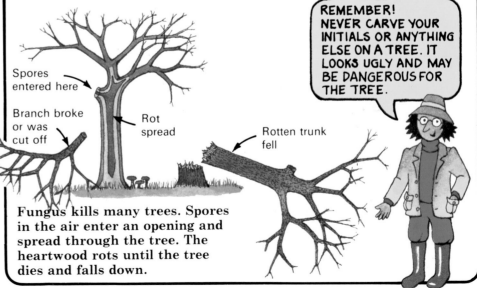

Spores entered here

Branch broke or was cut off

Rot spread

Rotten trunk fell

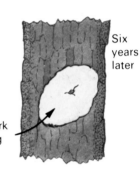

REMEMBER! NEVER CARVE YOUR INITIALS OR ANYTHING ELSE ON A TREE. IT LOOKS UGLY AND MAY BE DANGEROUS FOR THE TREE.

Fungus kills many trees. Spores in the air enter an opening and spread through the tree. The heartwood rots until the tree dies and falls down.

Woodland Life

When you walk in a forest, it may seem dead and deserted, but in its depths, the forest hides a wealth of life. Trees provide protection from bad weather, wind and too much sun. Tree roots help to hold the soil in place. Fallen leaves and twigs make a rich soil called humus. All this encourages plants to grow.

Trees also provide food and shelter for many animals. The plants and animals you find in coniferous and broadleaved forests are usually different, although they may overlap.

A Coniferous Forest

A coniferous forest is dark and dense. Few plants grow on the ground because of the thick layer of needles and the lack of light. Here are some animals and plants you might see in a coniferous forest.

Pine Marten

Squirrel's drey

Long-eared Owl's nest

Long-eared Owl

Great Spotted Woodpecker

Red Deer

Crossbill

Bracken

Fox

Black Grouse

Norway Spruce cones

Wood Ant-hill

Broad Buckler Fern

Timberman

Goldcrest

Fly Agaric

Red Squirrel

Lichen

Black Slug

Treecreeper

A Broadleaved Forest

A broadleaved forest is more light and open and so attracts many plants and animals. There are many flowers in spring before the trees' leaves have blocked out the light. As you can see, an Oak wood supports a great variety of life.

Mistletoe

Green Woodpecker

Nuthatch

Rook in nest

Tawny Owl

Long-eared Bat in tree

Poor Man's Beefsteak

Blue Tit

Oak

Roe Deer

Wood Anemone

Badger

Bluebells

Rabbit

Ivy

Pheasant

Hedgehog

Common Shrew

Primrose

Common Toad

Earthworm

Greater Stag Beetle

Speckled Wood Butterfly

Making a Tree Survey

Make a survey of the trees that grow around you. Choose a garden, street or park where you think there will be a variety of trees, but start with a small area first. It is easier and more fun to do this with a friend.

When you have decided on an area, make a rough map of it with any landmarks, such as roads or buildings. Try to work out a scale for your map. (It helps to use graph paper.) Work in a definite order so that you do not miss out any trees, and then go back to identify and measure them.

What to Take

Tape measure

Pencils

String

Tree field guide

Notebook

Identifying a Tree

Try to identify the trees using this book or a field guide. Remember that there are many clues to help you recognize them, so don't use just one clue.

Making a Map

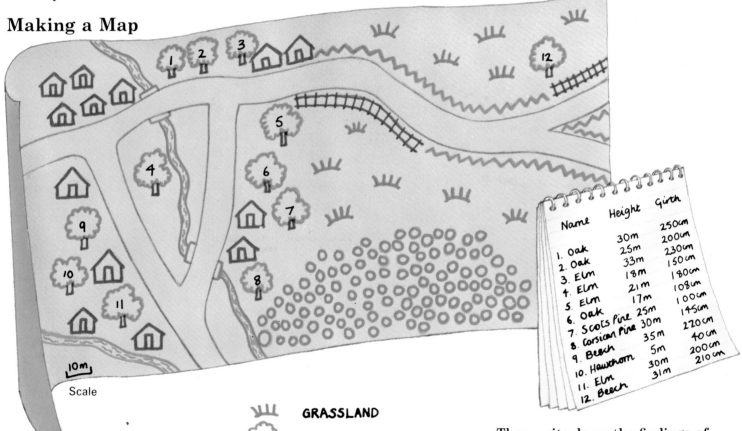

Name	Height	Girth
1. Oak	30m	250cm
2. Oak	25m	200cm
3. Elm	33m	230cm
4. Elm	18m	150cm
5. Elm	21m	180cm
6. Oak	17m	108cm
7. Scots Pine	25m	100cm
8. Corsican Pine	30m	145cm
9. Beech	35m	220cm
10. Hawthorn	5m	40cm
11. Elm	30m	200cm
12. Beech	31m	210cm

10m

Scale

After you have identified and measured the trees (as shown above), make a neater and more detailed copy of your map. Show the scale of your map. Then make a key to the symbols you used. Here are some suggestions:

GRASSLAND

TREE

WOODLAND

STREAM

BRIDGE

HOUSE

HEDGE

FENCE

Then write down the findings of your survey. Give the name, height and girth of each tree. Repeat the survey later to see if there are any new trees, or if anything has changed.

Measuring a Tree

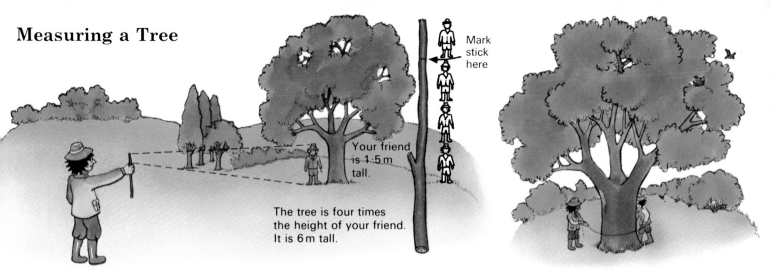

Mark stick here

Your friend is 1.5 m tall.

The tree is four times the height of your friend. It is 6 m tall.

Ask your friend to stand next to the tree. Hold a stick up vertically at arm's length, and move your thumb up the stick until it is in line with your friend's feet, while the tip of the stick is in line with the top of your friend's head.

Mark the stick where your thumb is. See how many times the part of the stick above the mark goes into the height of the tree (four times here). Then multiply your friend's height (1.5 m here) by this number to get the height of the tree (6 m).

Measure around the tree at chest height to find the girth. Ask your friend to hold one end of some string while you hold the other. Walk around the tree until you meet. Then measure the length of string.

1 Studying a Tree

Make a careful study of one tree all through the year. Choose a tree which you can get to easily and often. Make a notebook in which you keep a record of when it comes into leaf, when it flowers and fruits, and when it drops its leaves. Include sketches or photos of the tree at these different times and specimens from it.

2

Study the animals that live in or near your tree. Look for birds' nests and squirrels' dreys in the tree top. Look on the trunk for insects and on the ground for other traces of animals, such as owl pellets, and nuts or cones which have been eaten by animals. To examine the insects in the tree top, beat a sturdy branch with a stick. Catch the insects that fall on a white sheet.

3

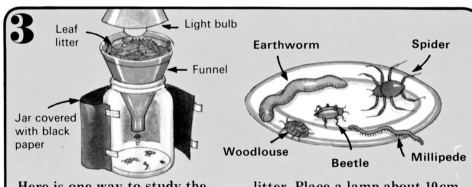

Leaf litter

Light bulb

Funnel

Jar covered with black paper

Earthworm

Spider

Woodlouse

Beetle

Millipede

Here is one way to study the animals which hide in the leaf litter on the ground. Take a large funnel (or make one out of tin foil), and place it in a jar. Cover the jar with black paper. Fill the funnel with damp leaf litter. Place a lamp about 10 cm above the leaves and switch it on. Wait a few hours. The heat and light from the lamp will drive the animals into the dark jar. You can take them out and study them.

Common Trees to Spot : Conifers

Lawson Cypress 25 m. Narrow shape. Drooping top shoot. Small, round cones. Common as hedge.

Western Red Cedar 30 m. Branches curve upwards. Tiny, flower-like cones. Hedges.

Yew 15 m. Dark green. Trunk gnarled. Bark reddish. Leaves and red-berried fruits poisonous.

Western Hemlock 35 m. Branches and top shoot droop. Small cones. Needles various lengths.

Norway Spruce 30 m. Christmas tree. Long, hanging cones. Parks, gardens, plantations.

Douglas Fir 40 m. Hanging, shaggy cones. Deep-ridged bark. Important timber tree.

European Silver Fir 40 m. Large, upright cones at top of tree. Parklands.

Scots Pine 35 m. Uneven crown. Bare trunk. Flaking bark. Common wild and planted.

Corsican Pine 36 m. Shape rounder and fuller than **Scots Pine**. Long, dark-green needles. Dark brown bark.

Blue Atlas Cedar 25 m. Broad shape. Barrel-shaped, upright cones. Blue-green needles. Parks.

European Larch 38 m. Upright cones egg-shaped. Soft, light-green needles fall off in winter.

Japanese Larch 35 m. Upright, rosette-like cones. Orange twigs. Blue-green needles fall off in winter.

Broadleaved Trees

Olive 10 m. Evergreen. Twisted grey trunk. Black edible fruits. Southern Europe.

Holm Oak 20 m. Evergreen. Shiny leaves resemble Holly. Grey bark. Parks and gardens.

Weeping Willow 20 m. Drooping shape. Near water and in gardens.

Japanese Cherry 9 m. Flowers April–May. Many varieties. Gardens and along streets.

Wild Cherry or **Gean** 15 m. Red-brown bark peels in ribbons. Flowers April–May. Fruits sour. Woods, thickets.

Almond 8 m. Flowers March–April before leaves. Edible nut inside green fruit. Gardens.

Holly 10 m. Evergreen. Leaves often variegated. Berries poisonous. Often shrub-like.

Sweet Chestnut 35 m. Spiral-ridged bark. Two edible nuts in prickly green case. Wide-spreading branches.

Crab Apple 10 m. Small tree. Flowers May. Fruits edible but sour. Wild in hedges and thickets.

Common Pear 15 m. Straight trunk. Flowers April–May. Edible fruits. Hedgerows and gardens.

Orange 9 m. Evergreen. Many varieties. Fragrant flowers in winter. Fruits edible. Southern Europe.

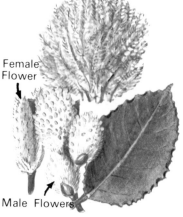

Goat or **Pussy Willow** 7 m. Catkins March–April. Separate male and female trees. Hedges and damp woodlands.

Broadleaved Trees

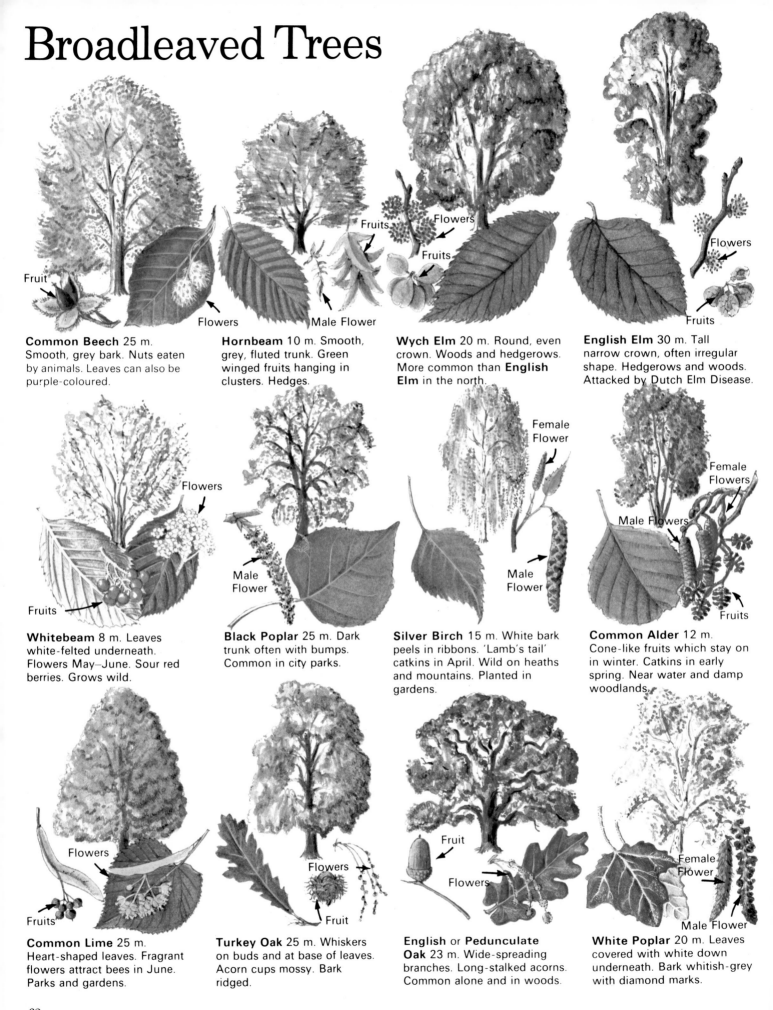

Common Beech 25 m. Smooth, grey bark. Nuts eaten by animals. Leaves can also be purple-coloured.

Fruit
Flowers

Hornbeam 10 m. Smooth, grey, fluted trunk. Green winged fruits hanging in clusters. Hedges.

Fruits
Male Flower

Wych Elm 20 m. Round, even crown. Woods and hedgerows. More common than **English Elm** in the north.

Flowers
Fruits

English Elm 30 m. Tall narrow crown, often irregular shape. Hedgerows and woods. Attacked by Dutch Elm Disease.

Flowers
Fruits

Whitebeam 8 m. Leaves white-felted underneath. Flowers May–June. Sour red berries. Grows wild.

Flowers
Fruits

Black Poplar 25 m. Dark trunk often with bumps. Common in city parks.

Male Flower

Silver Birch 15 m. White bark peels in ribbons. 'Lamb's tail' catkins in April. Wild on heaths and mountains. Planted in gardens.

Female Flower
Male Flower

Common Alder 12 m. Cone-like fruits which stay on in winter. Catkins in early spring. Near water and damp woodlands.

Female Flowers
Male Flowers
Fruits

Common Lime 25 m. Heart-shaped leaves. Fragrant flowers attract bees in June. Parks and gardens.

Flowers
Fruits

Turkey Oak 25 m. Whiskers on buds and at base of leaves. Acorn cups mossy. Bark ridged.

Flowers
Fruit

English or **Pedunculate Oak** 23 m. Wide-spreading branches. Long-stalked acorns. Common alone and in woods.

Fruit
Flowers

White Poplar 20 m. Leaves covered with white down underneath. Bark whitish-grey with diamond marks.

Female Flower
Male Flower

Tulip Tree 20 m. Tulip-like flowers June-July. Upright brown fruits. Parks, gardens.

Field Maple 10 m. Rounded crown. Narrow-ridged bark. Winged seeds almost form straight line. Hedges and woods.

Norway Maple 15 m. Seeds form wide angle. Autumn leaves colourful. Parks, streets.

Sycamore 20 m. Seeds form close angle. Smooth bark flakes off in plates. Parks, streets.

London Plane 30 m. Bark flakes off leaving white patches. Spiky fruits stay on in winter. City streets.

Fig 6 m. Flower inside a pear-shaped receptacle which becomes the fruit. Gardens.

Horse Chestnut 25 m. Compound leaves. Upright flowers May. Prickly fruits with 'conkers' inside.

Laburnum or **Golden Rain** 7 m. Compound leaves. Flowers May-June. Seeds poisonous. Gardens.

False Acacia or **Locust Tree** 20 m. Compound leaves. Ridged twigs spiny. Hanging flowers in June. Gardens, parks.

Walnut 15 m. Compound leaves. Deep-ridged bark. Hollow twigs. Edible nuts inside thick green fruits.

Rowan or **Mountain Ash** 7 m. Compound leaves. Flowers May. Sour orange berries September. Wild on mountains.

Common Ash 25 m. Compound leaves open late. Keys stay on in winter. Common in woods and parks.

Trees in Winter

Corsican
Pine

Norway
Spruce

Monkey
Puzzle
(Chile Pine)

Maidenhair
Tree
(Ginkgo)

Cedar of
Lebanon

Italian
Cypress

Strawberry
Tree

Big Tree
(Wellingtonia)

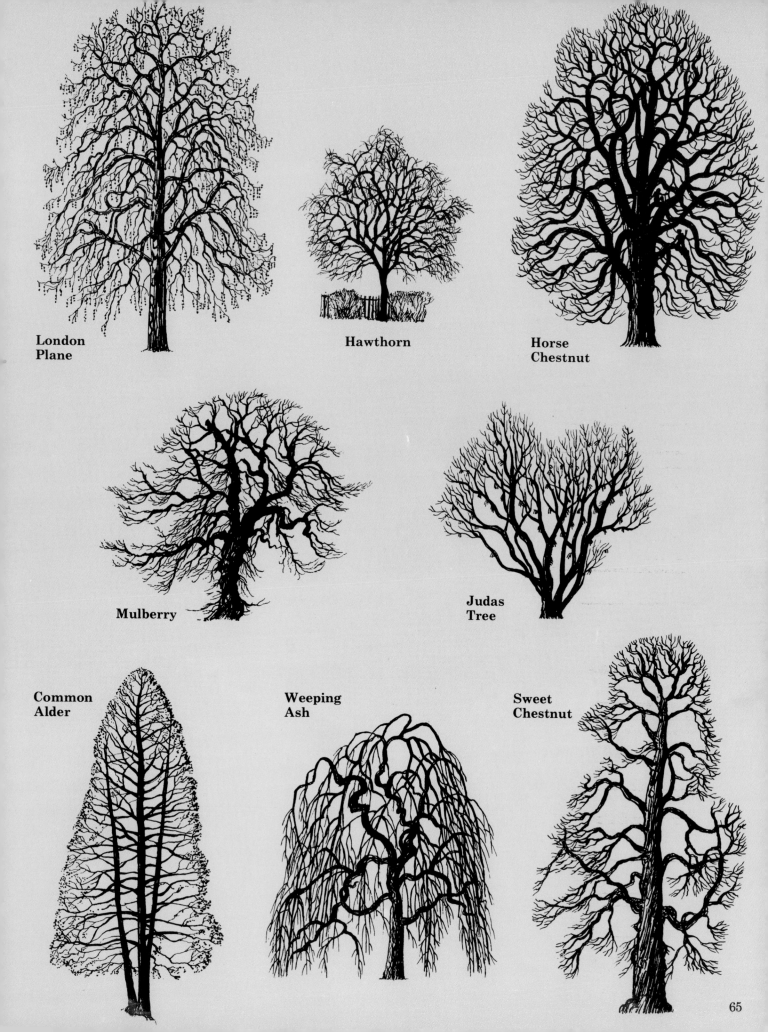

**London
Plane**

Hawthorn

**Horse
Chestnut**

Mulberry

**Judas
Tree**

**Common
Alder**

**Weeping
Ash**

**Sweet
Chestnut**

65

Foxglove

Marsh Marigold

Part 3 written by
Sue Tarsky

Consultant Editors
Sally Heathcote,
Jean Mellanby

**Wood
Anemone**

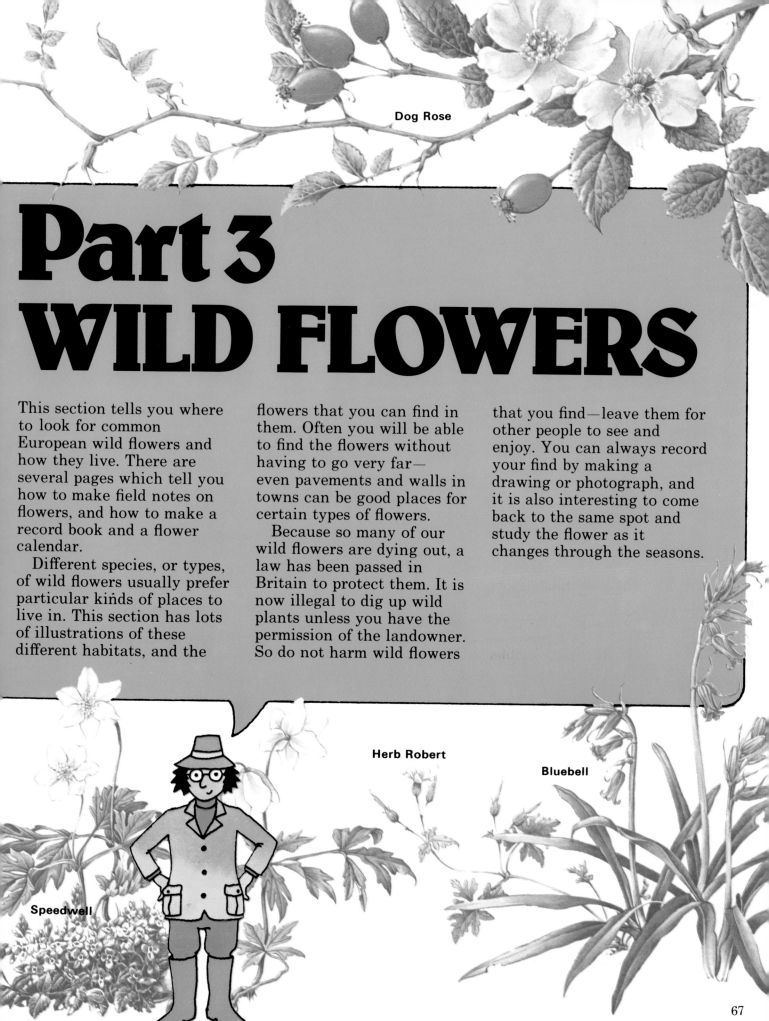

Dog Rose

Part 3
WILD FLOWERS

This section tells you where to look for common European wild flowers and how they live. There are several pages which tell you how to make field notes on flowers, and how to make a record book and a flower calendar.

Different species, or types, of wild flowers usually prefer particular kinds of places to live in. This section has lots of illustrations of these different habitats, and the

flowers that you can find in them. Often you will be able to find the flowers without having to go very far—even pavements and walls in towns can be good places for certain types of flowers.

Because so many of our wild flowers are dying out, a law has been passed in Britain to protect them. It is now illegal to dig up wild plants unless you have the permission of the landowner. So do not harm wild flowers

that you find—leave them for other people to see and enjoy. You can always record your find by making a drawing or photograph, and it is also interesting to come back to the same spot and study the flower as it changes through the seasons.

Herb Robert

Bluebell

Speedwell

Looking for Wild Flowers

When you go looking for wild flowers, take a notebook and two pencils with you for making quick sketches. Write down everything about a flower as soon as you see it. A magnifying glass is useful for looking at the small parts, and a tape measure for finding its height. Don't dig up flowers, and only pick them if you are sure they are common, and there are lots of the same kind growing together. Take sheets of newspaper to press the flowers. Use an outdoor thermometer to note the air temperature.

What You Need

Pencil

Notebook

Magnifying glass

Book with newspaper

Thermometer

Tape measure

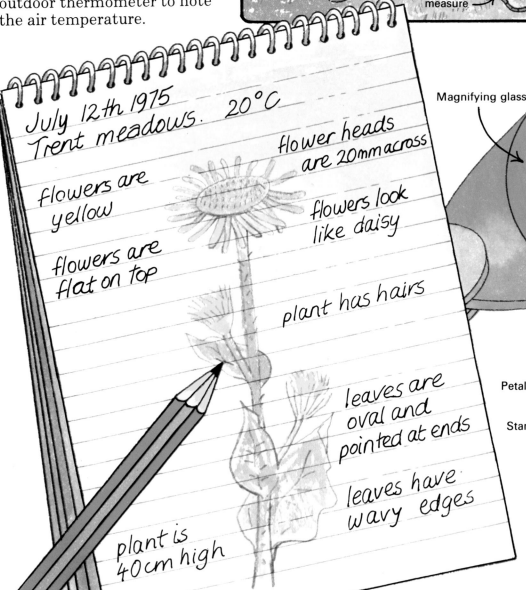

July 12th 1975
Trent meadows. 20°C

flowers are yellow

flower heads are 20mm across

flowers are flat on top

flowers look like daisy

plant has hairs

leaves are oval and pointed at ends

leaves have wavy edges

plant is 40cm high

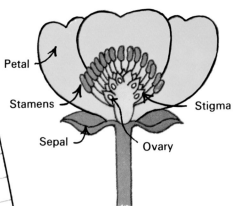

Magnifying glass

Petal

Stamens

Stigma

Sepal

Ovary

This is what the inside of a Buttercup looks like. Other flowers may look different. Try to draw what you see inside the flower you have found.

The three flowers shown on the right are very rare indeed. If you think you may have found a rare wild flower, do not pick it. If you do, it will die and be even more rare. Instead, draw the flower and show your drawing to an adult who knows about rare flowers.

If it is rare, you can report it to a conservation or nature club in your area. An expert may be able to gather some seeds when they fall from the flower and plant them carefully so that they will grow.

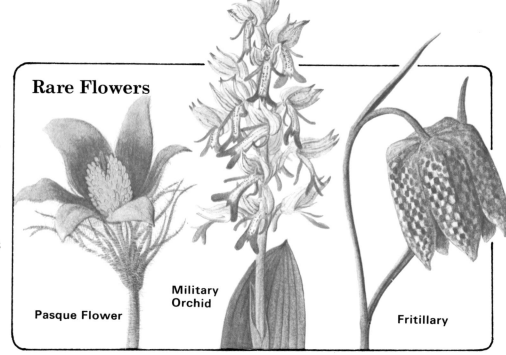

Rare Flowers

Pasque Flower

Military Orchid

Fritillary

Our Church

John's house

My school

My house

50 paces

Symbols for your map

⚘ FLOWERS

♇ WOODS

∿ STREAM

ⱳ GRASSLAND

⌂ HILLS

ⱳ MARSHES, WATER

▬ BRIDGE

⌂⌂ HOUSES

How to Make a Flower Map

The easiest way to make a map is to draw it as you walk along a route you know well. Draw lines for the road or path and make it turn in the same way that you do. Put in symbols for bridges, buildings and other special places. Wherever you find a wild flower, mark the place on your map with a star.

Draw the symbols and write what they stand for on the bottom of your map so that everyone can understand them. If you like, you can use a scale to show distance so that anyone can follow your map. You can choose any scale you want. This map shows that 2 cm. is equal to 50 paces.

How Plants Live

The Rosebay Willowherb and the Field Buttercup have flowers with petals and sepals, and also leaves, stems and roots. Most other plants have the same parts, but they are often different shapes and sizes.

Each part of the plant does at least one special thing that helps the plant to live. The leaves make food for the plant. During the day, they take in carbon dioxide, a gas in the air, and together with the green colouring of the leaves, water and sunlight, make food. The leaves take in gases and give out gases and water through holes that are so small that you cannot see them, even with a magnifying glass.

The flower is a very important part of the plant. It is here that the seeds grow.

The petals may be brightly coloured or scented to attract insects. Some flowers need insects to carry pollen to other flowers for pollination (see page 72), so the brighter the colours, the more insects the flower will attract.

The sepals protect the flower when it is in bud. When the flower opens, they lie underneath the petals. All the sepals together are called the calyx.

The leaves make food and "breathe" for the plant. They also get rid of any water that the plant does not need. Because leaves need light to make food, the whole plant grows towards light. Some plants close their leaves at night.

The stem carries water from the roots to the leaves, and carries food made in the leaves to the rest of the plant. It also holds the leaves up to the light.

Rosebay Willowherb

Field Buttercup

The roots hold the plant firmly in the ground, and take up water from the soil that the plant needs.

How to Recognize Flowers

Colour

The easiest thing to notice first about a flower is its colour. A few examples are shown below. But you should also look at the shape of its petals, sepals and leaves.

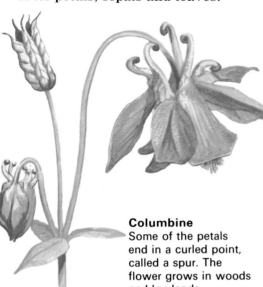

Columbine
Some of the petals end in a curled point, called a spur. The flower grows in woods and lowlands.

Bloody Cranesbill
The flowers are a bright purplish crimson and grow in dry, grassy places.

Bluebell
Bluebells are mostly blue, and sometimes white. They have a stalk with no leaves on it.

Petals

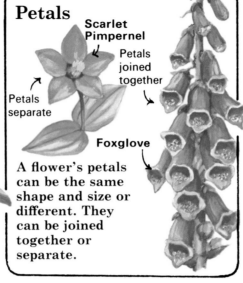

Scarlet Pimpernel

Petals separate

Petals joined together

Foxglove

A flower's petals can be the same shape and size or different. They can be joined together or separate.

Sepals

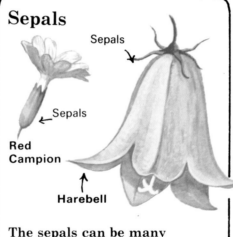

Sepals

Sepals

Red Campion

Harebell

The sepals can be many different shapes and sizes, joined together or separate.

Mouse-ear Hawkweed
The flowers are lemon-yellow and the plant has leafy runners which grow just above the ground.

Flowers and Stems

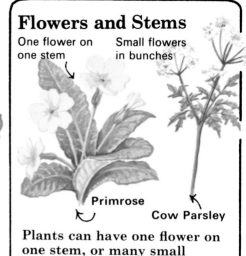

One flower on one stem

Small flowers in bunches

Primrose

Cow Parsley

Plants can have one flower on one stem, or many small flowers bunched together.

Leaves

Wood Anemone

Divided leaf, joined at base

Leaves can be single, as in the Bugle, or divided into separate parts. In the Wood Anemone, the separate parts are joined together at the base. Sometimes the parts are on little stalks on a larger stalk. These are called leaflets.

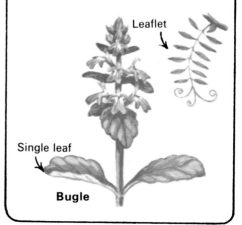

Leaflet

Single leaf

Bugle

How Flowers Grow

Almost every plant has a male part, called the stamen, and a female part, called the pistil. The Common Poppy has a group of stamens which grow around the pistil in the centre of the flower (see no. 3).

This page tells you how the stamens and the pistil in a Poppy together make seeds, which will later leave the plant and grow to form new plants. Not all plants make seeds in this way, but many do.

1

In the spring the new plant grows from a seed buried in the ground. There may be several flowers on one plant.

Bud

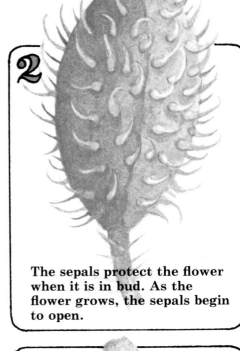

2

The sepals protect the flower when it is in bud. As the flower grows, the sepals begin to open.

6

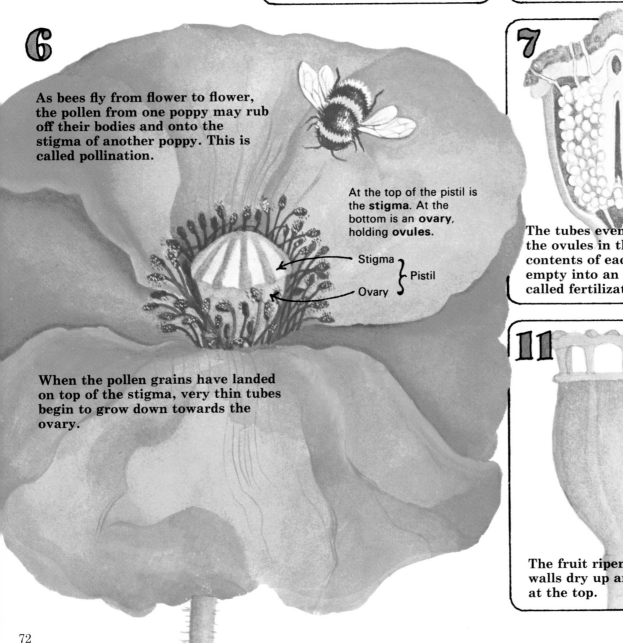

As bees fly from flower to flower, the pollen from one poppy may rub off their bodies and onto the stigma of another poppy. This is called pollination.

At the top of the pistil is the **stigma**. At the bottom is an **ovary**, holding **ovules**.

Stigma
Pistil
Ovary

When the pollen grains have landed on top of the stigma, very thin tubes begin to grow down towards the ovary.

7

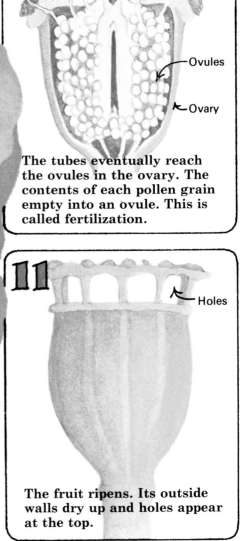

Pollen tube

Ovules

Ovary

The tubes eventually reach the ovules in the ovary. The contents of each pollen grain empty into an ovule. This is called fertilization.

11

Holes

The fruit ripens. Its outside walls dry up and holes appear at the top.

3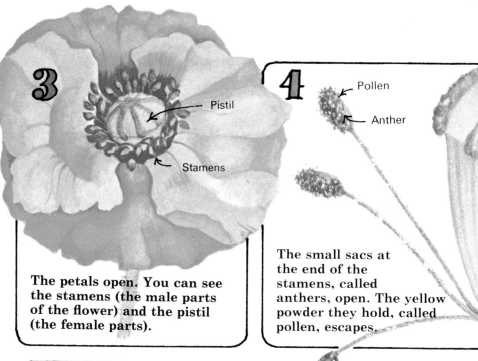

Pistil

Stamens

The petals open. You can see the stamens (the male parts of the flower) and the pistil (the female parts).

4

Pollen

Anther

The small sacs at the end of the stamens, called anthers, open. The yellow powder they hold, called pollen, escapes.

5

Bees visit the flower to feed. Pollen grains accidentally rub off on their hairy bodies or on their legs.

8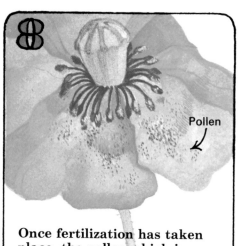

Pollen

Once fertilization has taken place, the pollen which is left is no longer needed, and it falls off.

9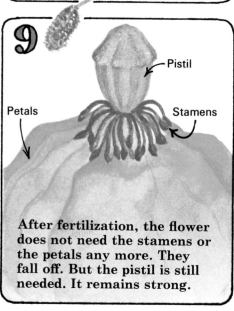

Pistil

Petals

Stamens

After fertilization, the flower does not need the stamens or the petals any more. They fall off. But the pistil is still needed. It remains strong.

10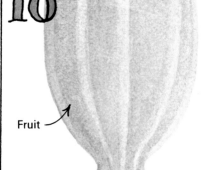

Fruit

Inside the pistil, the fertilized ovules are growing to form seeds. They are attached to the inside walls of the ovary. At this stage, the ovary is called the fruit.

12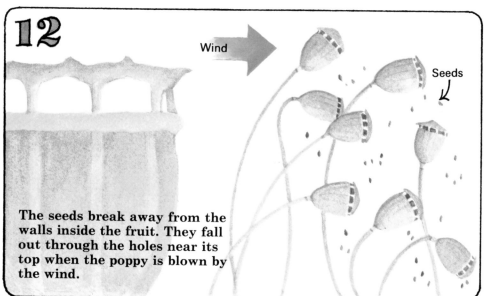

Wind

Seeds

The seeds break away from the walls inside the fruit. They fall out through the holes near its top when the poppy is blown by the wind.

The seeds which fall out of the fruit onto the soil in the autumn may grow into new plants the next spring.

How Pollen is Spread

In some plants, pollen from the stamens of one flower can make seeds grow in the ovary of the same flower. This is called self-pollination. In other plants, pollen must go from a flower of one plant to a flower of the same kind on a different plant. This is called cross-pollination. Pollen from a rose cannot make a seed grow in a daisy.

Most plants need insects to carry pollen, but some use the wind. Insects may go to a flower because of its scent or coloured petals. Some flowers have spots or lines on their petals called nectar guides. The insects follow these paths to find nectar.

Sometimes they must brush past the pollen, which sticks to their bodies. When they visit another flower, the pollen rubs off on the stigma.

Sometimes in summer the air is full of pollen, because the wind carries it from wind-pollinated flowers. It can make people sneeze, and give them hay-fever.

1 By Insects

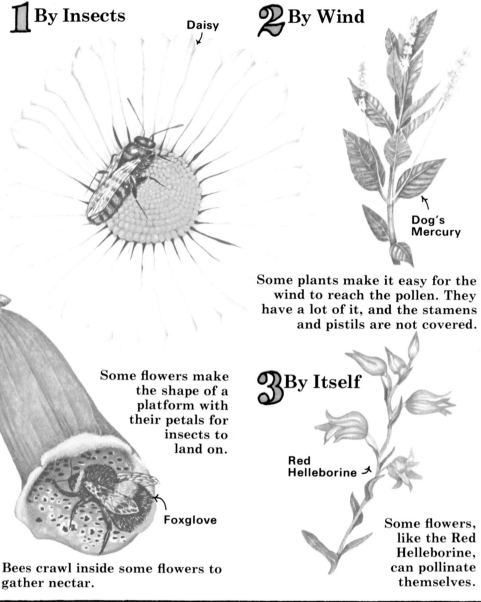

Daisy

Some flowers make the shape of a platform with their petals for insects to land on.

Foxglove

Bees crawl inside some flowers to gather nectar.

2 By Wind

Dog's Mercury

Some plants make it easy for the wind to reach the pollen. They have a lot of it, and the stamens and pistils are not covered.

3 By Itself

Red Helleborine

Some flowers, like the Red Helleborine, can pollinate themselves.

What Plants Need
Wild flowers need to grow, spread their pollen, and make sure that their seeds are carried away from the parent plant. To do these things, they often depend on the weather, the soil and other living creatures — even people.

SOME PLANTS NEED INSECTS TO CARRY POLLEN

PLANTS NEED A BALANCE OF WATER AND MINERAL SALTS IN THE SOIL TO HELP THEM GROW AND FLOWER

PLANTS NEED CERTAIN TEMPERATURES, WHETHER THEY GROW IN COOL OR HOT PLACES. MOST EUROPEAN FLOWERS BLOOM WHEN IT IS WARM

PLANTS NEED LIGHT TO MAKE FOOD FOR THEMSELVES AND TO GROW

74

How Seeds are Scattered

Plants cannot produce seeds until they have been pollinated. Then they scatter seeds in different ways. Some use the wind, some use animals, some use water and some scatter their seeds themselves. They produce seeds that will be spread easily in at least one way. New plants need light to grow, so seeds grow best away from their parent plant, which might otherwise shadow them.

By Animals

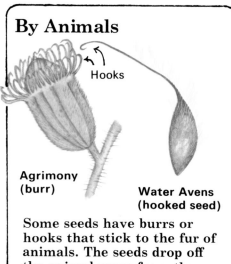

Hooks

Agrimony (burr)

Water Avens (hooked seed)

Some seeds have burrs or hooks that stick to the fur of animals. The seeds drop off the animal away from the parent plant.

By Wind

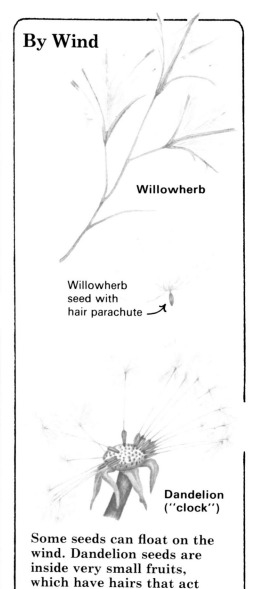

Willowherb

Willowherb seed with hair parachute

Dandelion ("clock")

Some seeds can float on the wind. Dandelion seeds are inside very small fruits, which have hairs that act like parachutes.

By Water

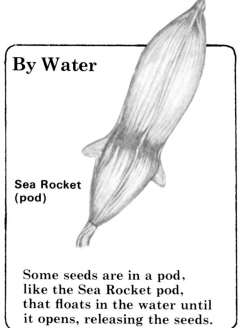

Sea Rocket (pod)

Some seeds are in a pod, like the Sea Rocket pod, that floats in the water until it opens, releasing the seeds.

By Explosion

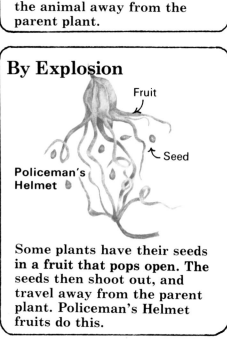

Fruit

Seed

Policeman's Helmet

Some plants have their seeds in a fruit that pops open. The seeds then shoot out, and travel away from the parent plant. Policeman's Helmet fruits do this.

SOME PLANTS NEED WATER TO CARRY SEEDS AWAY FROM THE PARENT PLANT

BIRDS MAY FLY FAR FROM WHERE THEY EAT FRUITS. THE SEEDS PASS THROUGH THEIR BODIES AND FALL ON THE GROUND

ANIMALS CARRY SEEDS AND NUTS AND DROP THEM AWAY FROM THE PARENT PLANT

PEOPLE OFTEN SPREAD SEEDS WITHOUT KNOW-ING. THEY GET SEEDS IN THE SOLES OF THEIR SHOES

Flower Record Book

Keep a record book of everything you discover about wild flowers. If you use a loose-leaf binder, you can add pages whenever you wish. This is a perfect place to put any maps you have made, or even any photographs you have taken. Remember—anything to do with wild flowers belongs in your record book. Take down the results of your experiments in your book. Draw each step of an experiment as it happens. Write down what you see happening.

A Simple Experiment

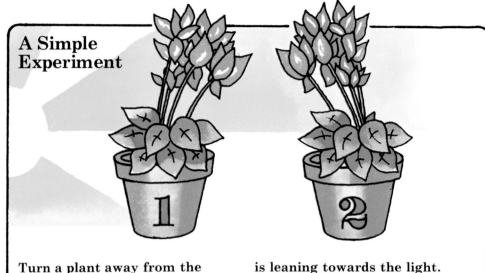

Turn a plant away from the light. Come back a few days later. You will see that the plant is leaning towards the light. It is growing towards it because it needs light to make food.

1 Pressing and Mounting

If you pick a common flower you can press it. Put it between two sheets of blotting paper. Rest some heavy books on top.

2

When the flower is completely dry, put a dab of glue on the stem. Stick it carefully to the inside of a clear plastic bag, so you can see both sides.

3

If you find any flower heads on the ground, put them in the plastic bag, too. Stick the bag to a page in your book with sticky tape. Write the name of the flower if you know it and the date and place where you found it.

Common Mallow
Found in a grassy field on July 26th.

1 Leaf Printing

Put a leaf onto a flat surface with its underside facing you.

2

Cover it with a piece of thin white paper. Rub back and forth over the paper with a coloured crayon until the shape and veins show through.

3

Stick your leaf prints into your record book.

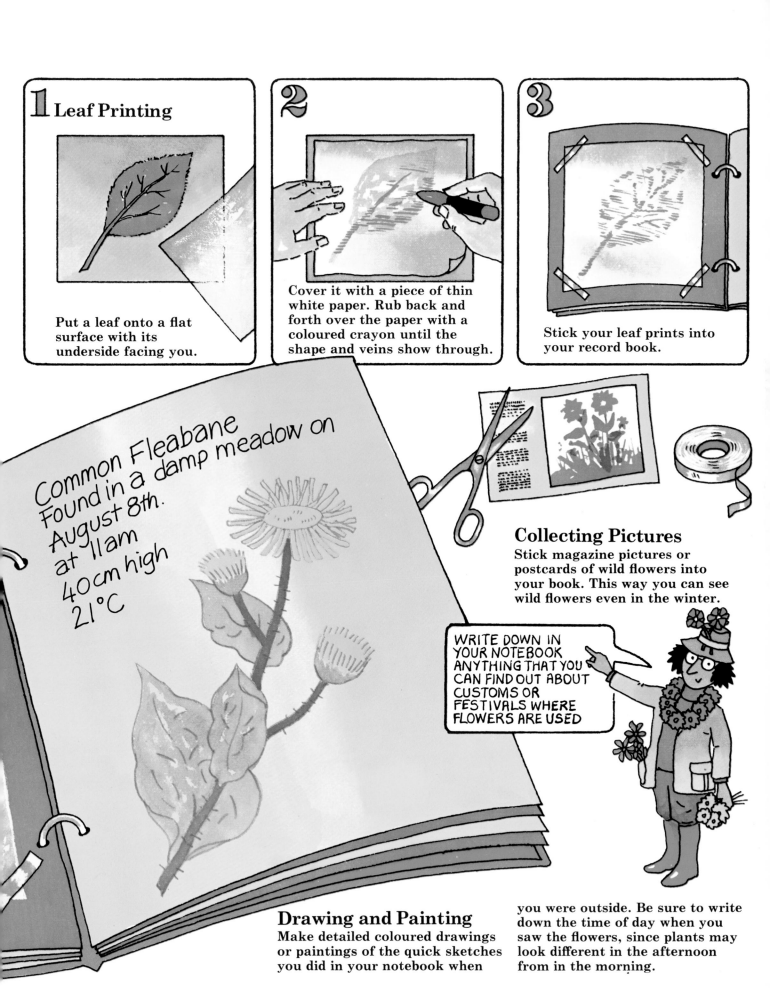

Common Fleabane
Found in a damp meadow on
August 8th.
at 11am
40cm high
21°C

Collecting Pictures
Stick magazine pictures or postcards of wild flowers into your book. This way you can see wild flowers even in the winter.

WRITE DOWN IN YOUR NOTEBOOK ANYTHING THAT YOU CAN FIND OUT ABOUT CUSTOMS OR FESTIVALS WHERE FLOWERS ARE USED

Drawing and Painting
Make detailed coloured drawings or paintings of the quick sketches you did in your notebook when you were outside. Be sure to write down the time of day when you saw the flowers, since plants may look different in the afternoon from in the morning.

Flower Calendar

You can see different flowers blooming in each season of the year. Make a calendar to help you remember them all. You can also see how a flower changes as the seasons change. Draw it once when it blooms and then draw it again a few months later.

The pictures of the Arum on the right show how different a flower can look at various stages in its life. (Two of the pictures show the inside of the flower.)

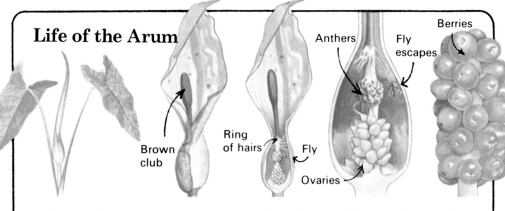

Life of the Arum

Anthers   Fly escapes   Berries

Brown club   Ring of hairs   Fly   Ovaries

At first, the Arum is green. When the flower opens, it has a brown club. This attracts flies with its smell, and they get trapped inside by a ring of hairs.

They drop pollen on the ovaries. The hairs wither and the flies escape. In autumn, the ovaries develop into very poisonous red berries.

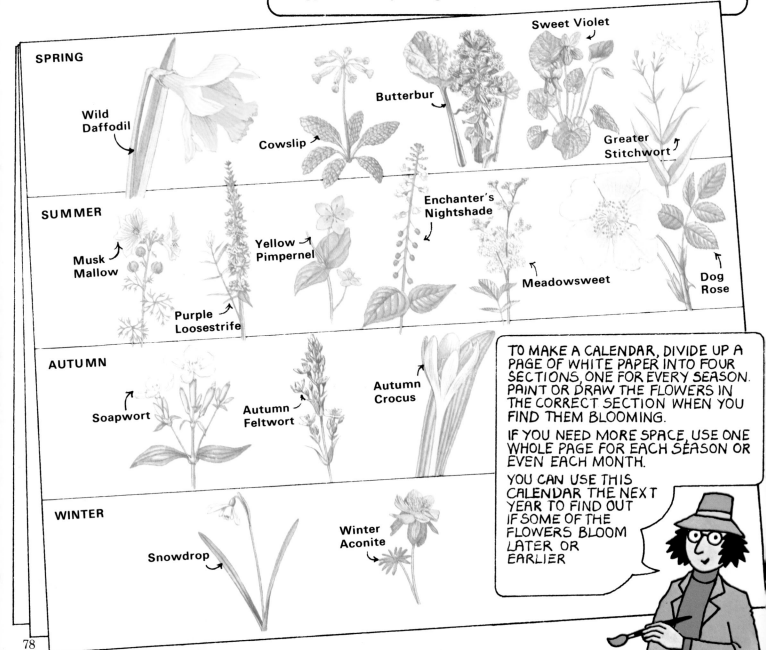

SPRING

Wild Daffodil   Cowslip   Butterbur   Sweet Violet   Greater Stitchwort

SUMMER

Musk Mallow   Purple Loosestrife   Yellow Pimpernel   Enchanter's Nightshade   Meadowsweet   Dog Rose

AUTUMN

Soapwort   Autumn Feltwort   Autumn Crocus

WINTER

Snowdrop   Winter Aconite

TO MAKE A CALENDAR, DIVIDE UP A PAGE OF WHITE PAPER INTO FOUR SECTIONS, ONE FOR EVERY SEASON. PAINT OR DRAW THE FLOWERS IN THE CORRECT SECTION WHEN YOU FIND THEM BLOOMING.

IF YOU NEED MORE SPACE, USE ONE WHOLE PAGE FOR EACH SEASON OR EVEN EACH MONTH.

YOU CAN USE THIS CALENDAR THE NEXT YEAR TO FIND OUT IF SOME OF THE FLOWERS BLOOM LATER OR EARLIER

Rivers and Ponds

Look for plants in different places near fresh water. If they grow in the water, they may be rooted to the bottom or have their roots floating. Their leaves may be under the water or floating on top of it. If plants are growing on the land, they may be at the water's edge, on the banks, or in swamps. Most water plants have their flowers above the surface of the water. They are usually pollinated by insects or wind, not by water.

Yellow Iris

The Yellow Iris has unusual petals and the leaves are very stiff and pointed. Look for stripes on the petals—they are nectar guides.

Frogbit

The Frogbit has shoots that grow sideways. New plants grow upwards from these shoots.

Duckweed

Duckweed can grow to cover a whole pond. It floats on top of still water.

Reedmace

Anthers

Seeds

The seeds of the Reedmace have silky parachutes that the wind carries. You can pick the flower for decoration, as this plant grows in large groups. Let them dry at home and then, if you wish, paint them.

Water Lily

The petals of the Water Lily give shade to pond creatures in hot weather. They can rest on the broad, thick leaves.

Policeman's Helmet

This flower has its seeds in a fruit. When the seeds are fully grown, the fruit explodes if anything touches it. You can collect these seeds in the late summer and plant them in the spring.

Pod

The Leaves of Water Plants

The leaves of plants growing in the water are of all shapes and sizes. They can be oval, round, short or long. This is because some grow under still water, some grow under fast-moving water and others grow on top of the water.

The Water Crowfoot has broad leaves above the water and thread-like leaves below the water.

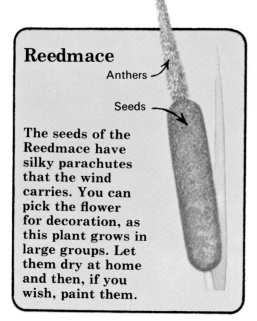
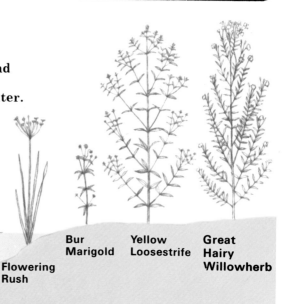

Spiked Water Milfoil

Water Soldier

Great Bladderwort

Water Crowfoot

Amphibious Bistort

Flowering Rush

Bur Marigold

Yellow Loosestrife

Great Hairy Willowherb

Fields, Meadows and Marshes

Fields vary from place to place and so do the flowers that grow in them. Fields can be used for pasturing animals or for growing crops. Meadows are used for growing hay, and marshes are grassy areas which are waterlogged all, or almost all, of the time.

You will find different flowers in different kinds of field, meadow or marsh, depending on what the area is used for, and how wet or dry the soil is. Wet soil is rich in many things that plants need, so you will usually find a lot of flowers.

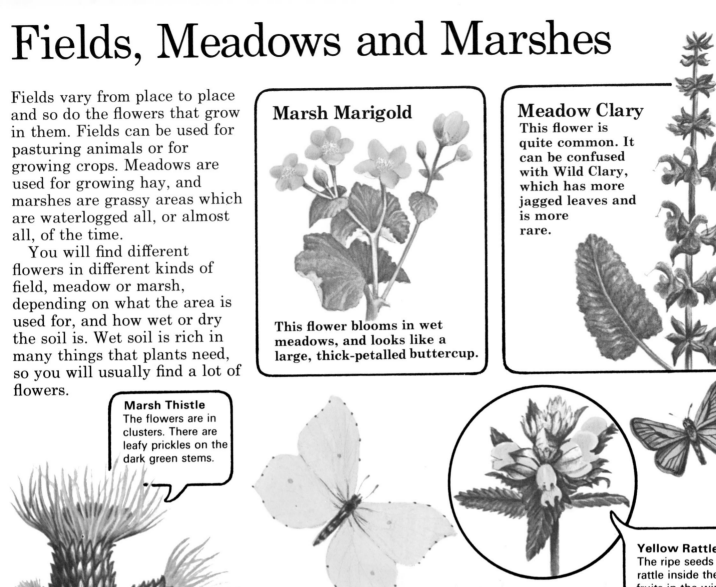

Marsh Marigold

This flower blooms in wet meadows, and looks like a large, thick-petalled buttercup.

Meadow Clary
This flower is quite common. It can be confused with Wild Clary, which has more jagged leaves and is more rare.

Marsh Thistle
The flowers are in clusters. There are leafy prickles on the dark green stems.

Yellow Rattle
The ripe seeds rattle inside their fruits in the wind.

Common Comfrey
The flowers are bell-shaped and hanging. You can make tea from the leaves.

Red Clover
The flower heads are made up of dozens of sweet-smelling flowers.

Wild Pansy
The flowers are violet or yellow, or a mixture of both colours.

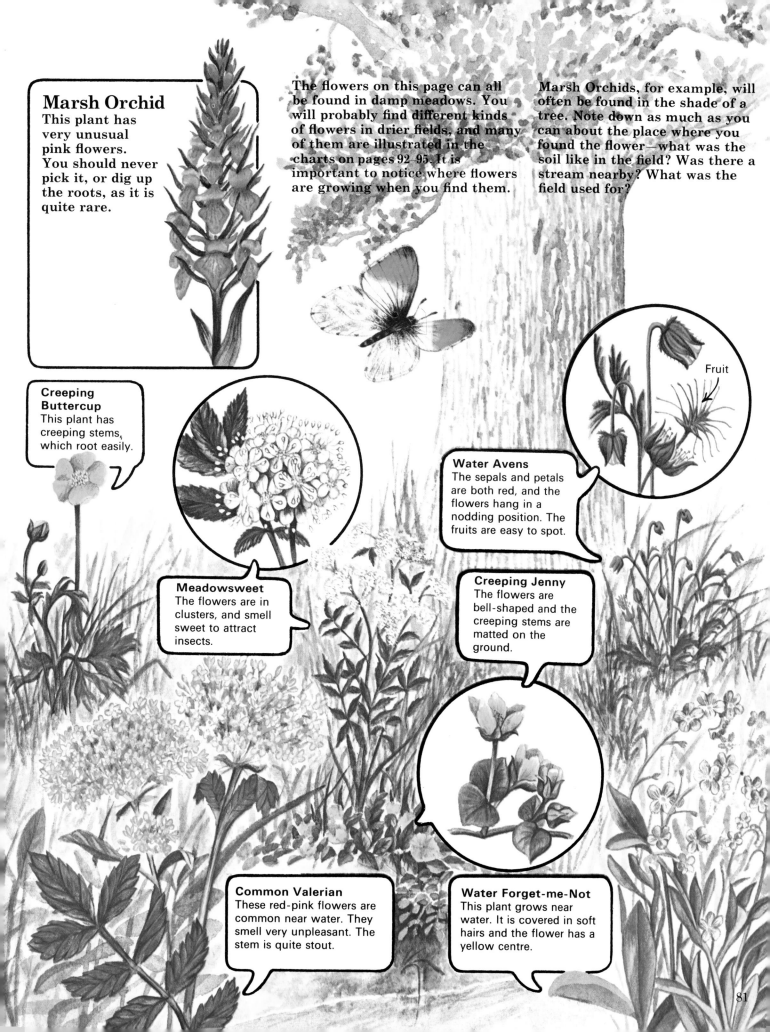

Marsh Orchid
This plant has very unusual pink flowers. You should never pick it, or dig up the roots, as it is quite rare.

The flowers on this page can all be found in damp meadows. You will probably find different kinds of flowers in drier fields, and many of them are illustrated in the charts on pages 92-95. It is important to notice where flowers are growing when you find them.

Marsh Orchids, for example, will often be found in the shade of a tree. Note down as much as you can about the place where you found the flower—what was the soil like in the field? Was there a stream nearby? What was the field used for?

Fruit

Creeping Buttercup
This plant has creeping stems, which root easily.

Water Avens
The sepals and petals are both red, and the flowers hang in a nodding position. The fruits are easy to spot.

Meadowsweet
The flowers are in clusters, and smell sweet to attract insects.

Creeping Jenny
The flowers are bell-shaped and the creeping stems are matted on the ground.

Common Valerian
These red-pink flowers are common near water. They smell very unpleasant. The stem is quite stout.

Water Forget-me-Not
This plant grows near water. It is covered in soft hairs and the flower has a yellow centre.

81

Hedgerows and Roadsides

A hedgerow is a line of scrub or bushes planted by man, but often other bushes start to grow in between the planted ones. Hedgerows are important because many plants, animals and birds live in them. As fields are mown or ploughed up, living things look for shelter and food there. Many hedges have been destroyed, but people are now trying to save the ones that remain.

Hedges provide shade and shelter for flowers. Look for plants that have grown from seeds trapped in the hedge. They are blown there by the wind.

Flowers growing at the roadside must be tough and strong. They have car exhaust fumes blown at them and litter dumped on them. Only plants that have learned how to spread and grow survive.

Dog Rose
Birds eat the red fruits, called rose hips.

Wild Clematis
The fruits have long white hairs.

Cow Parsley
The flowers form a landing platform for insects.

Honeysuckle
The flowers are pollinated at night by moths.

Greater Burdock
The fruits of this plant stick to the fur of animals.

Stinging Nettle
There are stinging hairs around the edge of the leaves The flowers are green.

Teasel
In winter, teasels are brown and brittle.

Foxglove
These flowers are very poisonous. Do not touch them.

Dandelion
The seeds form a feathery "clock", and float away when you blow them.

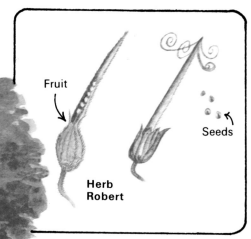

Fruit

Seeds

Herb Robert

Look for the fruit of the Herb Robert. When the seeds are fully grown, the fruit explodes, and the seeds shoot out.

Stinging Nettle

Tortoiseshell Butterfly

The Small Tortoiseshell butterfly lays its eggs on the leaves of the Stinging Nettle. If you find any eggs, do not touch them.

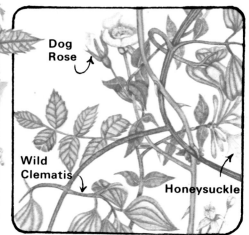

Dog Rose

Wild Clematis

Honeysuckle

Wild Clematis and Honeysuckle twine themselves round the Dog Rose. It has backward-pointing thorns like hooks, to help it climb.

Make a Scent Jar

Make a scent jar from the petals of any flowers whose smell you like. The Dog Rose, Honeysuckle and Wild Strawberry are good flowers to use. You can put them in a jar or sew little bags from scraps of fabric. Be sure to leave one side of the bag open until you have put the dried petals inside.

Put the petals between two sheets of blotting paper and press them under a pile of books. With a pencil, punch holes in a circle of tin foil to

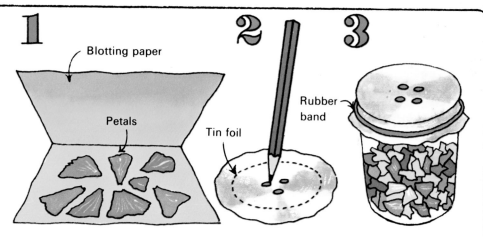

1

Blotting paper

Petals

2

Tin foil

3

Rubber band

make the lid. When the petals are dry, put them in the jar with some pieces of dried

orange and lemon peel, and a bay leaf. Fix the foil lid over the jar with a rubber band.

Creeping Cinquefoil
The creeping stems are called runners.

Greater Stitchwort
The delicate stem is square, not round.

Bird's-foot Trefoil

Wild Strawberry
You can eat the fruits.

Herb Robert
The flowers droop at night or in bad weather.

Coltsfoot
The seeds form a feathery "clock" like the dandelion's.

Woodlands

When you see big and healthy trees in woods, you may find that there are not many flowers beneath them. The roots of the trees are probably taking almost all the food from the soil and their leaves are blocking the sunlight from reaching the flowers. Some wild flowers that grow in woods bloom in early spring. This is before the leaves on the trees are fully out. The kinds of flowers you will find change with the type of wood you are in and the seasons. Remember to look at the edge of woods. There is enough sunlight there for flowers to grow. See for yourself how many flowers grow near the edge and how many grow where it is very shady. How much of the ground in a wood is covered with flowers?

OAK WOODS
OAK TREES MAY GROW TO BE VERY LARGE. IF THEY DO, VERY LITTLE LIGHT FILTERS DOWN BENEATH THEIR LEAVES. EVEN THE GRASSES NEARBY WOULD NOT GROW VERY HIGH. A GOOD PLACE TO SEARCH FOR FLOWERS IN AN OAK WOOD IS NEAR PATHS AT THE EDGE OF THE WOOD

BEECH WOODS
BEECH TREES GROW BEST WHERE THE SOIL DOES NOT HOLD MUCH WATER. THE FLOWERS YOU WILL FIND IN A BEECH WOOD ALSO PREFER SOIL THAT IS NOT TOO WET. SEE IF THE FLOWERS YOU FIND IN A BEECH WOOD ARE DIFFERENT FROM THOSE IN AN OAK WOOD

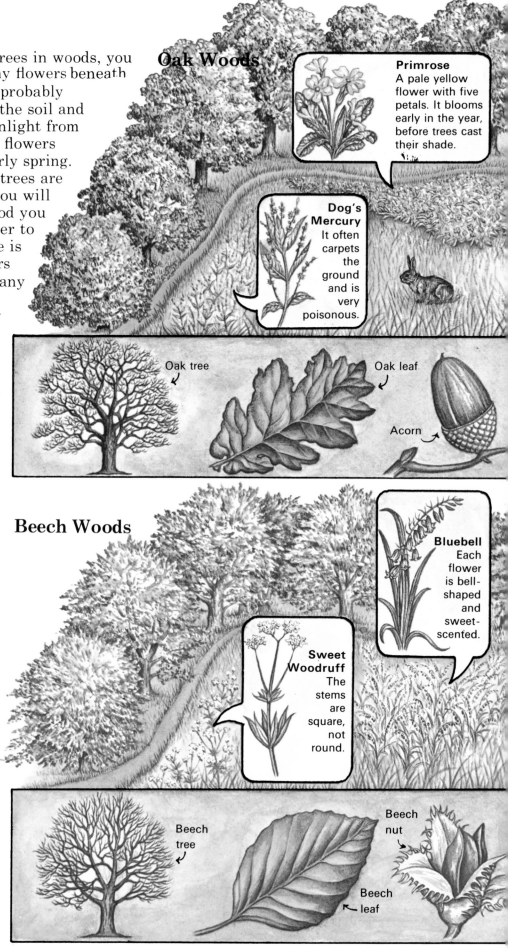

Oak Woods

Primrose
A pale yellow flower with five petals. It blooms early in the year, before trees cast their shade.

Dog's Mercury
It often carpets the ground and is very poisonous.

Oak tree

Oak leaf

Acorn

Beech Woods

Bluebell
Each flower is bell-shaped and sweet-scented.

Sweet Woodruff
The stems are square, not round.

Beech tree

Beech leaf

Beech nut

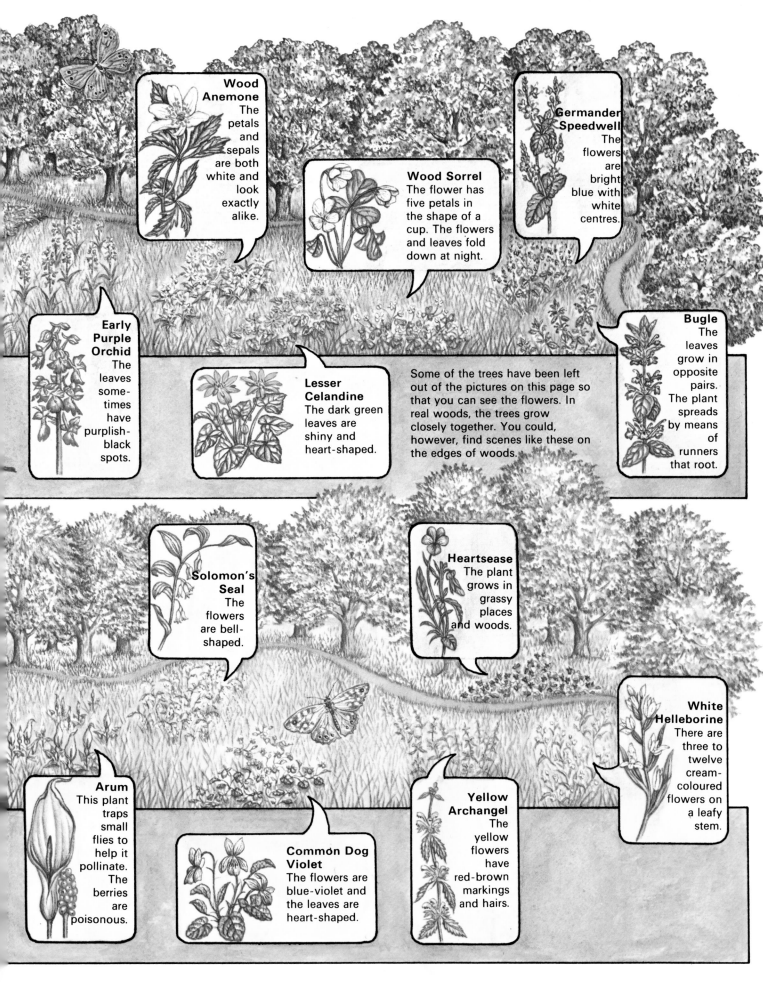

85

The Seashore

Plants near the sea must learn how to survive. They must find ways to get water and then stop it escaping. To do this, some plants grow a thick outer layer to trap the water, while others have a waxy coat over their leaves, or roll up their leaves when it is very hot and sunny.

Some plants have hairs on their leaves which shield them from the sun and other plants have very small leaves, or grow spines instead of leaves, so that water cannot escape.

Plants must be sturdy enough not to blow over in strong winds. They may have deep roots to grip the mud or stones. The roots also take up water.

Salt Marshes

Salt-Marshes are made of sand and mud. Be careful when you walk there. It is very easy to sink in. Go with a friend and wear rubber boots. The land in such places has slowly taken over from the sea. That is why the soil is salty.

There are different zones in marshes. Different plants grow in each zone. You will probably not find the plants that grow in marshes further inland.

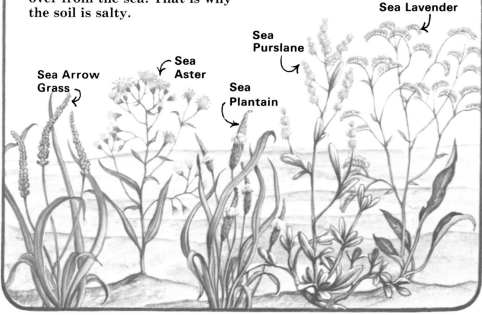

Sea Arrow Grass · Sea Aster · Sea Plantain · Sea Purslane · Sea Lavender

Sand Dunes

There are also different zones of sand dunes. They vary according to how far they are from the sea, and how much they have been built up or "fixed" by the growth of marram grass or other plants.

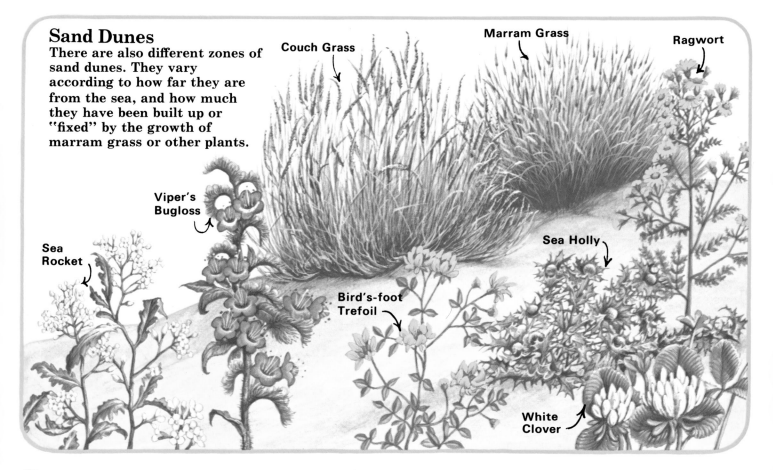

Couch Grass · Marram Grass · Ragwort · Viper's Bugloss · Sea Rocket · Bird's-foot Trefoil · Sea Holly · White Clover

Shingle Beaches

Not many plants can grow here. These beaches are made of pebbles that once were part of cliffs or rocks. They have been worn down by the pounding of the sea. There is some sand mixed in with the pebbles, but in many places they are constantly shifting. Plants like the Yellow Horned Poppy and the Sea Pea have deep roots that give them some anchorage in the shingle.

Shrubby Seablite

Sea Pea

Sea Bindweed

Yellow Horned Poppy

Cliffs

Plants must struggle to grow here. The wind blows almost all the time and tears up small plants whose roots are not deep. The water drains away quickly, leaving little for the plants and there is almost no soil. The plants must send their roots deep into cracks in the rock.

They sometimes grow along the steep angles of the cliff and are often sprayed with salty water from the sea. Sometimes cliffs have some soil towards the top where you will be able to find land plants.

Be careful when you look at flowers here. Do not climb any cliffs, and keep well back from the edge.

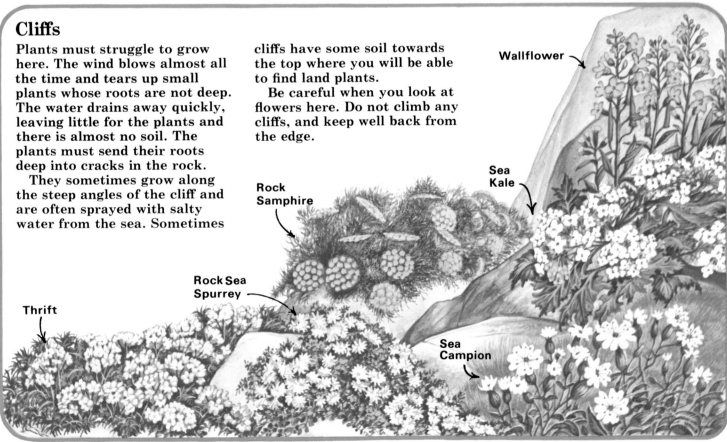

Wallflower

Sea Kale

Rock Samphire

Rock Sea Spurrey

Thrift

Sea Campion

Towns

Flowers grow in waste lands, walls, streets, car parks, gardens, churchyards or any other places in towns where they can find enough soil. Many flowers have learned how to spread in open ground. Some of these flowers are called weeds. Weeds are a problem to people growing other plants, because they take over the land. Many of the seeds of weed plants are spread by the wind, and some by water.

Seed Experiment

Heat some soil in an old pan in the stove to kill any seeds in the soil. Put the pan of soil outside. Do wild flowers start to grow? If so, how do you think they got there?

Ivy-leaved Toadflax
The plant is delicate and trailing, with tiny purple flowers, which have curved spurs. The stems are weak.

Common Toadflax
Each flower has an orange spot on the lower lip and a spur (a horn-shaped tube growing from a petal).

Spur

Rosebay Willowherb
The flowers have four bright pink petals, and the seeds have silky white hairs. It blooms June to September.

Golden Rod
The bright yellow flower heads are made up of dozens of tiny flowers. The seeds have hair parachutes.

Evening Primrose
The flower came originally from America and now grows wild in all parts of Europe.

Wild Chamomile
The plant spreads over wide areas, and has a nice smell when crushed. The petals may point down.

White Campion
This flower is pollinated by moths at night, and the plant has sticky hairs on it.

Oxford Ragwort
The leaves are toothed and the flower heads grow in clusters. The plant grows on bare or waste ground.

Daisy
One of the commonest European flowers. It also grows in short grass in fields. The flowers close up at night.

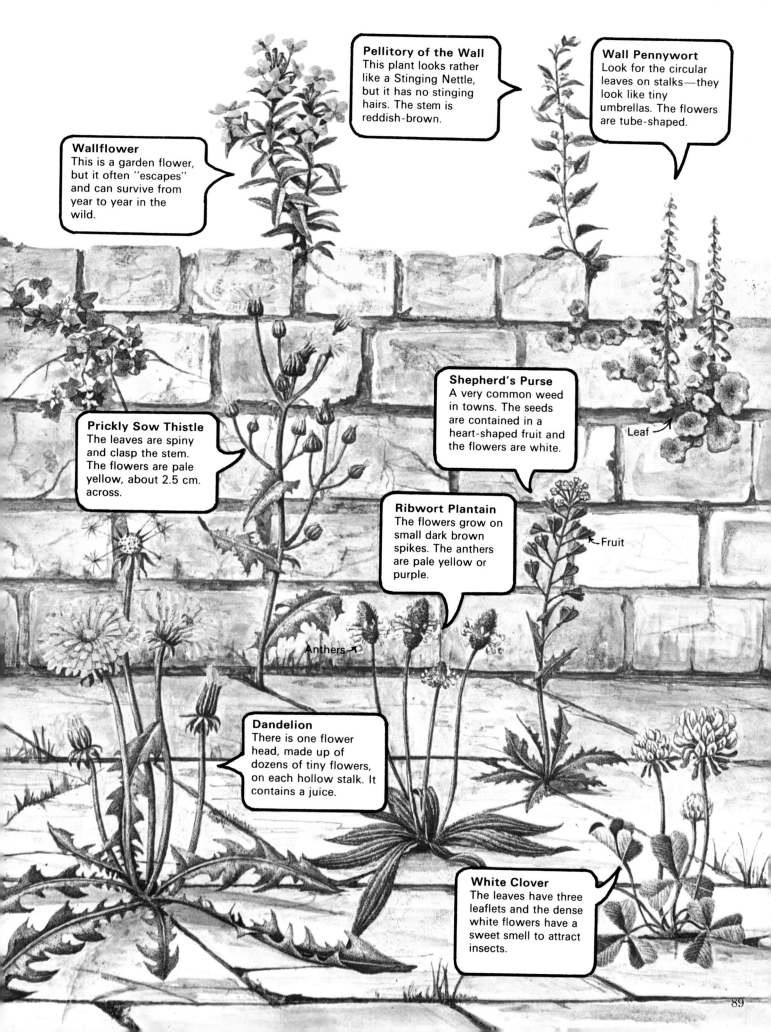

Moors and Mountains

Moors

There are fewer wild flowers that you will find growing on heaths and moors than in fields or meadows. The ones that are able to grow sometimes take over large areas of moorland.

Both heaths and moors are open lands that are swept by wind. Some are very dry and some are waterlogged from time to time. Water collects where the soil is very poor, such as in high land, or areas near the coast.

Different flowers grow on different types of moorland and heath. The most common plant of moorland is heather. It is sometimes burnt to encourage new shoots to grow.

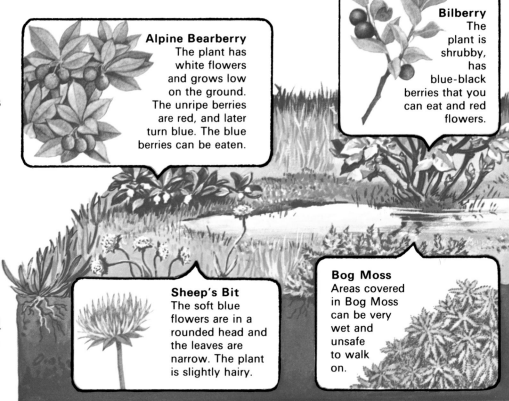

Alpine Bearberry
The plant has white flowers and grows low on the ground. The unripe berries are red, and later turn blue. The blue berries can be eaten.

Bilberry
The plant is shrubby, has blue-black berries that you can eat and red flowers.

Sheep's Bit
The soft blue flowers are in a rounded head and the leaves are narrow. The plant is slightly hairy.

Bog Moss
Areas covered in Bog Moss can be very wet and unsafe to walk on.

Mountains

The seeds of mountain flowers find it difficult to grow in the poor soils and cold, windy weather of mountain-sides. The higher up a mountain you go, the fewer flowers you will find growing. Trees cannot grow high up on mountains because of the strong winds and lack of soil.

Some plants, however, can grow high up the mountain-side. They are low ones that will not be blown away by high winds. Many flowers that grow on mountains spread by sending out creeping runner shoots which root.

Common Heather (Ling)
The plant usually takes over the area in which it grows. Its leaves are in opposite pairs and the flowers are pale purple. The plant also grows on moors and heaths and blooms in August.

Alpine Fleabane
The flowers have yellow centres with pale purple rays around them. The plant is short and hairy.

Common Butterwort
The leaves are broad and their edges roll up to trap and digest insects.

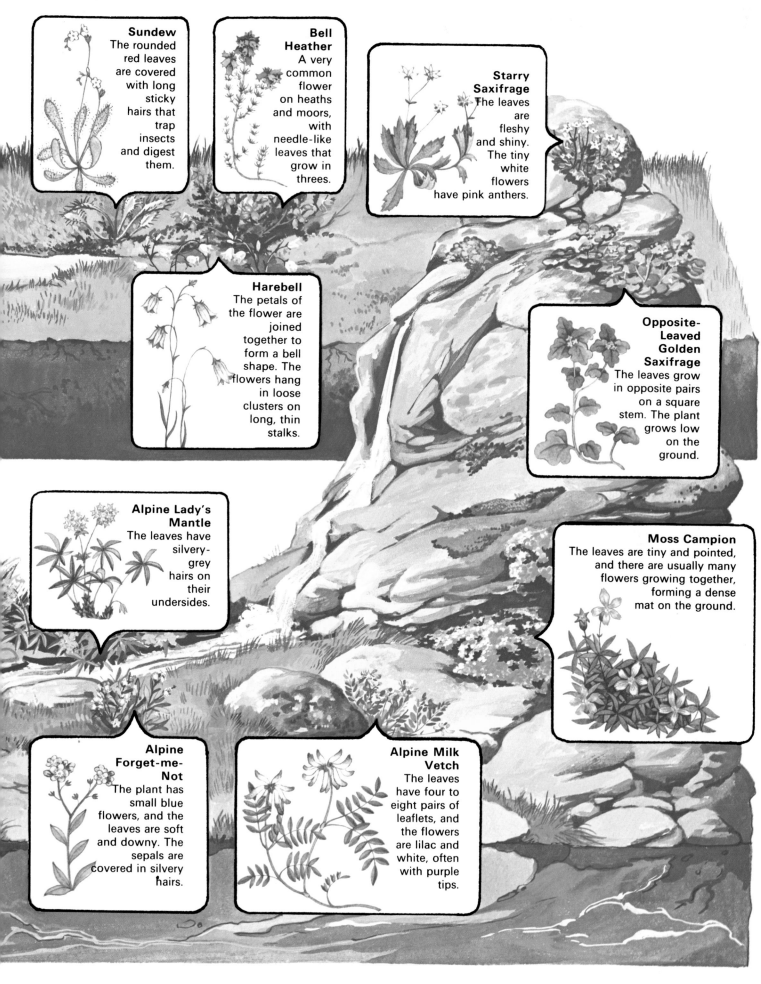

Sundew
The rounded red leaves are covered with long sticky hairs that trap insects and digest them.

Bell Heather
A very common flower on heaths and moors, with needle-like leaves that grow in threes.

Starry Saxifrage
The leaves are fleshy and shiny. The tiny white flowers have pink anthers.

Harebell
The petals of the flower are joined together to form a bell shape. The flowers hang in loose clusters on long, thin stalks.

Opposite-Leaved Golden Saxifrage
The leaves grow in opposite pairs on a square stem. The plant grows low on the ground.

Alpine Lady's Mantle
The leaves have silvery-grey hairs on their undersides.

Moss Campion
The leaves are tiny and pointed, and there are usually many flowers growing together, forming a dense mat on the ground.

Alpine Forget-me-Not
The plant has small blue flowers, and the leaves are soft and downy. The sepals are covered in silvery hairs.

Alpine Milk Vetch
The leaves have four to eight pairs of leaflets, and the flowers are lilac and white, often with purple tips.

91

Other Common Flowers to Spot

Field Pennycress
30 cm. Waste ground.
Summer.

Fruit (pod)

Sea Rocket
30 cm. Sandy coasts.
Summer.

Fruit

Bladder Campion
45 cm. Waste ground,
grassy places.
Spring/Summer.

Greater Stitchwort
20 cm. Woods, hedges,
fields. Spring.

Star-of-Bethlehem
15 cm. Grassy places.
Early Summer.

Cloudberry
15 cm. Upland bogs,
damp moors.
Summer.

White Stonecrop
Low and creeping.
Rocks, walls.
Summer.

White Bryony
Climbing to 4 m.
Hedges, scrub.
Spring/Summer.

White Dead Nettle
20 cm. Waysides,
waste places.
Spring to Autumn.

Feverfew
30 cm. Walls,
waste places.
Summer.

Cow Parsley
60 cm. Hedge-banks,
shady places.
Spring.

Flower

White Melilot
60 cm. Bare and
waste ground.
Summer.

Flower

Hogweed
Up to 3 m. Grassy
places, open woods.
Spring to Autumn.

Flower

Daisy
10 cm. Lawns,
short turf, fields.
All year.

Flower

Yarrow
30 cm.
Grassy places.
Summer/Autumn.

92 **Remember—if you cannot see a picture of the flower you want to identify here, look on the page earlier in the book which deals with the kind of place where you found it.**

The figure given in metres or centimetres is the average height of the flower from ground level to the top of the plant. The season given is when the plant is in flower. The captions also give the kind of place where the flower is most commonly found.

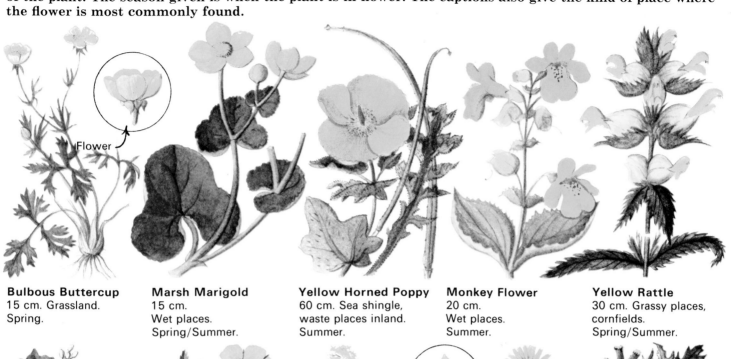

Bulbous Buttercup
15 cm. Grassland.
Spring.

Marsh Marigold
15 cm.
Wet places.
Spring/Summer.

Yellow Horned Poppy
60 cm. Sea shingle,
waste places inland.
Summer.

Monkey Flower
20 cm.
Wet places.
Summer.

Yellow Rattle
30 cm. Grassy places,
cornfields.
Spring/Summer.

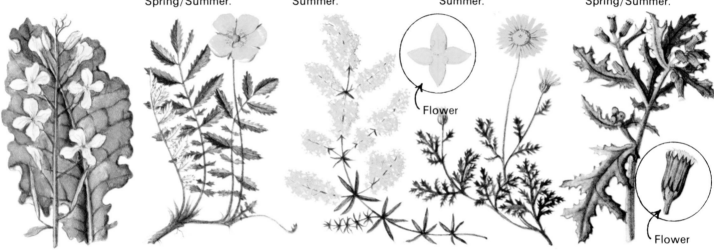

Wild Cabbage
60 cm.
Sea cliffs.
Summer.

Silverweed
Creeping with runners.
Damp, grassy places.
Spring/Summer.

Lady's Bedstraw
10 cm. Dry,
grassy places.
Summer.

Yellow Chamomile
30 cm. Dry, bare
and waste places.
Summer.

Groundsel
10 cm. Weed found in
gardens and on waste
ground. All year.

Common Gorse
Grows up to 2½ m.
Heaths, grassland.
All year.

Common Rockrose
Close to the ground.
Grassy and rocky places.
Summer.

Kidney Vetch
15 cm. Dry grassland.
by sea, on mountains.
Spring/Summer.

**Perforate St.
John's Wort**
45 cm. Grassy and
bushy places. Summer.

Yellow Waterlily
A few cms. above water.
Still water, slow streams.
Summer.

Remember—if you cannot see a picture of the flower you want to identify here, look on the page earlier in the book which deals with the kind of place where you found it.

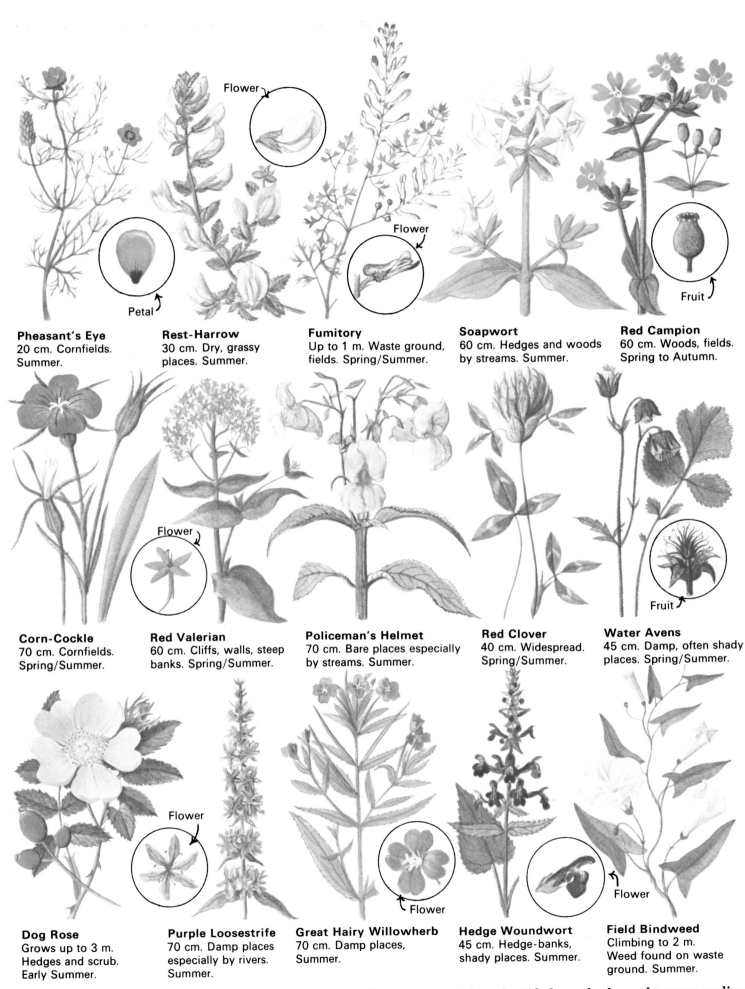

Pheasant's Eye
20 cm. Cornfields.
Summer.

Flower

Petal

Rest-Harrow
30 cm. Dry, grassy
places. Summer.

Flower

Fumitory
Up to 1 m. Waste ground,
fields. Spring/Summer.

Soapwort
60 cm. Hedges and woods
by streams. Summer.

Fruit

Red Campion
60 cm. Woods, fields.
Spring to Autumn.

Corn-Cockle
70 cm. Cornfields.
Spring/Summer.

Flower

Red Valerian
60 cm. Cliffs, walls, steep
banks. Spring/Summer.

Policeman's Helmet
70 cm. Bare places especially
by streams. Summer.

Red Clover
40 cm. Widespread.
Spring/Summer.

Fruit

Water Avens
45 cm. Damp, often shady
places. Spring/Summer.

Dog Rose
Grows up to 3 m.
Hedges and scrub.
Early Summer.

Flower

Purple Loosestrife
70 cm. Damp places
especially by rivers.
Summer.

Flower

Great Hairy Willowherb
70 cm. Damp places,
Summer.

Flower

Hedge Woundwort
45 cm. Hedge-banks,
shady places. Summer.

Flower

Field Bindweed
Climbing to 2 m.
Weed found on waste
ground. Summer.

Remember—if you cannot see a picture of the flower you want to identify here, look on the page earlier in the book which deals with the kind of place where you found it.

Some flowers are more widespread in some localities than others—you may be able to find several of one type growing in one area, and none at all in another.

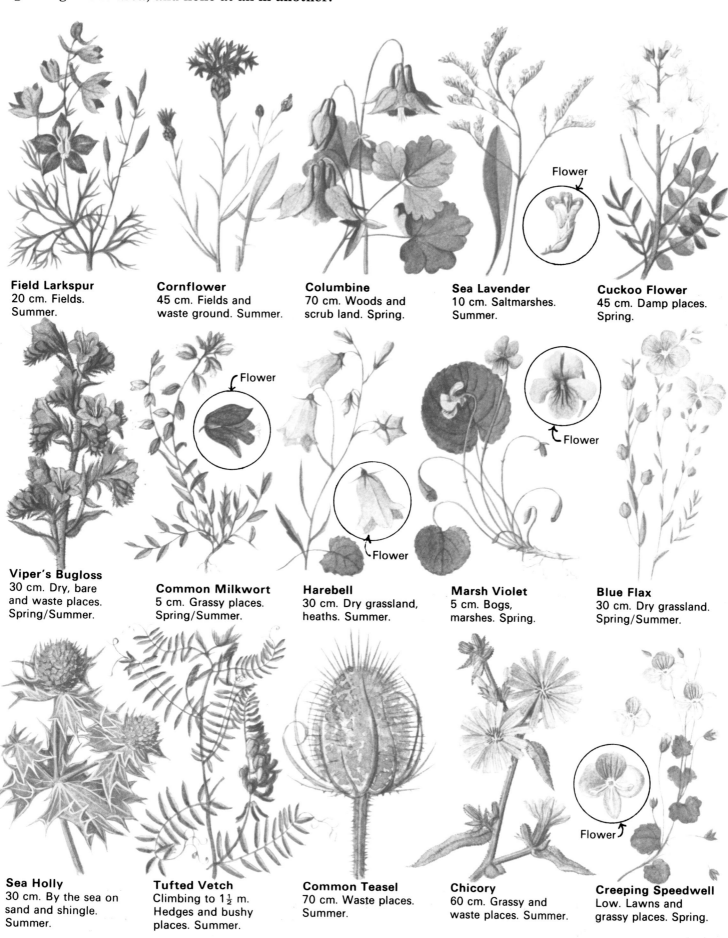

Field Larkspur
20 cm. Fields.
Summer.

Cornflower
45 cm. Fields and
waste ground. Summer.

Columbine
70 cm. Woods and
scrub land. Spring.

Sea Lavender
10 cm. Saltmarshes.
Summer.

Flower

Cuckoo Flower
45 cm. Damp places.
Spring.

Flower

Viper's Bugloss
30 cm. Dry, bare
and waste places.
Spring/Summer.

Common Milkwort
5 cm. Grassy places.
Spring/Summer.

Flower

Harebell
30 cm. Dry grassland,
heaths. Summer.

Flower

Marsh Violet
5 cm. Bogs,
marshes. Spring.

Blue Flax
30 cm. Dry grassland.
Spring/Summer.

Sea Holly
30 cm. By the sea on
sand and shingle.
Summer.

Tufted Vetch
Climbing to 1½ m.
Hedges and bushy
places. Summer.

Common Teasel
70 cm. Waste places.
Summer.

Chicory
60 cm. Grassy and
waste places. Summer.

Flower

Creeping Speedwell
Low. Lawns and
grassy places. Spring.

Remember—if you cannot see a picture of the flower you want to identify here, look on the page earlier in the book which deals with the kind of place where you found it.

Grasses, Sedges and Rushes

Grasses

Most grasses have round hollow stems, long narrow leaves and spikes or sprays of tiny flowers.

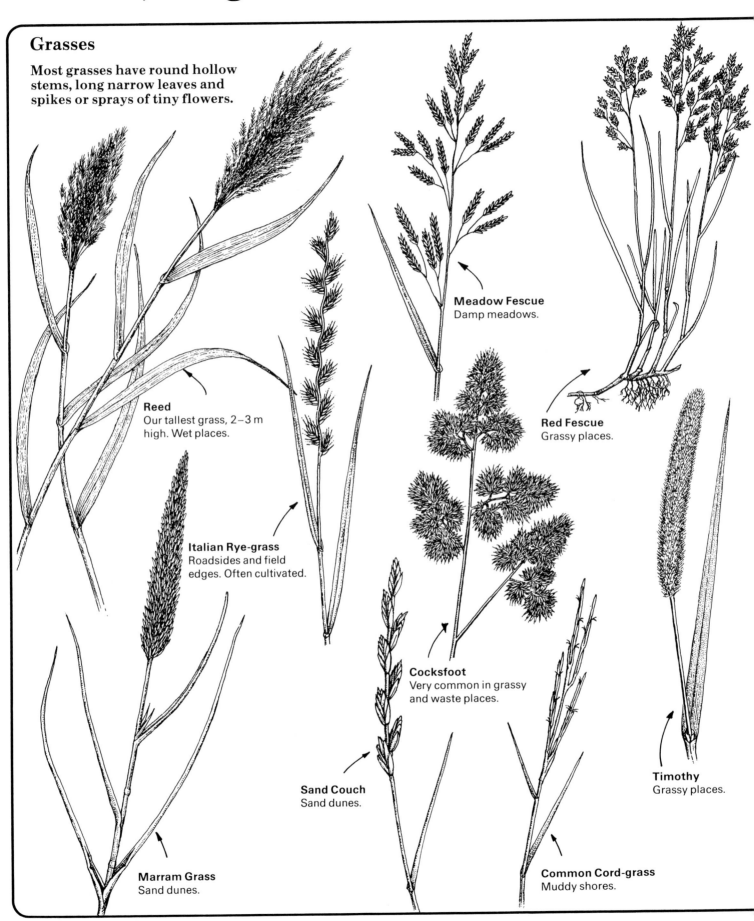

Reed
Our tallest grass, 2–3 m high. Wet places.

Italian Rye-grass
Roadsides and field edges. Often cultivated.

Marram Grass
Sand dunes.

Sand Couch
Sand dunes.

Meadow Fescue
Damp meadows.

Red Fescue
Grassy places.

Cocksfoot
Very common in grassy and waste places.

Common Cord-grass
Muddy shores.

Timothy
Grassy places.

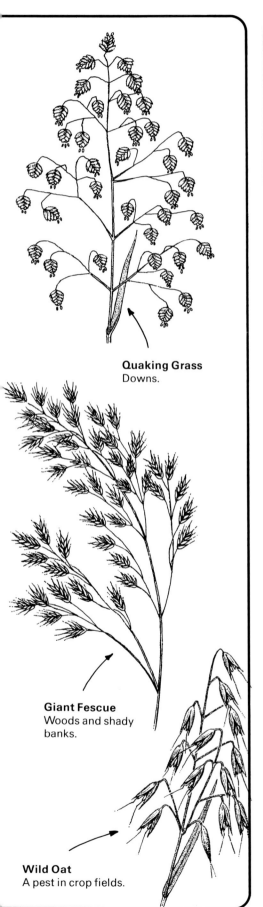

Quaking Grass
Downs.

Giant Fescue
Woods and shady banks.

Wild Oat
A pest in crop fields.

Sedges

Sedges look rather like grasses, but their stems are often three-sided, and never hollow like grass stems.

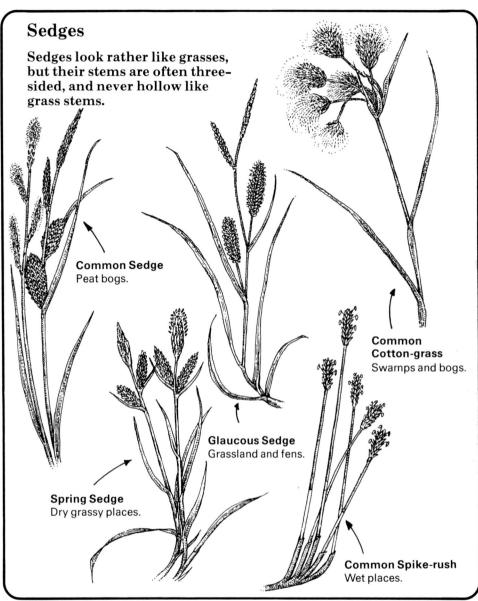

Common Sedge
Peat bogs.

Spring Sedge
Dry grassy places.

Glaucous Sedge
Grassland and fens.

Common Cotton-grass
Swamps and bogs.

Common Spike-rush
Wet places.

Rushes

Rushes often grow in tufts, in wet, marshy places.

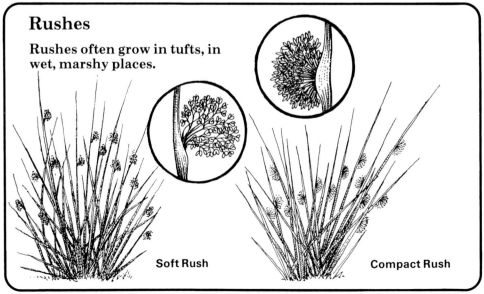

Soft Rush

Compact Rush

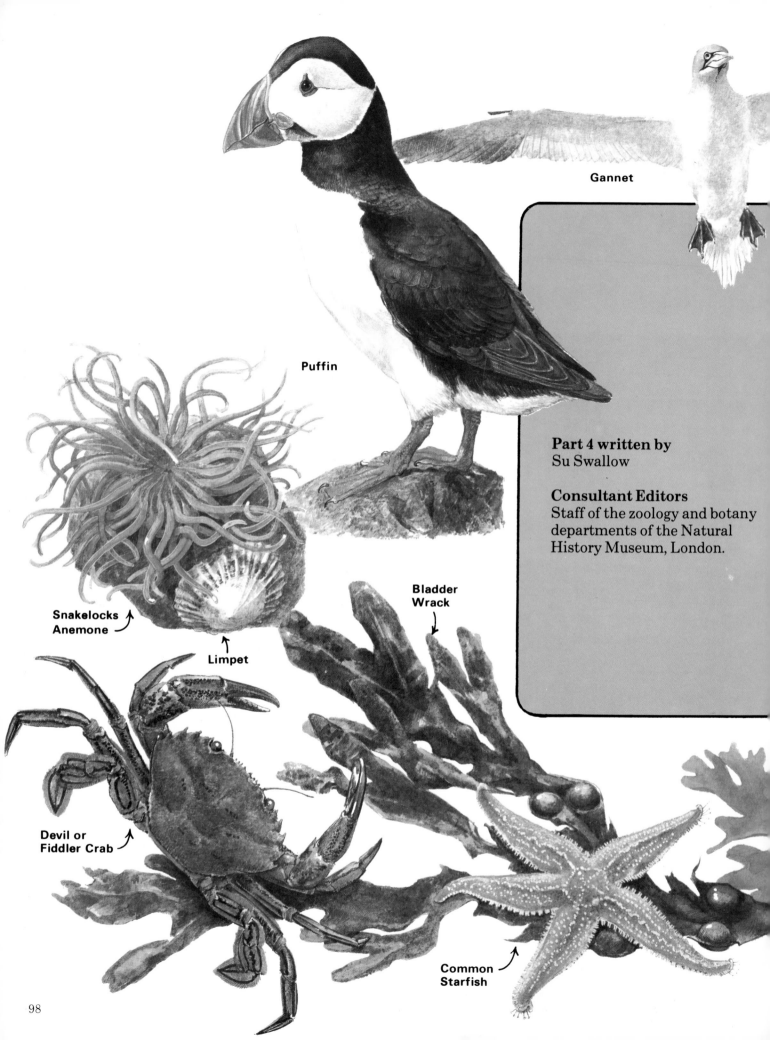

Gannet

Puffin

Snakelocks
Anemone

Limpet

Bladder
Wrack

Part 4 written by
Su Swallow

Consultant Editors
Staff of the zoology and botany
departments of the Natural
History Museum, London.

Devil or
Fiddler Crab

Common
Starfish

Part 4
SEASHORE LIFE

This section of the book tells you where to look for common animals, birds, fishes and plants on European coasts. It shows you lots of clues to look for, how animals and plants live in different kinds of places, and how to take notes and make collections.

Even if a beach looks deserted, you can still find out a lot about the animals that live there, by searching for tracks and other signs, such as lugworm casts.

If you want to identify something you have found, first look on the pages that deal with that kind of animal or plant. If you cannot see it there, then turn to the charts at the end of this section, where there are more species (kinds of animals or plants) to spot.

As with other hobbies, like birdwatching, a beachcomber needs some special equipment, and this is described over the page.

If you study seashore life, always be careful not to disturb animals, or pull up plants. Put shells back where you found them, and if you move rocks or stones to look under them, place them back in the same position.

In this way you will not only prevent any undue disturbance to the animals that live in the area, but you will also be able to go back to the same place and examine the same rocks for wildlife again.

Periwinkles

Common Mussel

Pelican's Foot Shell

Pod Razor Shell

Painted Top Shell

Queen Scallop

Hidden Life on the Beach...

This man may think he is alone on the beach, but in fact there are living creatures all around him. They have chosen places where they are difficult to spot, and where they are least likely to be disturbed by men or other animals. The numbers show you where six of them are hidden.

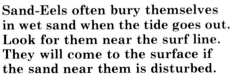

Sand-Eels often bury themselves in wet sand when the tide goes out. Look for them near the surf line. They will come to the surface if the sand near them is disturbed.

Common Starfish

Starfish usually live in the sea. If they get stranded on shore, they take shelter in pools of sea water among rocks. This one is opening a Scallop to eat it.

Herring Gull

Gulls always nest in places that are difficult for animals to get to. They usually choose ledges on cliffs. Watch out for birds flying to or from the nests.

...and How to Find it

Goose Barnacles

Goose Barnacles grow on stalks that look like the necks of geese. These were washed ashore on driftwood. They gather food with their fringe of tentacles.

Shore Crab

This Shore Crab is hiding in a clump of seaweed in a rock pool. Use a net to hunt for crabs, and put them back in sea water when you have finished with them.

What to Take

Fishing net

Magnifying glass

Trowel

Penknife

Notebook and pencil

Spade

Plastic screw-top containers

Bucket

Sieve

You will stand a better chance of finding the things that live on the beach if you take the right equipment with you. Whenever you make a discovery, note down the time and what part of the beach you were on. Wear what you want, but put on shoes or boots for wading in rock pools, so that you don't cut your feet.

Sea Anemone

Prawn

Barnacles under a rock

Periwinkles on seaweed

Lugworm casts on sand

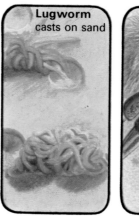

Hermit Crab in Whelk shell

Sea Anemones are flesh-eating animals that look like plants. They live on small fish and shellfish, like this prawn. Their tentacles can sting.

The best time for exploring the beach is when the tide is furthest out. Check the local newspaper for the times of tides. Look on rocks for Barnacles and Limpets; in seaweed for Periwinkles and shellfish; under marks on wet sand for burrowing animals; and in empty shells for Hermit Crabs.

101

Exploring the Seashore

The kinds of animals and plants you find on the seashore will depend very much on the kind of beach you are exploring. Rocky, sandy and muddy beaches are good places to look. Shingle, or pebble, beaches are usually rather bare because the pebbles keep shifting, and at low tide they are too dry to support life. If you visit different kinds of beaches close together, notice how the creatures you find change from one beach to another. See which has more seaweeds, or more shells, where you find birds feeding, and so on.

Tides and Zones

The sea creeps up the shore, and then down again, roughly twice every 24 hours. These movements of the sea are called tides. The tides in the Mediterranean Sea are very small, and hard to notice, while the tides in other seas, like the Atlantic, are more obvious.

The highest point on the shore reached by the water is called "high water", and the lowest is called "low water". Spring tides (nothing to do with the season) happen roughly once a fortnight. They rise higher and fall lower than neap tides, which occur in between each spring tide.

The seashore can be divided into zones between the different high and low water levels. The picture below shows you the common seaweeds and shells that live in each zone.

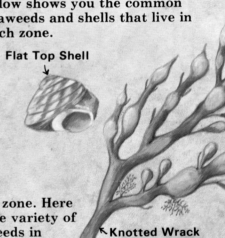

HIGH WATER Spring tides

HIGH WATER Neap tides

Small Periwinkles in rock crevice

Channel Wrack

Thick Top Shell

Rough Periwinkle on rock

Spiral Wrack

Flat Top Shell

Knotted Wrack

Lichens

Splash Zone
A few animals and plants live here. They are sprayed, but not covered, by water.

Upper Zone
This zone is uncovered for days at a time. Fewer creatures live here than in the middle zone.

Middle Zone
This is the largest zone. Here you will find a wide variety of animals and seaweeds in large numbers.

1 Types of Coastline— Rocky Shores

Purple Sandpiper

Ravens

Groynes

The movement of the sea changes the shape of rocky shores. The water wears cliffs away and pulls pieces of rock down the shore, leaving the heaviest at the top. Groynes stop the rocks being swept too far *along* the shore.

2 Sand Dunes

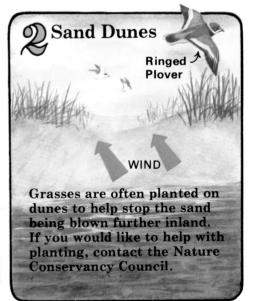

Ringed Plover

WIND

Grasses are often planted on dunes to help stop the sand being blown further inland. If you would like to help with planting, contact the Nature Conservancy Council.

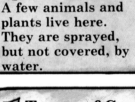

The Mediterranean Coast

Mediterranean Gulls

Blue Rock Thrush

You can sometimes see the tide mark on rocks in the Mediterranean.

60 cm.

The seashore on the Mediterranean Sea has all the zones shown on this page, but they are telescoped into a very narrow band. The tide in the Mediterranean never rises and falls more than about 60 cm., so it is difficult to see the different zones. You will still be able, however, to find many of the plants and animals shown in this book. Look, too, for animals that can live more or less out of water, such as Land Crabs.

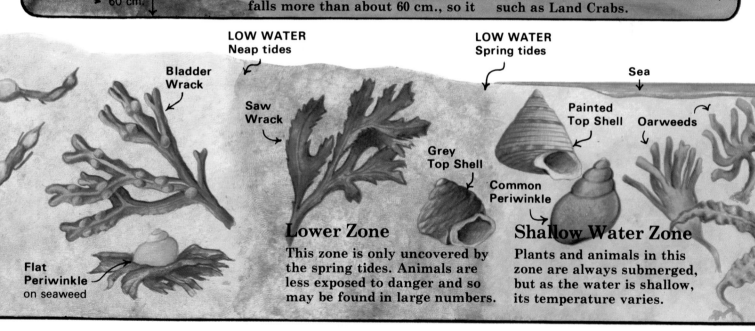

LOW WATER
Neap tides

LOW WATER
Spring tides

Sea

Bladder Wrack

Saw Wrack

Painted Top Shell

Oarweeds

Grey Top Shell

Common Periwinkle

Flat Periwinkle on seaweed

Lower Zone

This zone is only uncovered by the spring tides. Animals are less exposed to danger and so may be found in large numbers.

Shallow Water Zone

Plants and animals in this zone are always submerged, but as the water is shallow, its temperature varies.

③ Dykes

Brent Geese

Very flat coasts may be flooded by the sea. Dykes are built to hold back the water. A lot of wildlife may be found on these sheltered coasts.

Make your own Map of the Beach

String

WOOTTON BAY
2ND MAY 1976
LOW TIDE
Brown Seaweed + Periwinkles
3m. Splash Zone
Thick Top Shell
7m Upper Zone
15m middle Zone
Knotted Wrack
10m Lower Zone
Grey Top Shell

Stretch a piece of string, tied to rocks at both ends, down the beach, and mark on your map everything that you see near the line. See if you can work out, from the seaweeds and shells you find, where the different zones begin and end. Make your map at low tide.

Seaweeds and their Secrets

You can find many kinds of seaweed growing on the shore, especially on rocky shores, and large deep-water seaweeds are often washed up after a storm. Compare them with land plants to see how well they are suited to life in the sea. Instead of growing roots, they anchor themselves to rocks or stones against the action of the waves. They take in food from the water, not the ground. Some can live both in and out of water as the tide goes in and out.

Check: some seaweeds have a thick vein, or **midrib**, running up the frond.

Check: what colour are the leaf-like branches (called **fronds**)? Are they flat or wavy, or broken along the edges?

Check: how long is the stalk, or **stipe**?

Holdfast. Check: is it disk-shaped or branched?

Brown Seaweed

Bladder wrack is one of the most common brown seaweeds. Use the check points in the picture to help you identify other seaweeds.

Some seaweeds have **air bladders**. They help to keep the plant upright in the water. Check: are they growing singly or in pairs?

Check: do fronds divide, or **branch**, or do they grow straight up from the holdfast? You can work out roughly how old Bladder Wrack is by counting two branchings for each year.

Bladder Wrack

1 At low tide seaweed growing on the shore lies flat.

2 At high tide the water holds it up.

Red Seaweed

Most red seaweeds are smaller than brown seaweeds. Look for them on rocks and in deep rock pools on the lower zone. Some feel hard and brittle, and look like coral.

Green Seaweed

Most green seaweeds are small, but they often grow in large clumps and cover rocks like a carpet. Look for them under large brown seaweeds on the upper and middle zones.

How Many Frond Shapes Can You Find?

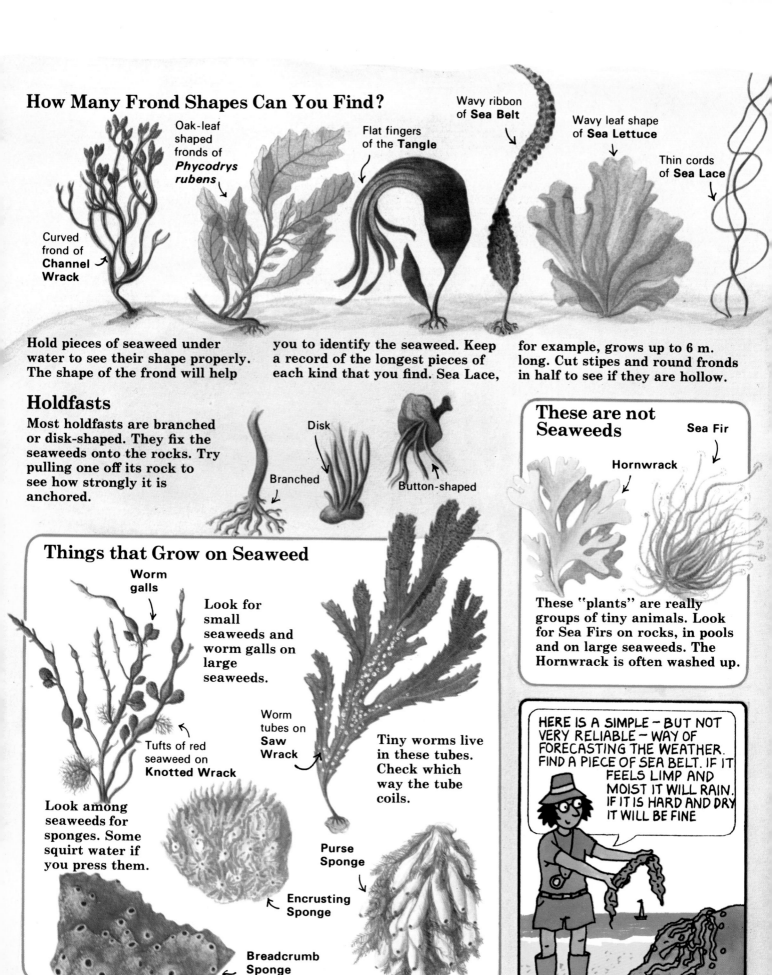

Curved frond of **Channel Wrack**

Oak-leaf shaped fronds of **Phycodrys rubens**

Flat fingers of the **Tangle**

Wavy ribbon of **Sea Belt**

Wavy leaf shape of **Sea Lettuce**

Thin cords of **Sea Lace**

Hold pieces of seaweed under water to see their shape properly. The shape of the frond will help you to identify the seaweed. Keep a record of the longest pieces of each kind that you find. Sea Lace, for example, grows up to 6 m. long. Cut stipes and round fronds in half to see if they are hollow.

Holdfasts

Most holdfasts are branched or disk-shaped. They fix the seaweeds onto the rocks. Try pulling one off its rock to see how strongly it is anchored.

Disk

Branched

Button-shaped

These are not Seaweeds

Sea Fir

Hornwrack

These "plants" are really groups of tiny animals. Look for Sea Firs on rocks, in pools and on large seaweeds. The Hornwrack is often washed up.

Things that Grow on Seaweed

Worm galls

Look for small seaweeds and worm galls on large seaweeds.

Tufts of red seaweed on **Knotted Wrack**

Worm tubes on **Saw Wrack**

Tiny worms live in these tubes. Check which way the tube coils.

Look among seaweeds for sponges. Some squirt water if you press them.

Purse Sponge

Encrusting Sponge

Breadcrumb Sponge

HERE IS A SIMPLE — BUT NOT VERY RELIABLE — WAY OF FORECASTING THE WEATHER. FIND A PIECE OF SEA BELT. IF IT FEELS LIMP AND MOIST IT WILL RAIN. IF IT IS HARD AND DRY IT WILL BE FINE

Rock Pools

A beach with rock pools can be one of the most exciting to explore. Here you will find animals that cannot survive out of water when the tide is out, as well as animals and plants that also live elsewhere on the shore. Look especially in pools with seaweed, which protects the animals from the sun and keeps the water temperature more even. Wear shoes that will not slip on wet rocks.

On windy days, when the surface of the rock pool is disturbed, look through the bottom of a clear plastic box to see into the pool. Keep very still and wait for animals to come out of hiding.

ALWAYS put rocks back the right way up to protect the animals living underneath.

Sea Anemones

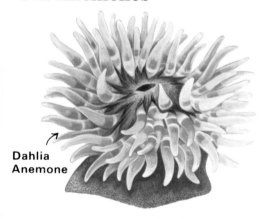

Dahlia Anemone

Sea anemones are animals. This one is usually camouflaged with bits of shell and gravel. If you prod it, it squirts water and contracts.

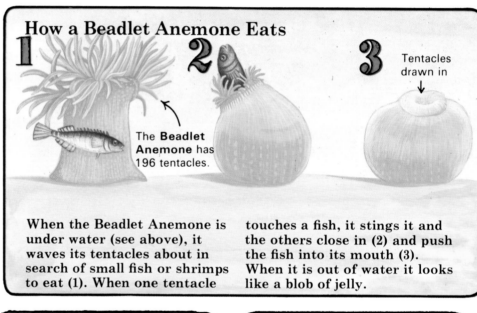

How a Beadlet Anemone Eats

1

The **Beadlet Anemone** has 196 tentacles.

2

3

Tentacles drawn in

When the Beadlet Anemone is under water (see above), it waves its tentacles about in search of small fish or shrimps to eat (1). When one tentacle touches a fish, it stings it and the others close in (2) and push the fish into its mouth (3). When it is out of water it looks like a blob of jelly.

Shore Crab

The Shore Crab is common on the middle and lower zones. A crab carries its tail under its body. Check how many joints it has. Some also hide their fourth pair of legs.

Spider Crab

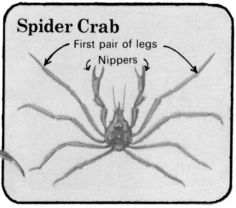

First pair of legs

Nippers

Look under stones and among seaweed on the lower zone for this crab. Its shell is about 1 cm. across. Notice the length of the first pair of legs.

Sea Urchin

The Sea Urchin's spines drop off when it dies. Some live on rocks and have a strong round shell. Other types burrow in the sand and have a more delicate, oval shell.

Lift aside thick clumps of seaweed to find the animals sheltering underneath.

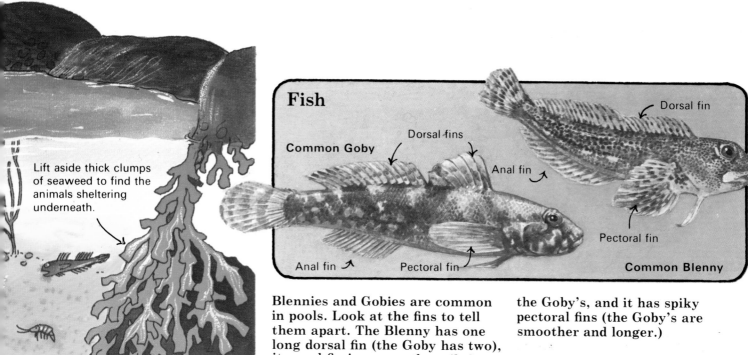

Fish

Common Goby

Dorsal fins

Anal fin

Anal fin

Pectoral fin

Dorsal fin

Pectoral fin

Common Blenny

Blennies and Gobies are common in pools. Look at the fins to tell them apart. The Blenny has one long dorsal fin (the Goby has two), its anal fin is nearer the tail than the Goby's, and it has spiky pectoral fins (the Goby's are smoother and longer.)

Shrimps and Prawns

Shrimps and prawns are hard to spot because of their pale colours. Use a net to catch them. Prawns are larger (up to 15 cm.) than shrimps (up to 5 cm.) with feelers longer than their bodies.

Common Prawn

Common Shrimp

Brittle Stars

Look in pools among Coralline seaweeds for Brittle Stars. Handle them gently as their long thin arms break off easily.

Sea Hare

This Sea Hare has its shell in its body. It changes colour with age, from red to brown, then dark green. In summer, look for strings of its orange spawn round Oarweeds.

Starfish

Common Starfish

Common Sunstar

Cushion Star

Most starfish have five arms, but the Common Sunstar has up to 13. Look on the lower zone.

Look through a lens to see the rows of tube-feet (suckers) which pull the starfish along. Look in shallow shaded pools for the short-armed Cushion Star.

Flowers and Grasses

Many plants that grow by the sea are also found inland, but the seashore plants have to protect themselves against the salt spray and strong winds. Look at the leaves, the roots and the shape of the plants to see the differences. Some flowers can grow on any beach—even on shingle. Make a note of where you find flowers, and see if you can find the same flower on a different kind of beach.

Hawthorn is one of the few trees that grows by the sea. The wind dries out the soil on one side of the tree, so that its roots and branches only develop on the side away from the wind. They look as though they are being swept away.

Dunes

The picture shows how plants help to form dunes. The grasses have very long roots which hold down the sand in ridges, and stop the wind blowing the sand away. Marram grass is the most common.

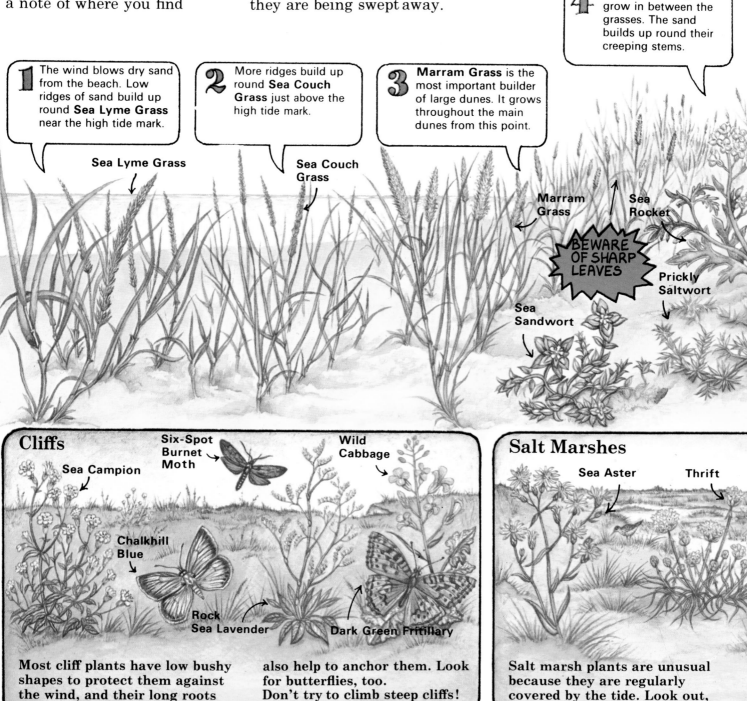

1 The wind blows dry sand from the beach. Low ridges of sand build up round **Sea Lyme Grass** near the high tide mark.

2 More ridges build up round **Sea Couch Grass** just above the high tide mark.

3 **Marram Grass** is the most important builder of large dunes. It grows throughout the main dunes from this point.

4 Small plants begin to grow in between the grasses. The sand builds up round their creeping stems.

Sea Lyme Grass

Sea Couch Grass

Marram Grass

Sea Rocket

BEWARE OF SHARP LEAVES

Prickly Saltwort

Sea Sandwort

Cliffs

Sea Campion

Six-Spot Burnet Moth

Wild Cabbage

Chalkhill Blue

Rock Sea Lavender

Dark Green Fritillary

Most cliff plants have low bushy shapes to protect them against the wind, and their long roots also help to anchor them. Look for butterflies, too.
Don't try to climb steep cliffs!

Salt Marshes

Sea Aster

Thrift

Salt marsh plants are unusual because they are regularly covered by the tide. Look out,

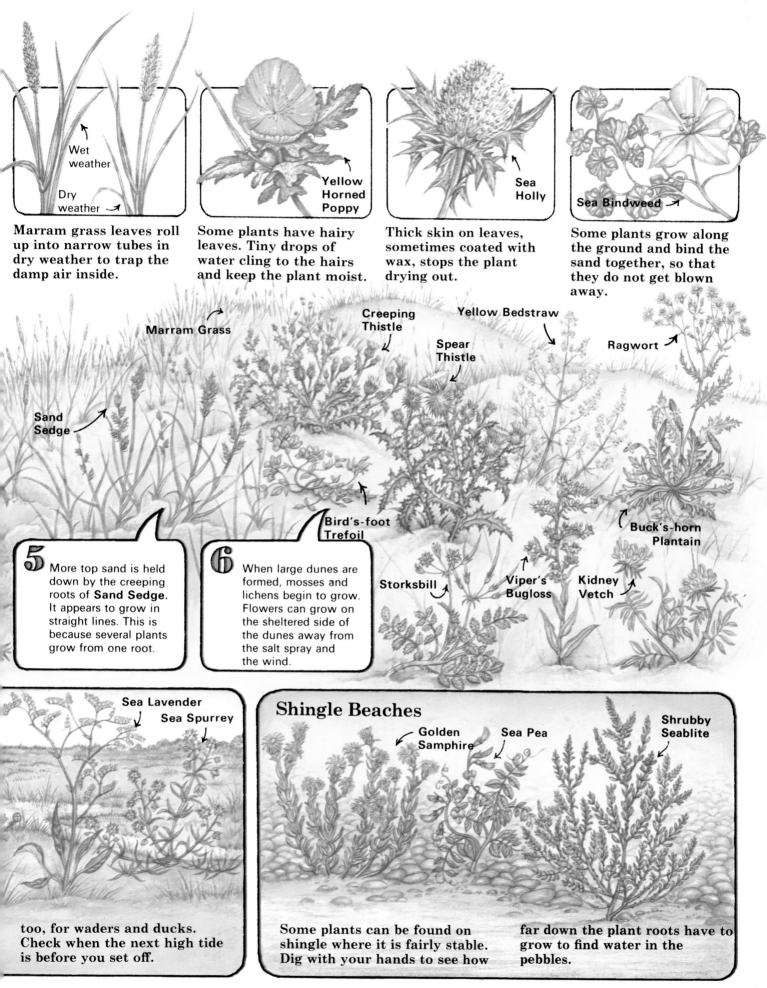

Marram grass leaves roll up into narrow tubes in dry weather to trap the damp air inside.

Some plants have hairy leaves. Tiny drops of water cling to the hairs and keep the plant moist.

Thick skin on leaves, sometimes coated with wax, stops the plant drying out.

Some plants grow along the ground and bind the sand together, so that they do not get blown away.

5 More top sand is held down by the creeping roots of **Sand Sedge**. It appears to grow in straight lines. This is because several plants grow from one root.

6 When large dunes are formed, mosses and lichens begin to grow. Flowers can grow on the sheltered side of the dunes away from the salt spray and the wind.

too, for waders and ducks. Check when the next high tide is before you set off.

Shingle Beaches

Some plants can be found on shingle where it is fairly stable. Dig with your hands to see how far down the plant roots have to grow to find water in the pebbles.

Collecting Shells

The empty shells you find on the beach once belonged to molluscs—soft-bodied animals without internal skeletons. Some molluscs live on the shore. Others live in the sea, but you may find their shells washed up on the shore. To identify your shell, you must first decide which group of molluscs it belongs to. Some will be gastropods, which have a single, usually coiled shell, like Whelks and Periwinkles.

Check whether your gastropod shell coils clockwise or anti-clockwise as you look down on its pointed top.

Bivalves are molluscs with two (bi) shells (or valves), held together by muscles. Empty bivalve shells often break apart in the sea, but if you find both halves together, see if they are the same shape and size, as in Mussels, or unequal, as in Scallops.

Shapes and Colours

Shell colours show up best when the shells are wet. Some shells vary in colour. You could make a collection of shells of the same kind with different colours. The shape of shells can vary, too, depending on where they live.

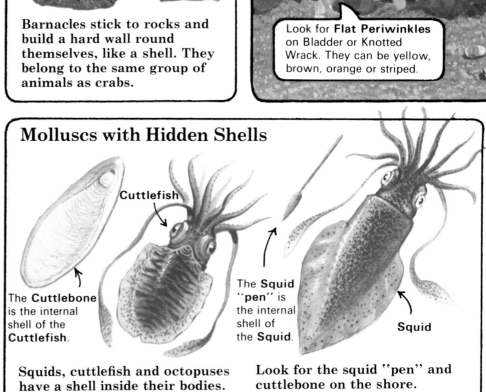

Look for **Flat Periwinkles** on Bladder or Knotted Wrack. They can be yellow, brown, orange or striped.

Gastropods

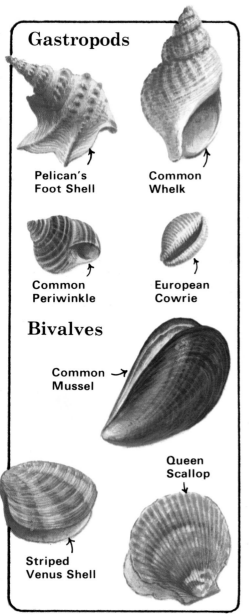

Pelican's Foot Shell

Common Whelk

Common Periwinkle

European Cowrie

Bivalves

Common Mussel

Queen Scallop

Striped Venus Shell

These are not Molluscs

Acorn Barnacles

Barnacles stick to rocks and build a hard wall round themselves, like a shell. They belong to the same group of animals as crabs.

Molluscs with Hidden Shells

Cuttlefish

The **Cuttlebone** is the internal shell of the **Cuttlefish**.

The **Squid "pen"** is the internal shell of the **Squid**.

Squid

Squids, cuttlefish and octopuses have a shell inside their bodies.

Look for the squid "pen" and cuttlebone on the shore.

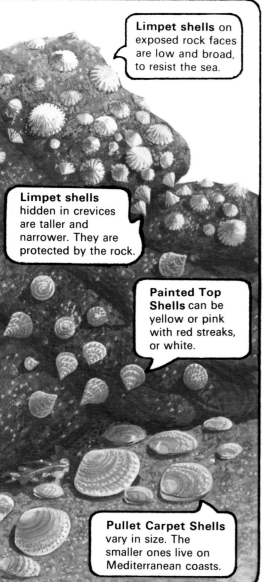

Limpet shells on exposed rock faces are low and broad, to resist the sea.

Limpet shells hidden in crevices are taller and narrower. They are protected by the rock.

Painted Top Shells can be yellow or pink with red streaks, or white.

Pullet Carpet Shells vary in size. The smaller ones live on Mediterranean coasts.

Shells with Holes

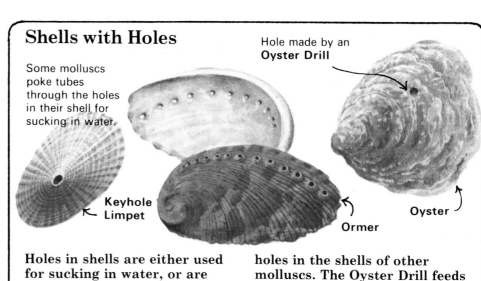

Some molluscs poke tubes through the holes in their shell for sucking in water.

Hole made by an **Oyster Drill**

Keyhole Limpet

Ormer

Oyster

Holes in shells are either used for sucking in water, or are made by molluscs that drill holes in the shells of other molluscs. The Oyster Drill feeds on Oysters in this way.

1 How to Collect Shells

Thick paper for labels

Magnifying glass

Pen

Plastic bags

Bucket

Trowel

Take these things with you. Search low down on the shore, on rocks, under seaweed and stones, in pools and in the sand.

2

Label

Put each shell in a separate bag, with a label saying where you found it.

3

Newspaper

Warm water

When you get home, clean your shells in warm water with a soft brush. Leave them to dry on newspaper.

4

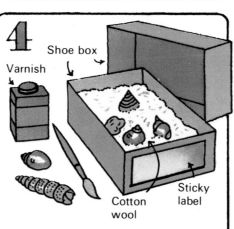

Shoe box

Varnish

Cotton wool

Sticky label

Brush a thin coat of varnish on each shell. Keep your collection *either* in a shoe box lined with cotton wool . . .

5

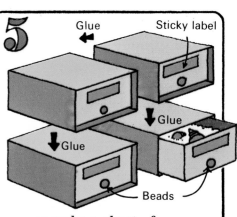

Glue

Sticky label

Glue

Glue

Beads

. . . *or* make a chest of drawers by sticking together several large matchboxes. Label the fronts and sew on beads for handles.

Looking at Shells

This picture shows where molluscs live, how they feed, how they fix themselves to rocks so they are not washed away by the sea, and how some can live both in and out of the water. Some gastropods eat seaweed. They file off bits of the plant with their rough "tongue". Others use the "tongue" to drill a hole in the shells of other molluscs, and scrape off bits of the animal inside. Most bivalves suck in sea water and feed off the tiny plants and animals in it.

Follow the Limpet

Mark some Limpets and the rock next to them with quick-drying paint. When you go back in a few hours, you will be able to see how far they have moved.

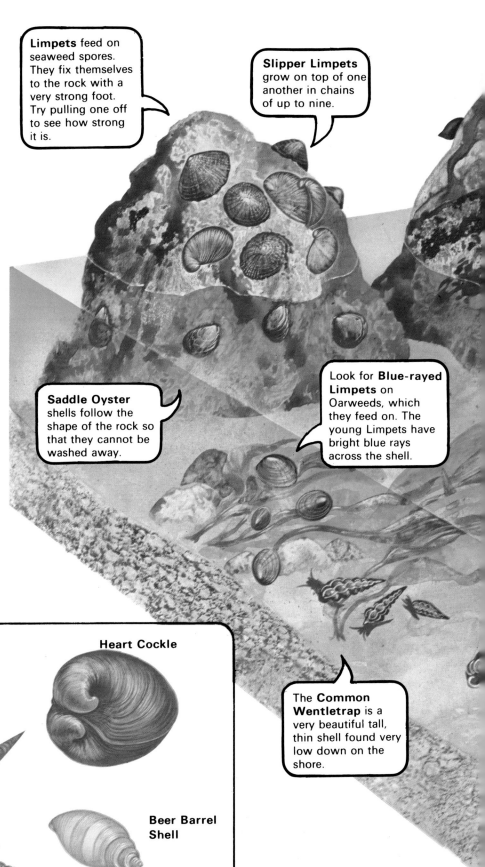

Limpets feed on seaweed spores. They fix themselves to the rock with a very strong foot. Try pulling one off to see how strong it is.

Slipper Limpets grow on top of one another in chains of up to nine.

Saddle Oyster shells follow the shape of the rock so that they cannot be washed away.

Look for **Blue-rayed Limpets** on Oarweeds, which they feed on. The young Limpets have bright blue rays across the shell.

The **Common Wentletrap** is a very beautiful tall, thin shell found very low down on the shore.

Rarer Shells
These shells are rather less common than the ones in the main picture.

Chinaman's Hat

Smooth Venus

Tower Shell

Pheasant Shell

Heart Cockle

Beer Barrel Shell

Common Periwinkles come off the rocks easily, but the rounded shape of their shell prevents them being smashed by the waves.

The **Rough Periwinkle** hides in cracks. When the tide is out, Periwinkles stick their shells to the rock, trapping a little water inside to keep them damp.

Piddocks are bivalves with rows of spines on their shells. They bore into rocks for protection.

Dog Whelks that feed on Mussels, their favourite food, become dark-coloured. Those that feed on Barnacles become white.

Mussels attach themselves to rocks by thin brown threads, to resist the beating of the waves.

Hermit Crabs have no shell of their own. Instead they live in empty gastropod shells, moving to a bigger shell as they grow.

Edible Cockles are bivalves that live in the sand. They have tubes, rather like small vacuum cleaners, for feeding on tiny bits of dead animals and plants lying on the sand.

Thin Tellins live in the sand and feed through siphons which they push above the surface. The siphons filter plankton from the sea water.

Look for small yellow and pink **Banded Chink Shells** on seaweed well down on the lower shore.

Look in muddy gravel for the **Baltic Tellin.** Like all Tellins, it has very long siphons for feeding off the surface of the sea bottom.

REMEMBER! PUT LIVE SHELLS BACK – THE RIGHT WAY UP – AS QUICKLY AS POSSIBLE, OTHERWISE YOU MIGHT KILL THEM. ONLY COLLECT EMPTY SHELLS

Watching Cliff Birds

How Seabirds Soar

Wind from the sea is pushed up as it hits cliffs. Seabirds "soar" in these up-currents of air, almost without moving their wings.

Wind

The **Kittiwake** has shorter legs than other gulls. Note the triangular black wing tips and black legs.

Ravens glide, dive and can even turn upside down. They eat shellfish, grain and small animals.

Herring Gulls nest in colonies. They nest on cliff ledges, on the ground, and even on buildings.

Cormorants can often be seen standing with their wings spread out. They sometimes fly many miles inland.

The **Great Black-backed Gull** is a very large gull, with a wing span of 1.5 m. It is very fierce, and sometimes kills and eats other seabirds.

Puffins nest in soft parts of the cliff. They use their large bills for burrowing and fighting. In winter the bill loses its brightly coloured outer layer.

Gannets build large nests (up to 60 cm. high) of seaweed, feathers, grass and earth. This is a chick.

The **Razorbill** has a stout body with short wings. It flies fast and swims well.

Manx Shearwaters almost touch the water as they glide over the sea. They are easy to recognize as they are black on top, white underneath.

Guillemots dive from the surface to catch fish. They can stay under water for up to a minute.

Gannets dive 30 m. or more to catch fish, which they swallow whole. Note the black wing tips, snowy white plumage, and strong flight with regular wing beats.

The **Storm Petrel**, our smallest seabird, flutters over the water looking for plankton and small fish. Note the square-shaped tail.

The **Fulmar** is fatter and fluffier than gulls. It glides on stiff wings, using the wind currents along the cliff face.

The **Shag** is very like the Cormorant, but it is smaller and thinner. It has a fast, direct flight, and often perches on rocks.

REMEMBER! DON'T GO NEAR THE CLIFF EDGE OR TRY TO CLIMB CLIFFS. NEVER TAKE BIRDS' EGGS OR DISTURB THEIR NESTING PLACES

The **Kittiwake**, a small gull, makes a nest of green seaweed stuck to the cliff with mud.

Guillemots lay a single egg on bare rock. The egg is pear-shaped, so it rolls round instead of falling off the cliff.

Razorbills nest in colonies, laying their single egg in a crevice or under a boulder on the cliff.

All these birds nest on cliffs or rocky islands. Some nest in groups, called colonies, which you may be able to visit. But even if you cannot get very close to the birds, it is still interesting to watch them in flight, and possible to identify many of them.

Birds on the Beach

Salt marshes and muddy shores are good places to look for waders, ducks and geese. Look for waders, gulls, and terns on sandy beaches. Some of these birds migrate from the far north in winter to find better feeding places. Notice especially how the birds you see move on the ground, and how they feed, to help you to identify them. Remember that many birds change their plumage in winter, often becoming duller in colour.

1 Keeping Safe

Little Tern's egg

Birds that nest on the shore have eggs that are patterned to blend in with the sand or stones where they are laid.

2

Redshank on nest

Some birds build nests that blend in with the background to hide them from enemies. The Redshank builds its nest with grass in a tuft of grass.

The **Herring Gull** drops shells from the air onto rocks to burst them open.

The **Sanderling** darts along the tide line looking for shrimps, molluscs and worms.

Black-headed Gulls paddle in wet sand to bring animals to the surface.

The **Common Tern** dives to catch small fish, especially Sand-Eels.

The **Redshank** probes in the sand for worms and small molluscs.

The male **Little Tern**, like other terns, gives Sand-Eels to the female in the courtship ceremony.

A baby **Herring Gull** will beg for food by pecking at a red spot on the parent's bill.

Turnstones use their short sharp bills to find animals under stones and seaweed.

The **Bar-tailed Godwit** probes wet mud for insects and molluscs to eat.

The **Oystercatcher** uses its bill to dislodge Limpets and prise open Mussels to eat.

116

3

Ringed Plover dragging its wing

Some birds pretend to be hurt if their eggs or chicks are in danger. The enemy then follows the parent bird, instead of attacking the nest.

Danger from Oil

When birds get covered in oil emptied into the sea from tankers, they cannot fly or swim, and many starve to death or swallow the oil when preening, and poison themselves. The oil mats the bird's feathers together. Then the bird can no longer keep a layer of warm air under its feathers, so many die of cold.

Sometimes, however, they can be saved. If you find a live bird coated in oil, contact the local RSPCA clinic. Do not try to clean the bird yourself.

Cormorant

1 Identifying Birds

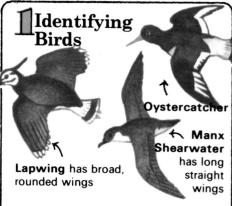

Oystercatcher

Manx Shearwater has long straight wings

Lapwing has broad, rounded wings

What shape are the bird's wings? Look to see if they are long or short, pointed or rounded, if the feathers are separated at the wing tips.

2

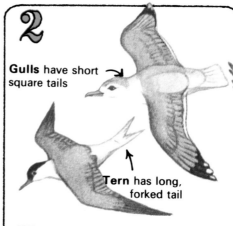

Gulls have short square tails

Tern has long, forked tail

What shape is the tail? It might be long or short, square or rounded, forked or cleft.

3

Guillemot flies straight and fast

Fulmar glides on stiff wings

How does it fly? In a straight or wavy line? Does it glide? If it is a diving bird, does it dive from the air or from the water's surface?

4

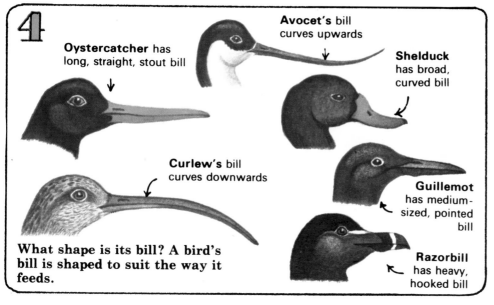

Oystercatcher has long, straight, stout bill

Avocet's bill curves upwards

Shelduck has broad, curved bill

Curlew's bill curves downwards

Guillemot has medium-sized, pointed bill

Razorbill has heavy, hooked bill

What shape is its bill? A bird's bill is shaped to suit the way it feeds.

5

Grey Plover has black patches under wings in winter

Dunlin has black belly

Kittiwake has black wing-tips and legs

Has it any special marks? Look on top and underneath for patches or stripes of colour. What colours are the bill and legs?

Animal Life in the Sand and Mud

At first sight a sandy beach may look empty. But if you dig down you can find many animals that burrow, especially on sheltered beaches where the sand is stable. There are no clear zones in the sand, because the conditions stay the same in spite of the tides. The animals simply burrow deeper to find moisture when the tide is out. You will find more animals near the surface if you dig along the low tide mark.

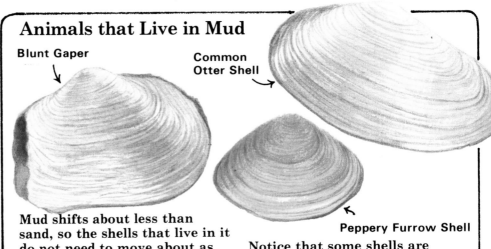

Animals that Live in Mud

Blunt Gaper

Common Otter Shell

Peppery Furrow Shell

Mud shifts about less than sand, so the shells that live in it do not need to move about as much as sand-dwellers. This makes them easier to dig up.

Notice that some shells are strong and thick to withstand the weight of the mud.

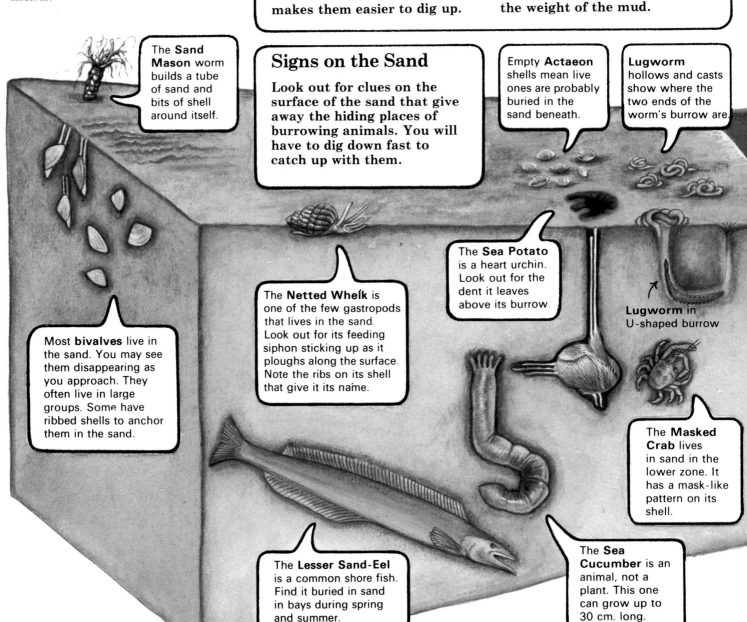

The **Sand Mason** worm builds a tube of sand and bits of shell around itself.

Signs on the Sand

Look out for clues on the surface of the sand that give away the hiding places of burrowing animals. You will have to dig down fast to catch up with them.

Empty **Actaeon** shells mean live ones are probably buried in the sand beneath.

Lugworm hollows and casts show where the two ends of the worm's burrow are.

Most **bivalves** live in the sand. You may see them disappearing as you approach. They often live in large groups. Some have ribbed shells to anchor them in the sand.

The **Netted Whelk** is one of the few gastropods that lives in the sand. Look out for its feeding siphon sticking up as it ploughs along the surface. Note the ribs on its shell that give it its name.

The **Sea Potato** is a heart urchin. Look out for the dent it leaves above its burrow.

Lugworm in U-shaped burrow

The **Masked Crab** lives in sand in the lower zone. It has a mask-like pattern on its shell.

The **Lesser Sand-Eel** is a common shore fish. Find it buried in sand in bays during spring and summer.

The **Sea Cucumber** is an animal, not a plant. This one can grow up to 30 cm. long.

Lesser Weever Fish ↗

DON'T TOUCH!
WATCH OUT FOR THIS FISH ON OR IN SAND, ESPECIALLY WHERE THERE'ARE A LOT OF SHRIMPS ON WHICH IT FEEDS. THE SPINES ON ITS FINS ARE POISONOUS

A Burrowing Starfish

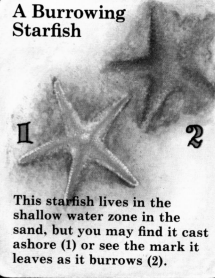

This starfish lives in the shallow water zone in the sand, but you may find it cast ashore (1) or see the mark it leaves as it burrows (2).

Look Under Heart Urchins

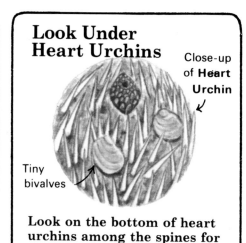

Close-up of **Heart Urchin** ↙

Tiny bivalves ↗

Look on the bottom of heart urchins among the spines for tiny bivalves that live there. Handle urchins gently as their spines rub off easily.

How Razor Shells Burrow

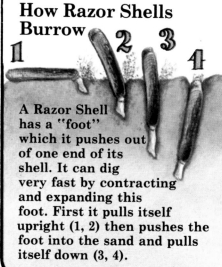

A Razor Shell has a "foot" which it pushes out of one end of its shell. It can dig very fast by contracting and expanding this foot. First it pulls itself upright (1, 2) then pushes the foot into the sand and pulls itself down (3, 4).

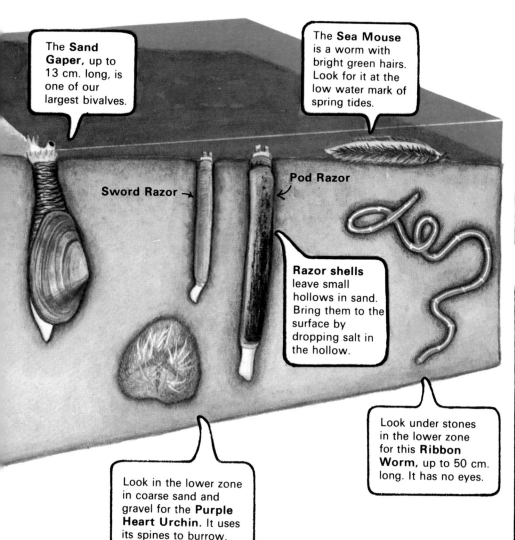

The **Sand Gaper,** up to 13 cm. long, is one of our largest bivalves.

The **Sea Mouse** is a worm with bright green hairs. Look for it at the low water mark of spring tides.

Sword Razor →

Pod Razor

Razor shells leave small hollows in sand. Bring them to the surface by dropping salt in the hollow.

Look in the lower zone in coarse sand and gravel for the **Purple Heart Urchin**. It uses its spines to burrow.

Look under stones in the lower zone for this **Ribbon Worm**, up to 50 cm. long. It has no eyes.

Worms in the Sand

Bootlace Worm ↙

The Bootlace Worm is usually 5 m. long. It lies in coils under stones on muddy shingle.

Fishes

Some kinds of fish are more difficult to identify than others because their colours vary between the male and female, and between adults and young. Look for fish in pools, estuaries, and shallow water in bays. Remember that some, like eels, spend part of their life in the sea and part in fresh water. Some fish feed on seaweed and plankton, others on worms, molluscs and other fish.

Flat Fish

Look in the shallow water zone for these flat fish. You will only find small specimens —the larger ones live in deep water. Notice how their colours act as a camouflage. They hide by flapping their fins on the sea bottom to cover themselves with sand.

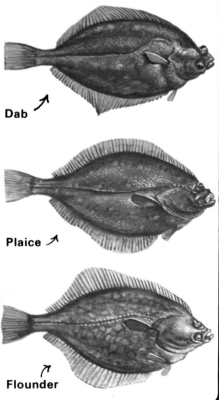

Dab

Plaice

Flounder

The **Lumpsucker** has a large, strong sucker on its underside for fixing itself to rocks. It has no scales, but notice the rows of lumps, called tubercles, on its body.

The **Spotted Goby** swims in shoals among seaweed just below low tide mark, and in harbours.

Lesser Sand-Eels swim in large shoals over sand. Their silvery colour makes them hard to see.

Look in weedy rock pools for the **15-Spined Stickleback**. In spring the male builds, guards and cleans its nest.

The **Grey Gurnard** lives on the seabed. It probes the bottom with feelers to find worms and crustaceans to eat.

Montagu's Sea Snail has a sucker, but no scales or tubercles. Look under seaweed. It lays its eggs on Oarweed holdfasts and rocks.

The Tompot Blenny is found low down on rocky shores. It grows to about 30 cm. long.

The Butterfish (or Gunnel) is a relative of the Blenny. It has a flat body and rounded tail, and a very slippery skin. It lives under rocks.

The Sand or Common Goby is patterned like the sand. Notice the dark spot on its dorsal fin. Gobies have a fin underneath which forms a weak sucker.

Conger Eels, up to 2 m. long, hide in cracks and under stones in the lower zone of rocky shores. They come out at night to feed. Beware of their sharp teeth!

Look in eelgrass very low down on the shore for the Greater Pipe-Fish. It has a long snout.

Look under seaweed in small pools for the Long-Spined Sea Scorpion. Its spines are sharp, but not poisonous.

The Cornish Sucker hides under stones. It has a strong sucker on its underside.

The Corkwing Wrasse hides in crevices. Wrasses are very colourful, heavily-built fish with thick lips and strong teeth.

Beachcombing

Above or on the high water level, you will see a line of dead seaweed and rubbish thrown up by the sea onto the beach. This is called the strand line. If you look more closely, you may find some interesting things, some alive, others dead. It is also a good place to look for animals and birds that find their food among this rubbish, like Sandhoppers, beetles, flies, gulls and Turnstones.

Some beachcombers hunt along the strand line for shipping objects, like cork and glass floats, old bottles, and fishing nets.

Things that Look like Stones

Ammonite

Belemnite

This is the fossil of an animal related to squids and octopuses.

Bean

This coiled fossil is the remains of an animal that lived millions of years ago. It shows the shape of the animal's shell.

This bean-shaped object is the fruit of a West Indian plant, up to 5 cm. across.

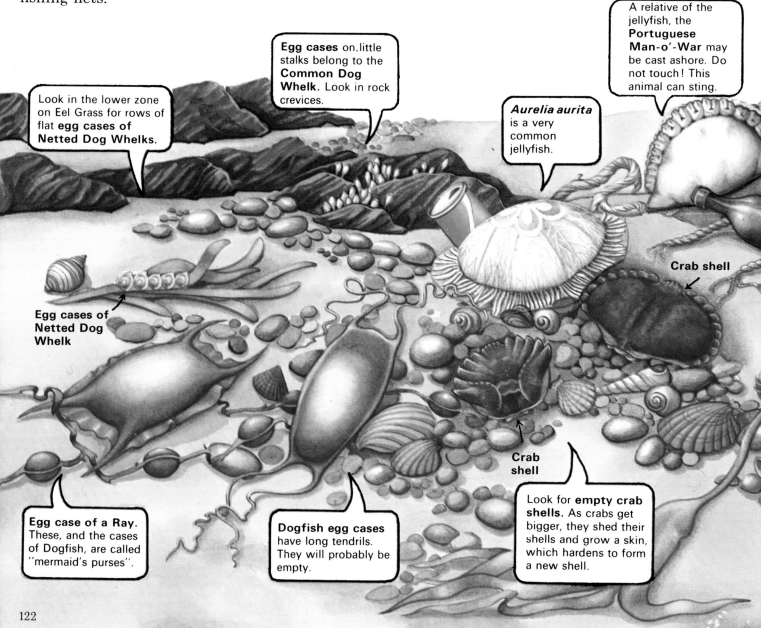

Look in the lower zone on Eel Grass for rows of flat **egg cases of Netted Dog Whelks**.

Egg cases on little stalks belong to the **Common Dog Whelk**. Look in rock crevices.

A relative of the jellyfish, the **Portuguese Man-o'-War** may be cast ashore. Do not touch! This animal can sting.

Aurelia aurita is a very common jellyfish.

Crab shell

Egg cases of Netted Dog Whelk

Crab shell

Egg case of a Ray. These, and the cases of Dogfish, are called "mermaid's purses".

Dogfish egg cases have long tendrils. They will probably be empty.

Look for **empty crab shells**. As crabs get bigger, they shed their shells and grow a skin, which hardens to form a new shell.

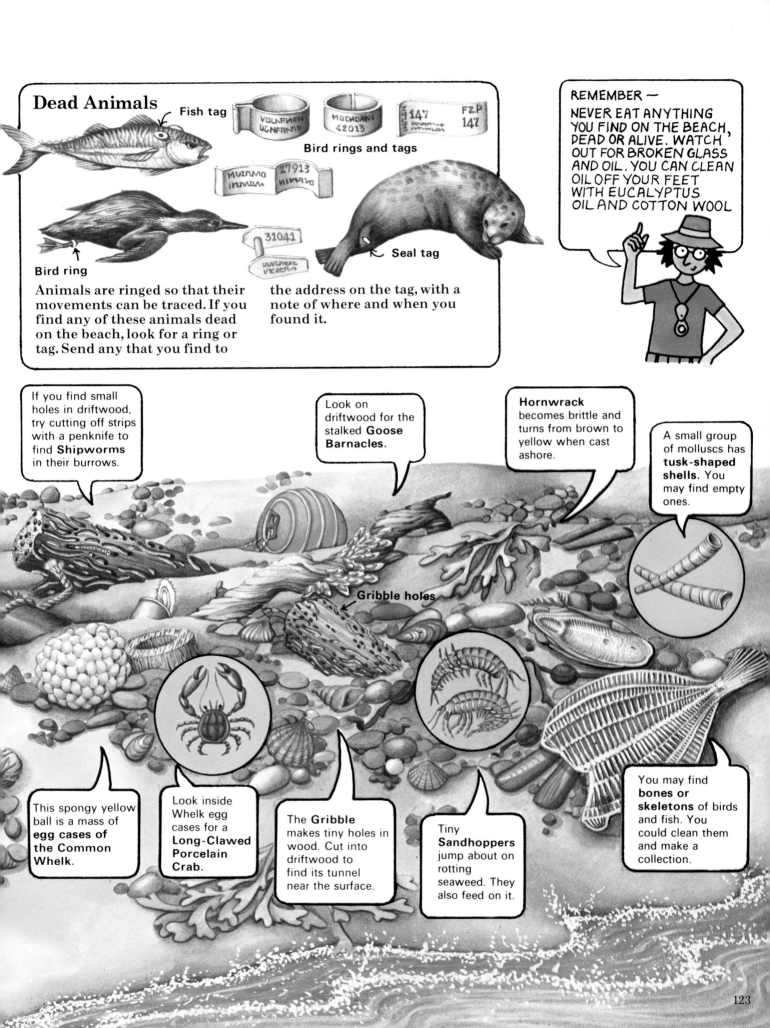

Dead Animals

Fish tag

Bird rings and tags

147

FZP
147

27913

31041

Bird ring

Seal tag

Animals are ringed so that their movements can be traced. If you find any of these animals dead on the beach, look for a ring or tag. Send any that you find to the address on the tag, with a note of where and when you found it.

REMEMBER — NEVER EAT ANYTHING YOU FIND ON THE BEACH, DEAD OR ALIVE. WATCH OUT FOR BROKEN GLASS AND OIL. YOU CAN CLEAN OIL OFF YOUR FEET WITH EUCALYPTUS OIL AND COTTON WOOL

If you find small holes in driftwood, try cutting off strips with a penknife to find **Shipworms** in their burrows.

Look on driftwood for the stalked **Goose Barnacles**.

Hornwrack becomes brittle and turns from brown to yellow when cast ashore.

A small group of molluscs has **tusk-shaped shells**. You may find empty ones.

Gribble holes

This spongy yellow ball is a mass of **egg cases of the Common Whelk**.

Look inside Whelk egg cases for a **Long-Clawed Porcelain Crab**.

The **Gribble** makes tiny holes in wood. Cut into driftwood to find its tunnel near the surface.

Tiny **Sandhoppers** jump about on rotting seaweed. They also feed on it.

You may find **bones or skeletons** of birds and fish. You could clean them and make a collection.

123

More Seashore Life to Spot

Fishes

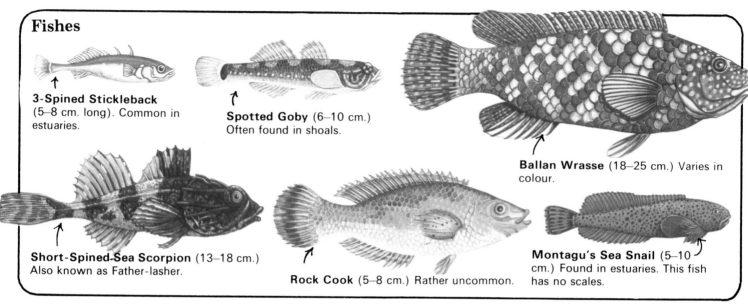

3-Spined Stickleback (5–8 cm. long). Common in estuaries.

Spotted Goby (6–10 cm.) Often found in shoals.

Ballan Wrasse (18–25 cm.) Varies in colour.

Short-Spined Sea Scorpion (13–18 cm.) Also known as Father-lasher.

Rock Cook (5–8 cm.) Rather uncommon.

Montagu's Sea Snail (5–10 cm.) Found in estuaries. This fish has no scales.

Jellyfish

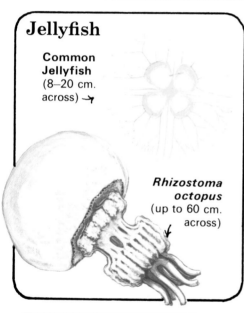

Common Jellyfish (8–20 cm. across) →

Rhizostoma octopus (up to 60 cm. across)

Anemones and Corals

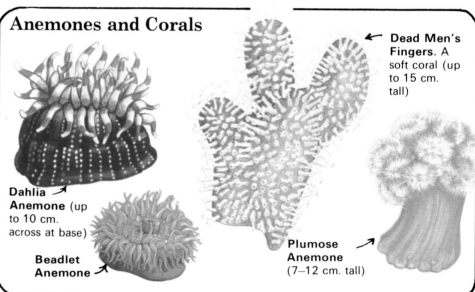

Dead Men's Fingers. A soft coral (up to 15 cm. tall)

Dahlia Anemone (up to 10 cm. across at base)

Beadlet Anemone

Plumose Anemone (7–12 cm. tall)

Sponges

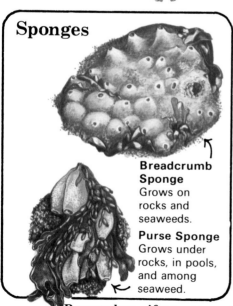

Breadcrumb Sponge Grows on rocks and seaweeds.

Purse Sponge Grows under rocks, in pools, and among seaweed.

Worms

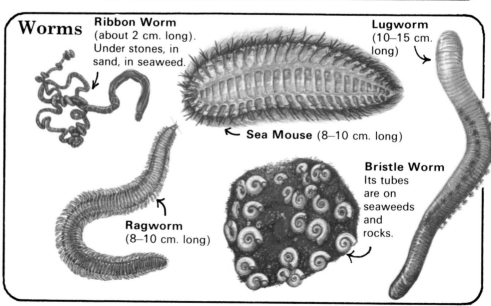

Ribbon Worm (about 2 cm. long). Under stones, in sand, in seaweed.

Lugworm (10–15 cm. long)

Sea Mouse (8–10 cm. long)

Ragworm (8–10 cm. long)

Bristle Worm Its tubes are on seaweeds and rocks.

Remember—if you cannot see a picture of the thing that you want to identify on these pages, turn to the page earlier in the book that deals with that kind of animal or plant.

Note: the animals in these boxes are not drawn to scale.

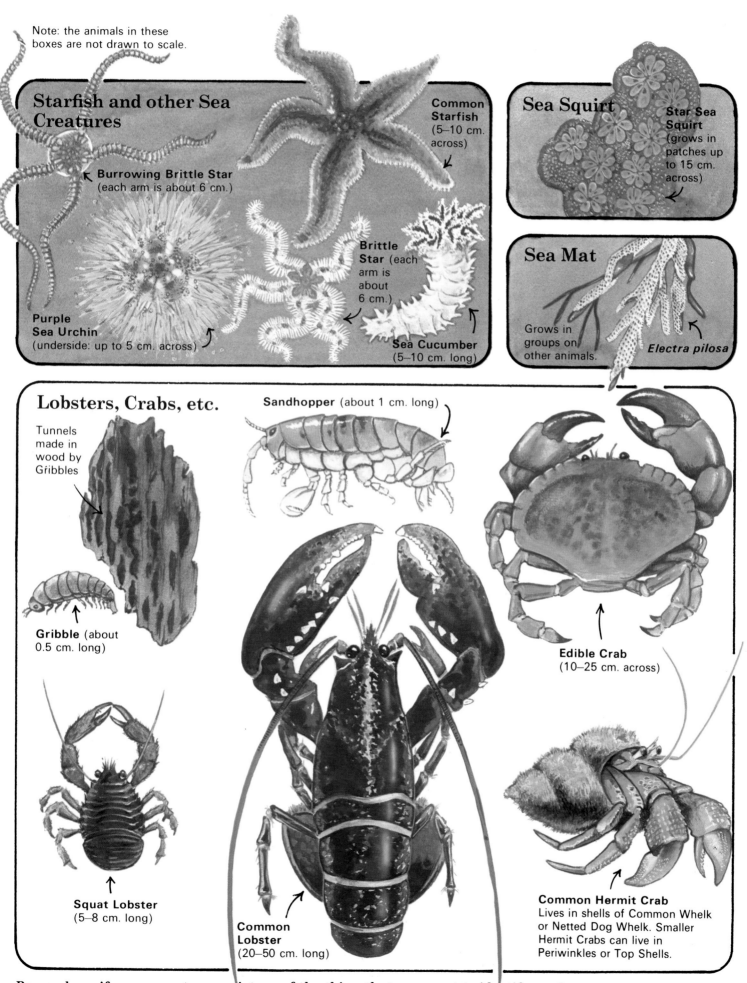

Starfish and other Sea Creatures

Common Starfish (5–10 cm. across)

Burrowing Brittle Star (each arm is about 6 cm.)

Brittle Star (each arm is about 6 cm.)

Purple Sea Urchin (underside: up to 5 cm. across)

Sea Cucumber (5–10 cm. long)

Sea Squirt

Star Sea Squirt (grows in patches up to 15 cm. across)

Sea Mat

Grows in groups on other animals.

Electra pilosa

Lobsters, Crabs, etc.

Sandhopper (about 1 cm. long)

Tunnels made in wood by Gribbles

Gribble (about 0.5 cm. long)

Edible Crab (10–25 cm. across)

Squat Lobster (5–8 cm. long)

Common Lobster (20–50 cm. long)

Common Hermit Crab
Lives in shells of Common Whelk or Netted Dog Whelk. Smaller Hermit Crabs can live in Periwinkles or Top Shells.

Remember—if you cannot see a picture of the thing that you want to identify on these pages, turn to the page earlier in the book that deals with that kind of animal or plant.

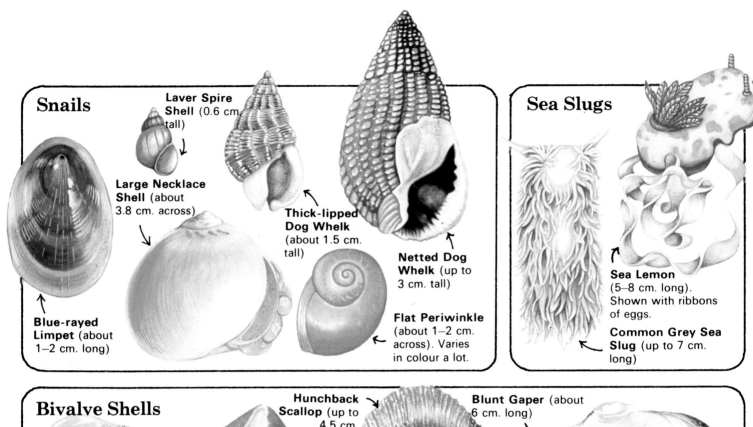

Snails

Laver Spire Shell (0.6 cm. tall)

Large Necklace Shell (about 3.8 cm. across)

Thick-lipped Dog Whelk (about 1.5 cm. tall)

Netted Dog Whelk (up to 3 cm. tall)

Blue-rayed Limpet (about 1–2 cm. long)

Flat Periwinkle (about 1–2 cm. across). Varies in colour a lot.

Sea Slugs

Sea Lemon (5–8 cm. long). Shown with ribbons of eggs.

Common Grey Sea Slug (up to 7 cm. long)

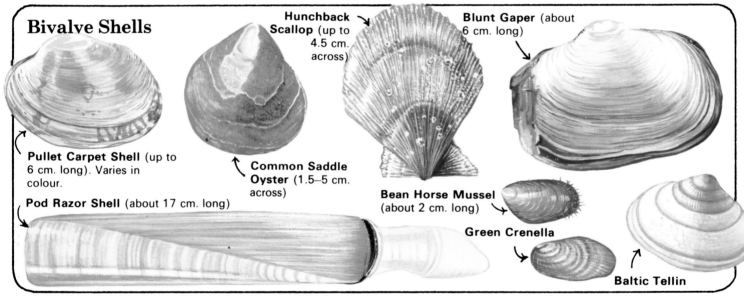

Bivalve Shells

Hunchback Scallop (up to 4.5 cm. across)

Blunt Gaper (about 6 cm. long)

Pullet Carpet Shell (up to 6 cm. long). Varies in colour.

Common Saddle Oyster (1.5–5 cm. across)

Pod Razor Shell (about 17 cm. long)

Bean Horse Mussel (about 2 cm. long)

Green Crenella

Baltic Tellin

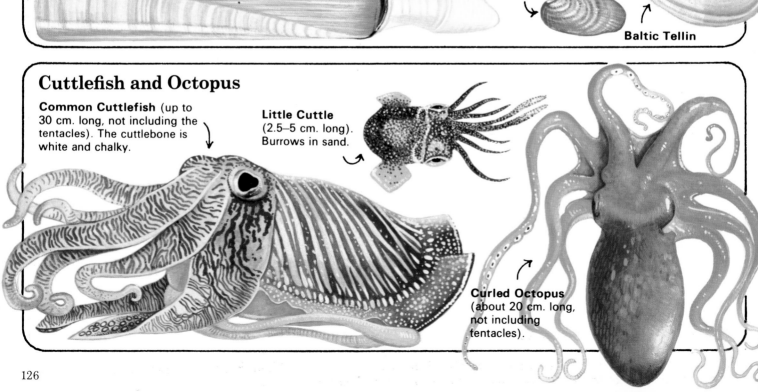

Cuttlefish and Octopus

Common Cuttlefish (up to 30 cm. long, not including the tentacles). The cuttlebone is white and chalky.

Little Cuttle (2.5–5 cm. long). Burrows in sand.

Curled Octopus (about 20 cm. long, not including tentacles).

Birds

Fulmar. Nests on cliffs in summer.

Shelduck

Scaup Estuaries and bays in winter.

Common Scoter

Male   Female

Eider Duck Rocky and sandy sea coasts.

Knot. Has grey plumage in winter.

Sanderling. Has pale plumage in winter.

Grey Plover. Has greyer appearance in winter.

Oyster-catcher Shores, islands, estuaries.

Curlew Sand dunes and grassy coasts.

Greenshank Marshes, estuaries, and mud flats.

Lesser Black-Backed Gull. Coasts and estuaries. Nests on cliffs.

Male

Stonechat Sea cliffs

Female

Wheatear

Plants

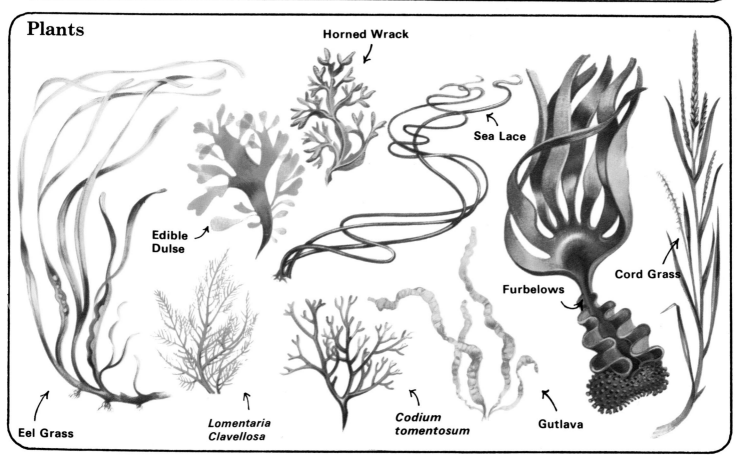

Horned Wrack

Sea Lace

Edible Dulse

Cord Grass

Furbelows

Eel Grass

Lomentaria Clavellosa

Codium tomentosum

Gutlava

Remember—if you cannot see a picture of the thing that you want to identify on these pages, turn to the page earlier in the book that deals with that kind of animal or plant.

Near the Seashore

Whales and dolphins

Dolphins and porpoises are small whales. You may see whales near the coast, and dolphins when they leap out of the water.

Whales are mammals, and have a blow-hole on top of their heads for breathing air. You may see a "spout" or "blow" from a whale; this is when it comes to the surface to breathe out. It blows out not water, but moist air. The moisture condenses when it meets the cold air, and forms a jet of droplets.

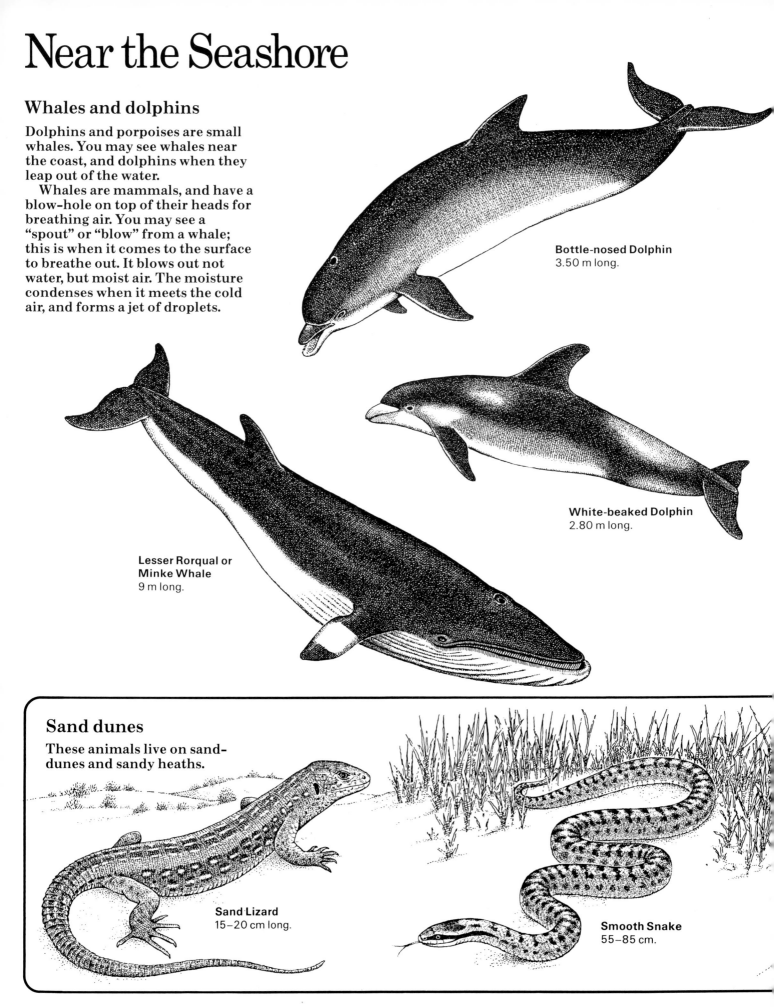

Bottle-nosed Dolphin
3.50 m long.

White-beaked Dolphin
2.80 m long.

Lesser Rorqual or Minke Whale
9 m long.

Sand dunes

These animals live on sand-dunes and sandy heaths.

Sand Lizard
15–20 cm long.

Smooth Snake
55–85 cm.

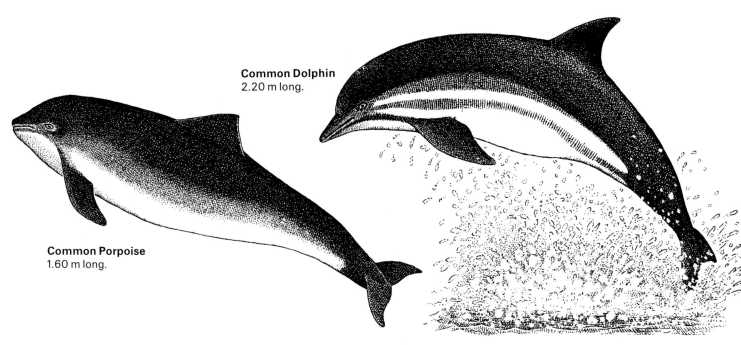

Common Dolphin
2.20 m long.

Common Porpoise
1.60 m long.

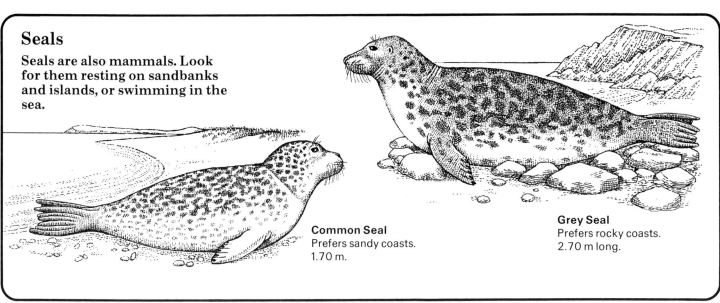

Seals

Seals are also mammals. Look for them resting on sandbanks and islands, or swimming in the sea.

Common Seal
Prefers sandy coasts.
1.70 m.

Grey Seal
Prefers rocky coasts.
2.70 m long.

Natterjack Toad
Rare. 6–8 cm.

Rabbit
Body length 40 cm.

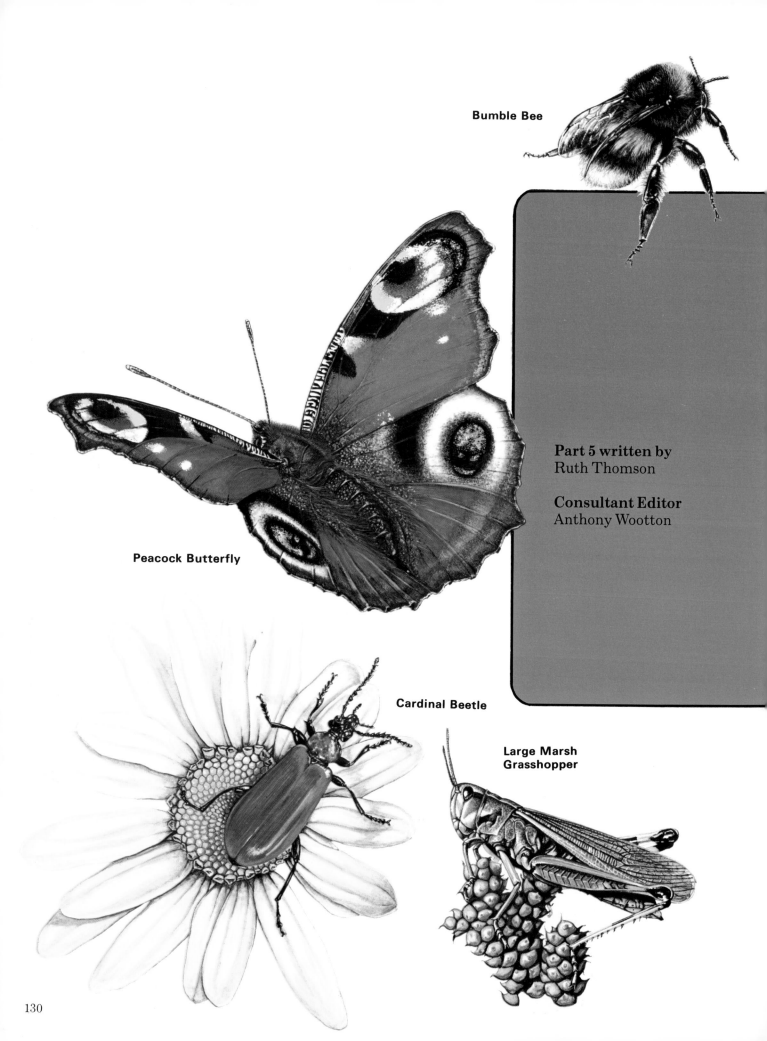

Bumble Bee

Peacock Butterfly

Part 5 written by
Ruth Thomson

Consultant Editor
Anthony Wootton

Cardinal Beetle

Large Marsh
Grasshopper

**Small Tortoiseshell
Butterfly**

Part 5
INSECTS

This section of the book tells you where to look for common European insects. It explains how insects live in different kinds of places, like gardens, ponds and in trees and how to recognize them.

It also shows you how to make notes, how to collect insects, and how to look after your collection. There are even details on breeding certain kinds of insects, and on making a garden of flowers to attract butterflies.

Other parts of this section describe how insects move, feed and sense things. At the end of the section are some charts showing lots of common insects to spot.

Wherever possible, the insects have been drawn life size. Where lengths are given, they refer to the length of the insect from the tip of its abdomen to its head, not including the antennae. The sizes given for winged insects refer to their wing span (from wing-tip to wing-tip).

If you would like to study insects further, try to find out if there is an entomological section in your local natural history society. Your library will probably have details.

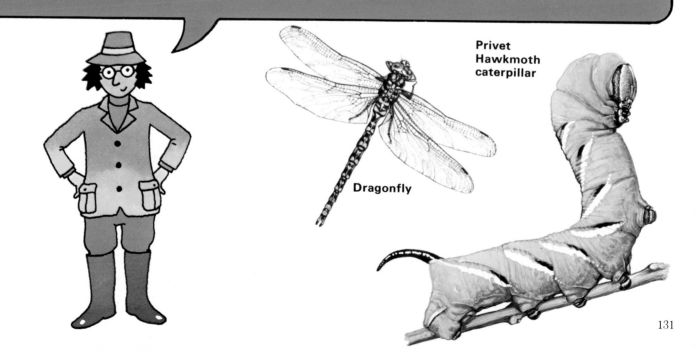

**Privet
Hawkmoth
caterpillar**

Dragonfly

Becoming an Insect Watcher

You can find insects almost anywhere, so it is easy to start watching them. Look first at as many kinds of insects as you can find so that you learn how they differ from other animals. Later you may want to study one or two kinds in more detail.

There are more *kinds* of insects (called *species*) than all the different kinds of mammals, fish, birds and reptiles put together. People are still discovering new species and finding out more about ones already known.

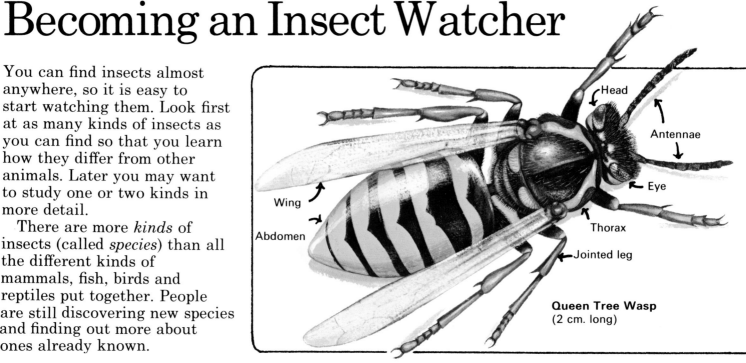

Queen Tree Wasp
(2 cm. long)

Head
Antennae
Eye
Thorax
Jointed leg
Wing
Abdomen

What You Need

These are some of the things it is useful to have if you want to be an insect-watcher. You will need a good pocket lens and a field notebook for recording what you see. Choose a lens which magnifies 8 or 10 times. It is a good idea to fix it on some string round your neck, to keep it handy. You may not need all the things shown: it depends on where you want to look for insects.

LAY A WHITE SHEET UNDER A BUSH. BEAT THE BUSH WITH A STICK. THE SHEET WILL CATCH FALLING INSECTS

A BUTTERFLY NET MAY BE USEFUL. STALK THE INSECT SLOWLY AND QUIETLY. TRY NOT TO HARM IT

A SMALL TROWEL IS USEFUL FOR DIGGING UP EARTH. SIEVE THE SOIL TO FIND INSECTS

Quick Sketches

Make quick sketches of the insects you find. When you get home, look them up and try to identify them.

1 Draw three ovals for the head, thorax and abdomen.

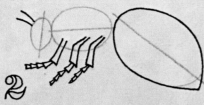

2 Draw the insect's legs and antennae in position.

3 Draw in the wings, if the insect has any.

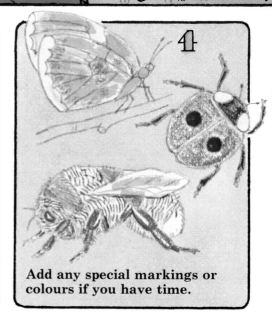

4 Add any special markings or colours if you have time.

What is an Insect?

All adult insects have three parts to their bodies: a head, a thorax (middle) and an abdomen (lower part). On their heads they have a pair of antennae, used mainly for smelling and feeling. Most insects have a pair of large eyes and all insects have three pairs of jointed legs (at some time in their lives) attached to the thorax. Most adult insects have wings. Apart from birds and bats, insects are the only other kind of animals that can fly properly.

These are not Insects

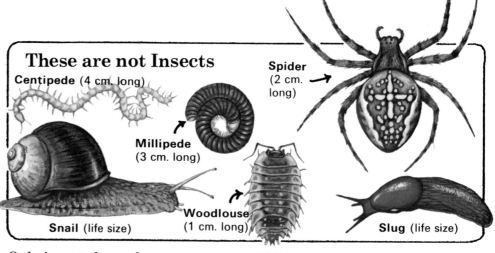

Centipede (4 cm. long)

Millipede (3 cm. long)

Spider (2 cm. long)

Woodlouse (1 cm. long)

Snail (life size)

Slug (life size)

Only insects have three parts to their body and three pairs of legs. Slugs and snails have no legs at all, and spiders have eight legs.

Millipedes, centipedes and woodlice have bodies made up of lots of parts, called segments, and have legs on every segment.

THE MOST IMPORTANT THING YOU NEED IS A NOTEBOOK. USE A NEW PAGE FOR EACH INSECT YOU FIND

YOU COULD MARK OFF AN AREA WITH STRING AND SEE HOW MANY INSECTS YOU FIND THERE

TAKE A BAG WITH POCKETS TO CARRY YOUR EQUIPMENT IN

CARRY INSECTS IN SCREW-TOP JARS OR BOXES LINED WITH PAPER OR MOSS

July 13th Heron Meadow 2pm Sunny

Cinnabar Caterpillars on leaves and stem of Ragwort. Colour-Yellow and black stripes.

HERON MEADOW gate

Cinnabar Caterpillars on Ragwort

bush

Ants' nest under stones

Keeping a Notebook

It is best to use a spiral-bound notebook for your notes. Then you can tear off pages and keep together all the notes you gather at different times on a particular insect. Make rough notes while you are watching; you can always make more careful ones later. Write down the date and the time when you saw the insect and what the weather was like. Try to describe the insect and the plant you found it on as fully as possible. If you find something that you want to look at again, make a map of where you found it.

133

Differences to Spot

QUICK CHECK LIST

WHEN YOU FIND AN INSECT, LOOK FIRST TO SEE WHETHER IT HAS WINGS AND, IF SO, HOW MANY.

IF IT HAS ONE PAIR OF WINGS, LOOK AT CHART A.

IF IT HAS TWO PAIRS OF WINGS, LOOK AT CHART B.

IF IT HAS NO WINGS, LOOK AT CHART C.

IF IT HAS HARD WING-CASES, LOOK AT CHART D.

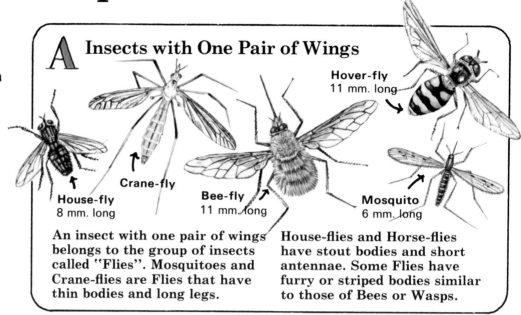

A Insects with One Pair of Wings

Hover-fly 11 mm. long

Crane-fly

House-fly 8 mm. long

Bee-fly 11 mm. long

Mosquito 6 mm. long

An insect with one pair of wings belongs to the group of insects called "Flies". Mosquitoes and Crane-flies are Flies that have thin bodies and long legs.

House-flies and Horse-flies have stout bodies and short antennae. Some Flies have furry or striped bodies similar to those of Bees or Wasps.

It is not always easy to tell one insect from another. Some Flies look very like Bees, while many Bugs look like Beetles. There are many different species of insects—perhaps a million in the world. Only a few are shown here–there are more later in the book.

When you are taking notes on an insect you have found, try to make a habit of asking yourself several questions about it. Does it have wings? How many pairs? Does the insect have hard wing-cases? The charts on this page show some of the insects which have these features.

This is not a scientific method of classifying insects, but it will help you to group them in your own mind. Take notes on anything else that you notice about the insect. Does it have antennae? How long are they? Does the insect have legs, and if so, how many? Remember that insects change colour and shape as they grow into adults, and that the male of a species is sometimes a different colour from the female.

B Insects with Two Pairs of Wings

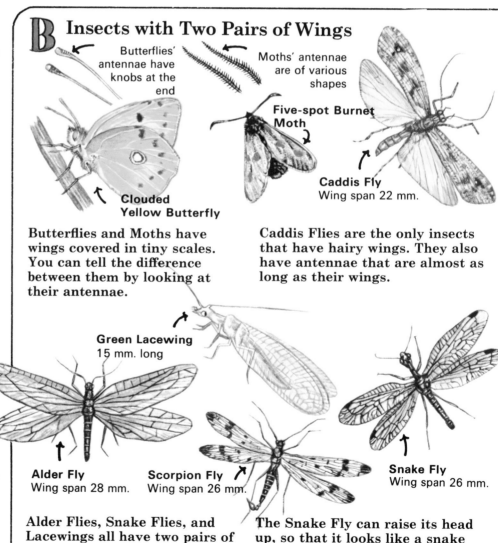

Butterflies' antennae have knobs at the end

Moths' antennae are of various shapes

Five-spot Burnet Moth

Clouded Yellow Butterfly

Caddis Fly Wing span 22 mm.

Butterflies and Moths have wings covered in tiny scales. You can tell the difference between them by looking at their antennae.

Caddis Flies are the only insects that have hairy wings. They also have antennae that are almost as long as their wings.

Green Lacewing 15 mm. long

Alder Fly Wing span 28 mm.

Scorpion Fly Wing span 26 mm.

Snake Fly Wing span 26 mm.

Alder Flies, Snake Flies, and Lacewings all have two pairs of wings that are both similar in size. Lacewings have long antennae and translucent wings.

The Snake Fly can raise its head up, so that it looks like a snake about to strike. You can recognize a male Scorpion Fly by its up-turned tail.

Where no size is given in a label, the insect is drawn life size.

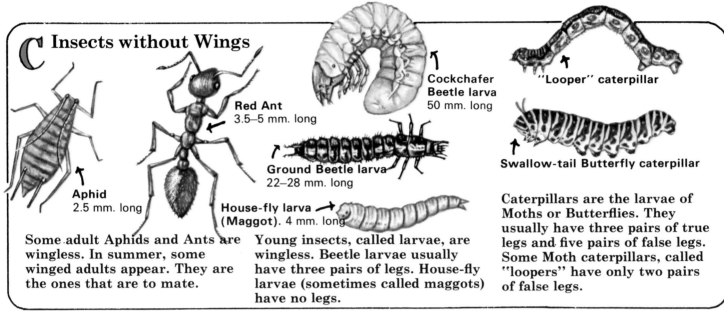

C Insects without Wings

Cockchafer Beetle larva 50 mm. long

"Looper" caterpillar

Red Ant 3.5–5 mm. long

Ground Beetle larva 22–28 mm. long

Swallow-tail Butterfly caterpillar

Aphid 2.5 mm. long

House-fly larva (Maggot). 4 mm. long

Some adult Aphids and Ants are wingless. In summer, some winged adults appear. They are the ones that are to mate.

Young insects, called larvae, are wingless. Beetle larvae usually have three pairs of legs. House-fly larvae (sometimes called maggots) have no legs.

Caterpillars are the larvae of Moths or Butterflies. They usually have three pairs of true legs and five pairs of false legs. Some Moth caterpillars, called "loopers" have only two pairs of false legs.

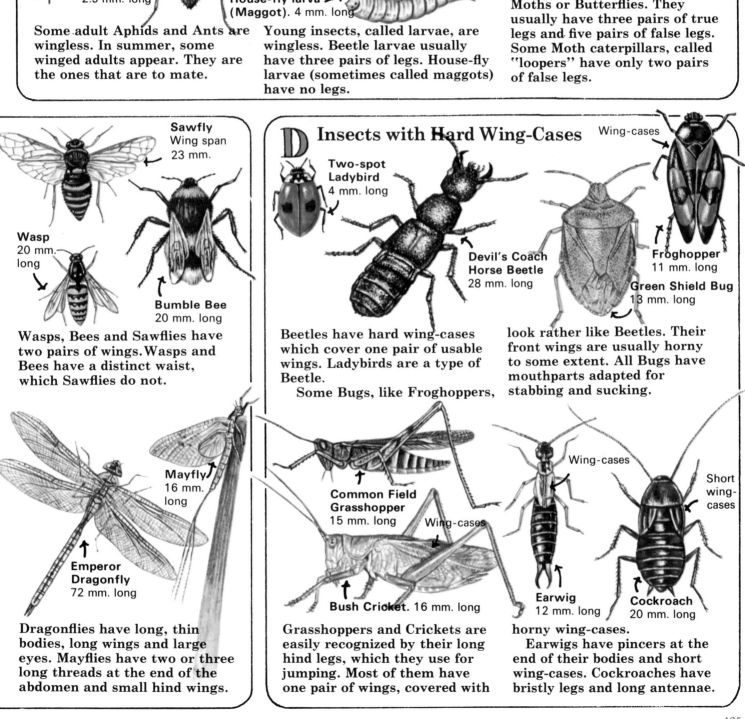

Sawfly Wing span 23 mm.

D Insects with Hard Wing-Cases

Wing-cases

Two-spot Ladybird 4 mm. long

Wasp 20 mm. long

Bumble Bee 20 mm. long

Devil's Coach Horse Beetle 28 mm. long

Froghopper 11 mm. long

Green Shield Bug 13 mm. long

Wasps, Bees and Sawflies have two pairs of wings. Wasps and Bees have a distinct waist, which Sawflies do not.

Beetles have hard wing-cases which cover one pair of usable wings. Ladybirds are a type of Beetle.

Some Bugs, like Froghoppers,

look rather like Beetles. Their front wings are usually horny to some extent. All Bugs have mouthparts adapted for stabbing and sucking.

Mayfly 16 mm. long

Common Field Grasshopper 15 mm. long

Wing-cases

Wing-cases

Short wing-cases

Emperor Dragonfly 72 mm. long

Bush Cricket. 16 mm. long

Earwig 12 mm. long

Cockroach 20 mm. long

Dragonflies have long, thin bodies, long wings and large eyes. Mayflies have two or three long threads at the end of the abdomen and small hind wings.

Grasshoppers and Crickets are easily recognized by their long hind legs, which they use for jumping. Most of them have one pair of wings, covered with

horny wing-cases.
Earwigs have pincers at the end of their bodies and short wing-cases. Cockroaches have bristly legs and long antennae.

Breeding, Growing and Changing

Almost all insects grow from eggs. The eggs hatch into young insects. Before they become adults, young insects must go through different stages of growth. Some young insects change shape completely. Others just get bigger. The ones on this page do not change their shape very much, only their size. The ones on the opposite page go through a further very different stage of growth after they hatch, before they become adult insects.

All insects have a soft skin at first, but this hardens and then cannot stretch. As they grow, insects have to change their skin. This is called moulting. A new skin grows under the old one. The old skin splits and the insect wriggles out, covered in its new, larger skin. Once the insect has become adult, it does not grow any more.

Some insects, like Crickets, Earwigs, Grasshoppers and Bugs, hatch from the eggs looking like smaller versions of the adults. They have no wings when they

hatch. These young insects are called nymphs. They moult several times, growing each time. The wings appear as small wing buds. At the last moult, the wing buds expand into wings.

The young of other insects, like Butterflies, Moths, Beetles, Flies, Ants, Bees and Gnats are called larvae. When they hatch from the eggs, they do not look like the adults they will become. They moult several times as they grow.

When these larvae have grown to a certain size, they

Dragonflies

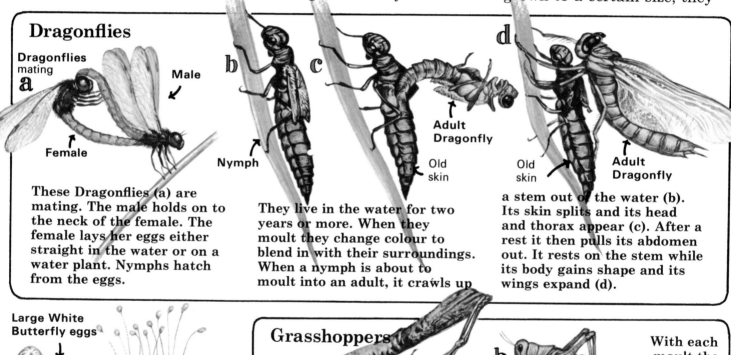

Dragonflies mating a — **Male** — **Female**

b **Nymph**

c **Old skin** — **Adult Dragonfly**

d **Old skin** — **Adult Dragonfly**

These Dragonflies (a) are mating. The male holds on to the neck of the female. The female lays her eggs either straight in the water or on a water plant. Nymphs hatch from the eggs.

They live in the water for two years or more. When they moult they change colour to blend in with their surroundings. When a nymph is about to moult into an adult, it crawls up

a stem out of the water (b). Its skin splits and its head and thorax appear (c). After a rest it then pulls its abdomen out. It rests on the stem while its body gains shape and its wings expand (d).

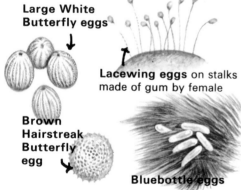

Large White Butterfly eggs

Lacewing eggs on stalks made of gum by female

Brown Hairstreak Butterfly egg

Bluebottle eggs

Female insects lay eggs, either singly or in clusters. A few insects, like the Earwig, look after their eggs and guard them, but most insects leave the eggs once they are laid.

Grasshoppers

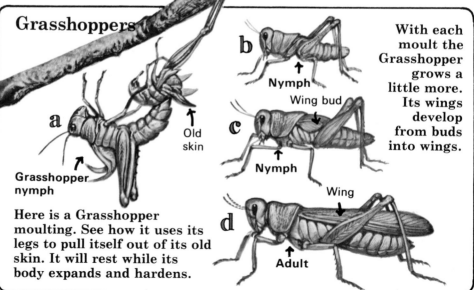

a **Grasshopper nymph** — **Old skin**

b **Nymph**

c **Wing bud** — **Nymph**

d **Wing** — **Adult**

With each moult the Grasshopper grows a little more. Its wings develop from buds into wings.

Here is a Grasshopper moulting. See how it uses its legs to pull itself out of its old skin. It will rest while its body expands and hardens.

shed their skin for the last time and become pupae. Pupae cannot feed and usually do not move. Inside the pupa, the body of the young insect changes into the adult insect.

When the adult is ready to emerge, the skin of the pupa splits and the adult struggles out. It does not grow any more after this.

The adult mates with an insect of the same species. Then the females look for places to lay their eggs. Some are laid on stems, some in or on the ground, and some in water.

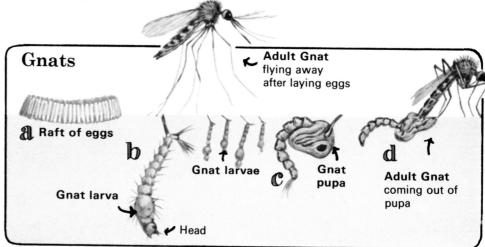

Gnats

a Raft of eggs

b Gnat larva — Head

Gnat larvae

c Gnat pupa

d Adult Gnat coming out of pupa

Adult Gnat flying away after laying eggs

Gnats lay their eggs in groups, which float like a raft on the water's surface (a). The larvae (b) hatch out, and then hang from the surface, breathing air through a siphon. Each larva turns into a pupa (c), which also lives near the surface. When the adult insect has formed inside the pupa, the skin splits and the Gnat crawls out (d).

Butterflies

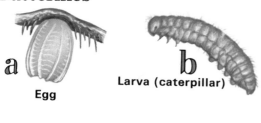

a Egg

b Larva (caterpillar)

c Pupa

d Adult Butterfly

The Meadow Brown Butterfly lays a single egg on grass (a). The caterpillar (b) comes out of the egg and spends the winter in this form. Early the next summer, it turns into a pupa (c). Inside the pupa, or chrysalis, the body of the caterpillar breaks down and reforms into the body of the Butterfly. This takes about four weeks. Then the pupa splits, and the adult emerges. It rests while its crumpled wings spread out and dry. Then it is ready to fly (d).

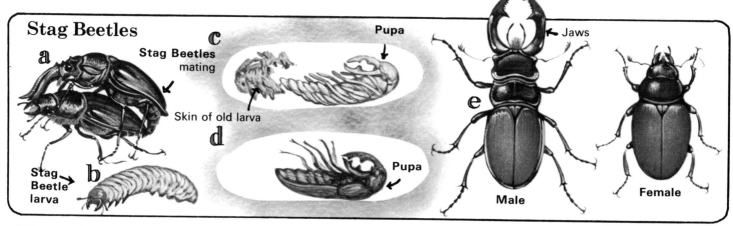

Stag Beetles

a Stag Beetles mating

b Stag Beetle larva

c Skin of old larva — Pupa

d Pupa

e Jaws — Male

Female

After mating (a), the female Stag Beetle lays her eggs in holes in rotten trees. The young larva (b) lives for three years burrowing through the soft wood of the tree. Then, the larva stops feeding, makes a pupal cell in the wood and becomes a pupa (c). It lies on its back to protect the newly-formed limbs until they harden (d). It emerges as an adult Beetle (e). The males have large jaws which look like a stag's antlers. They use them for fighting and to attract the female.

Insects in the Garden

A good place to start a study of insects is in your own garden. If you do not have a garden then look in your nearest park or open space. Make a chart of the insects you find there each month. In winter, look under stones, the bark of tree stumps and dead leaves. It is even worth looking in a garden shed. Some insects spend the winter without moving or feeding. This is called hibernation. If you find a hibernating insect, do not disturb it.

WHEN LOOKING FOR INSECTS REMEMBER THE INSECT-WATCHER'S CODE. ALWAYS REPLACE LOGS AND STONES EXACTLY AS YOU FOUND THEM. THEY ARE OFTEN INSECTS' HOMES. SEARCH CAREFULLY AND TRY NOT TO DAMAGE FLOWERS AND TWIGS MORE THAN YOU NEED. YOU HAVE A BETTER CHANCE OF FINDING INSECTS IF YOU MOVE SLOWLY AND QUIETLY. YOU CAN DISCOVER A LOT JUST BY WAITING AND WATCHING

1 On Tree Trunks

Engrailed Moth

Puss Moth pupa

Convolvulus Hawkmoth

Snipe Fly

Moths, especially those with colours like bark, rest on trees. In winter look for pupae in bark crevices.

5 On Grasses

Drinker Moth caterpillar

Meadow Brown Butterfly caterpillar

Meadow Grasshopper

Cuckoo-spit (made by Froghoppers as a protection)

Search carefully for insects on grasses. Many of them are green and so are difficult to see.

9 On the Ground

Devil's Coach Horse Beetle

Ground Beetle

Black Ant

Watch ants and beetles scuttling over the ground in summer. See if you can follow where they go.

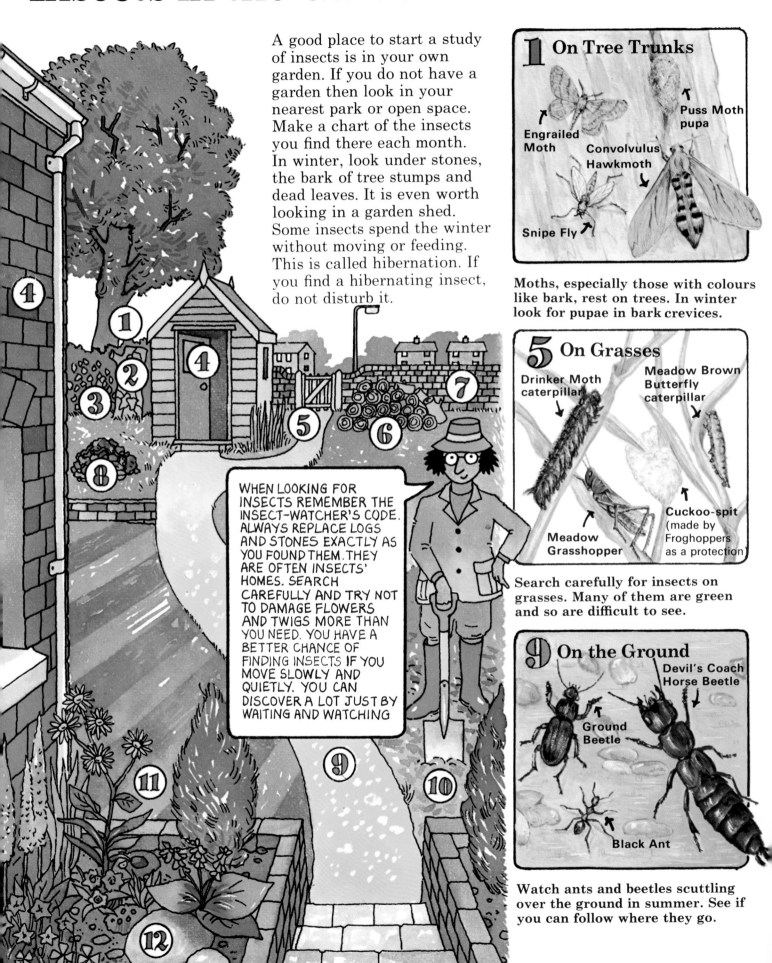

2 Under Bark

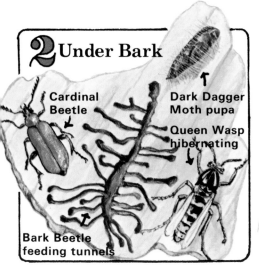

Cardinal Beetle

Dark Dagger Moth pupa

Queen Wasp hibernating

Bark Beetle feeding tunnels

Queen Wasps and Beetles sometimes hibernate under loose bark. Look for Bark Beetle tunnels.

3 On Leaves and Stems

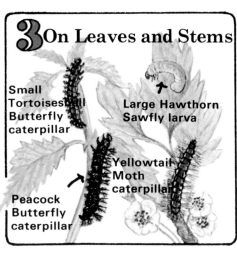

Small Tortoiseshell Butterfly caterpillar

Large Hawthorn Sawfly larva

Yellowtail Moth caterpillar

Peacock Butterfly caterpillar

Most caterpillars feed on leaves. Look for them in spring and summer, particularly on hedges.

4 House and Outhouse

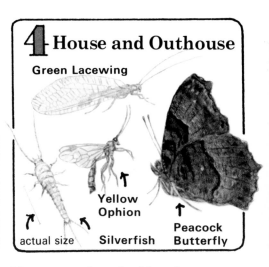

Green Lacewing

Yellow Ophion

actual size

Silverfish

Peacock Butterfly

If you search a shed in winter, you may find a Peacock Butterfly or a Lacewing.

6 In Woodpiles

Butterfly pupae

Herald Moth

Large Yellow Underwing Moth

In winter, these insects hibernate in sheltered places such as wood piles. Never disturb them there.

7 On Walls

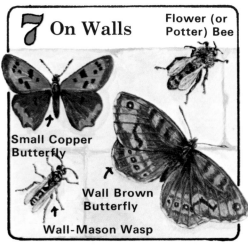

Flower (or Potter) Bee

Small Copper Butterfly

Wall Brown Butterfly

Wall-Mason Wasp

These insects like to settle on walls, particularly if the walls face the sun.

8 In the Rubbish Heap

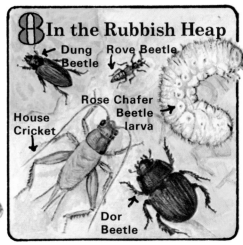

Dung Beetle

Rove Beetle

Rose Chafer Beetle larva

House Cricket

Dor Beetle

These insects feed on waste matter. You are most likely to find them in a rubbish heap.

10 In the Soil

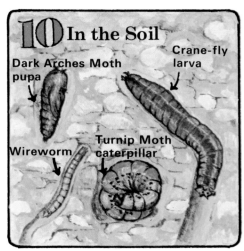

Dark Arches Moth pupa

Crane-fly larva

Turnip Moth caterpillar

Wireworm

You will have to dig in the ground to find these insects. The larvae (young insects) feed on roots.

11 On Flowers

Silver-Washed Fritillary

Hornet

In summer, look for insects like these feeding on the nectar and pollen of flowers.

12 Under Stones

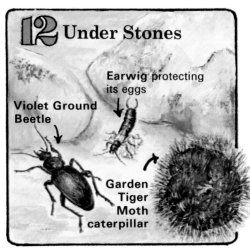

Earwig protecting its eggs

Violet Ground Beetle

Garden Tiger Moth caterpillar

Lift up large stones to discover these insects. They like to live in dark, damp places.

139

Insects in a Tree

Weevils

Nut Weevil

In autumn, look for acorns with holes in them. These are where Weevils have laid eggs.

Oak Apple Galls

Galls

Gall-Wasp (winged male) leaving Gall.

In May, you may see Oak Apples like these. They are swellings called galls, and are made by Gall-Wasp grubs. The Wasps emerge in mid-summer.

Greenfly

Greenfly

Look for leaves with yellow patches. These are caused by Greenfly feeding.

Bugs

Capsid Bug

There are many types of Capsid Bugs, and some of them like to live on oak trees. They feed on the sap of the leaves, or on young acorns.

Watch for birds eating insects on trees.

The **Four-Spot Carrion Beetle** feeds on Green Oak-Roller Moth caterpillars.

Common Goldeneye Lacewing

10-Spot Ladybird

Lacewings and Ladybirds feed on the Aphids, such as Greenfly, that live on oak trees.

Moth Caterpillars

Oak Beauty Moth caterpillar

Red-green Carpet Moth caterpillar

Maiden's Blush Moth caterpillar

Mottled Umber Moth caterpillar

These Moth caterpillars feed on oak leaves. Some of them can look like twigs, by holding on to a twig with their hind legs and stretching their bodies out stiff.

Green Oak-Roller

Green Oak-Roller Moth

If disturbed, the caterpillar can lower itself on a silken thread.

The caterpillar of this Moth hides and feeds inside an oak leaf, which it rolls over and binds with silk.

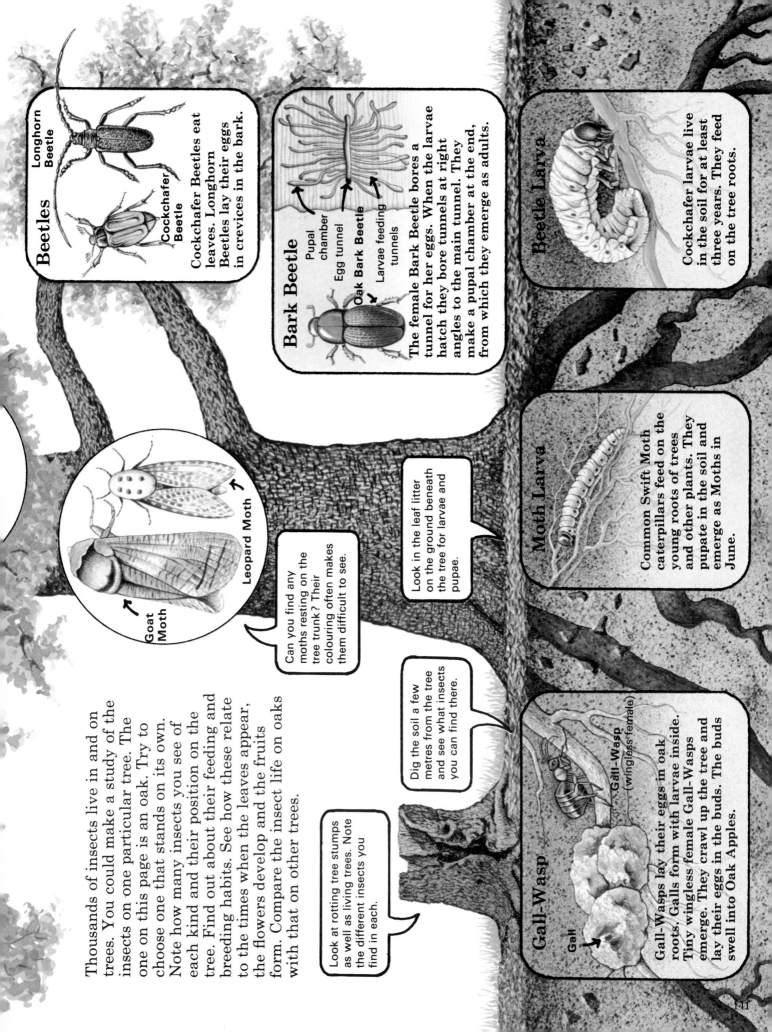

Beetles

Longhorn Beetle

Cockchafer Beetle

Cockchafer Beetles eat leaves. Longhorn Beetles lay their eggs in crevices in the bark.

Bark Beetle

Pupal chamber

Egg tunnel

Oak Bark Beetle

Larvae feeding tunnels

The female Bark Beetle bores a tunnel for her eggs. When the larvae hatch they bore tunnels at right angles to the main tunnel. They make a pupal chamber at the end, from which they emerge as adults.

Beetle Larva

Cockchafer larvae live in the soil for at least three years. They feed on the tree roots.

Goat Moth

Leopard Moth

Can you find any moths resting on the tree trunk? Their colouring often makes them difficult to see.

Look in the leaf litter on the ground beneath the tree for larvae and pupae.

Moth Larva

Common Swift Moth caterpillars feed on the young roots of trees and other plants. They pupate in the soil and emerge as Moths in June.

Thousands of insects live in and on trees. You could make a study of the insects on one particular tree. The one on this page is an oak. Try to choose one that stands on its own. Note how many insects you see of each kind and their position on the tree. Find out about their feeding and breeding habits. See how these relate to the times when the leaves appear, the flowers develop and the fruits form. Compare the insect life on oaks with that on other trees.

Look at rotting tree stumps as well as living trees. Note the different insects you find in each.

Dig the soil a few metres from the tree and see what insects you can find there.

Gall-Wasp

Gall-Wasp (wingless female)

Gall

Gall-Wasps lay their eggs in oak roots. Galls form with larvae inside. Tiny wingless female Gall-Wasps emerge. They crawl up the tree and lay their eggs in the buds. The buds swell into Oak Apples.

141

Pond Insects

The best time of year to find all these pond insects is in early summer. This is the time when the Dragonflies and other flying insects change from being nymphs, larvae and pupae living in the water. Look in different places around the pond. Watch the insects that fly over the pond and those that are on the surface. Search among the water weeds and dip with your net to find insects that live in the water.

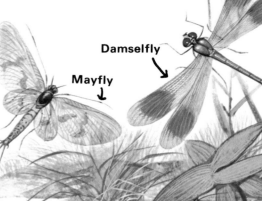

Damselfly

Mayfly

Common Damselfly

Whirligig Beetles can fly, swim on the surface and dive underwater.

Gnat

Alder-fly

Saucer Bug

Pond Skaters and **Water Crickets** live on the water's surface. They are both Bugs.

Water Measurer

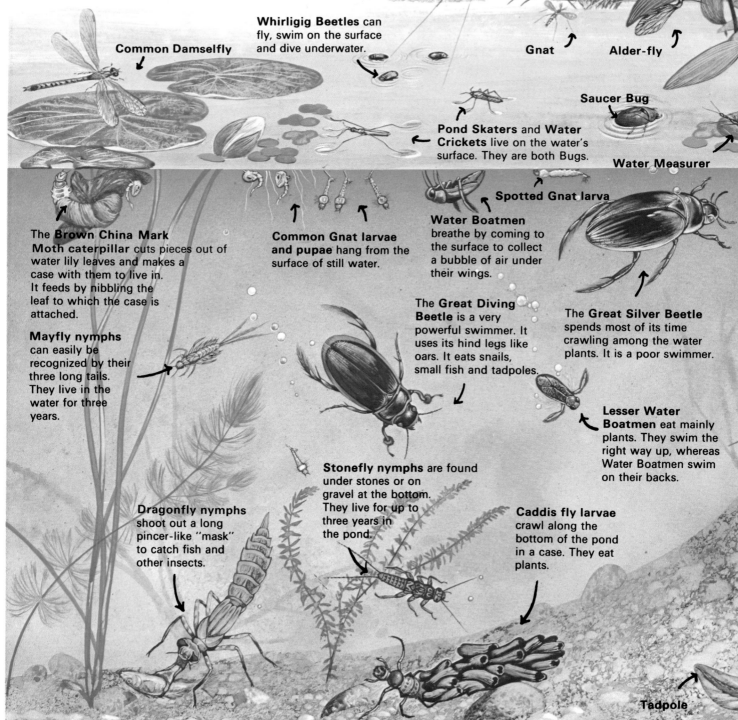

Spotted Gnat larva

The **Brown China Mark Moth caterpillar** cuts pieces out of water lily leaves and makes a case with them to live in. It feeds by nibbling the leaf to which the case is attached.

Common Gnat larvae and pupae hang from the surface of still water.

Water Boatmen breathe by coming to the surface to collect a bubble of air under their wings.

Mayfly nymphs can easily be recognized by their three long tails. They live in the water for three years.

The **Great Diving Beetle** is a very powerful swimmer. It uses its hind legs like oars. It eats snails, small fish and tadpoles.

The **Great Silver Beetle** spends most of its time crawling among the water plants. It is a poor swimmer.

Lesser Water Boatmen eat mainly plants. They swim the right way up, whereas Water Boatmen swim on their backs.

Dragonfly nymphs shoot out a long pincer-like "mask" to catch fish and other insects.

Stonefly nymphs are found under stones or on gravel at the bottom. They live for up to three years in the pond.

Caddis fly larvae crawl along the bottom of the pond in a case. They eat plants.

Tadpole

Caddis Fly

Midge

Brown China Mark Moth

Look for **Water Scorpions** by the edge of the pond. They look like dead leaves.

Rat-tailed maggots (the larvae of Hover-flies) live in the mud of stagnant ponds. They breathe air through a tube, which can be made longer or shorter according to how deep the maggot is.

The **Great Diving Beetle larva** is very fierce. It eats other pond animals.

TAKE A POND NET FOR CATCHING INSECTS THAT LIVE IN THE WATER OR ON THE SURFACE. YOU CAN USE A PLASTIC SIEVE IN SHALLOW WATER

What You Need

YOU ALSO NEED A SHALLOW WHITE DISH TO TIP YOUR CATCH INTO AND A TEASPOON FOR PUTTING IT INTO A SCREW-TOPPED CONTAINER. A TROWEL IS USEFUL FOR SCOOPING MUD BY THE POND'S EDGE

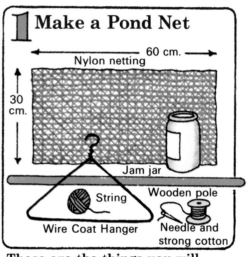

1 Make a Pond Net

60 cm.

Nylon netting

30 cm.

Jam jar

String

Wire Coat Hanger

Wooden pole

Needle and strong cotton

These are the things you will need for making a pond net.

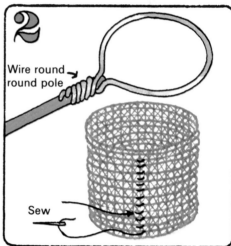

2

Wire round round pole

Sew

Bend the hanger into a hoop with pliers and wind the ends round the pole. Sew the edges of the netting.

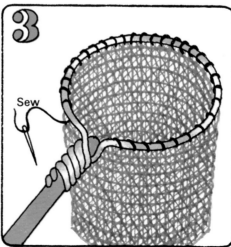

3

Sew

Sew the long edge of the netting over the wire frame.

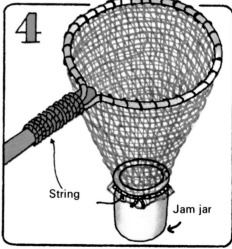

4

String

Jam jar

Fix the jar to the netting with string. Tie the string over the wire on the pole to strengthen it.

Insect Senses

Insects do not sense things in the same way that we do. They do not have a nose for smelling. However, insects can feel, smell and taste with their antennae. Some can also taste with their feet, while the hairs on an insect's body help it to feel.

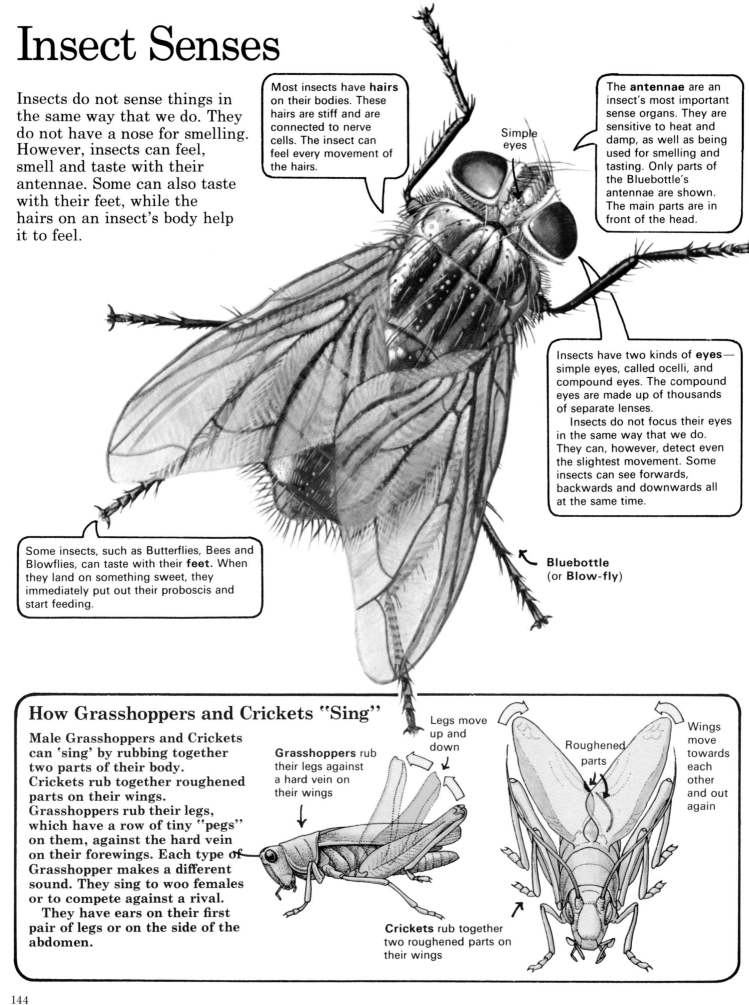

Most insects have **hairs** on their bodies. These hairs are stiff and are connected to nerve cells. The insect can feel every movement of the hairs.

Simple eyes

The **antennae** are an insect's most important sense organs. They are sensitive to heat and damp, as well as being used for smelling and tasting. Only parts of the Bluebottle's antennae are shown. The main parts are in front of the head.

Insects have two kinds of **eyes**—simple eyes, called ocelli, and compound eyes. The compound eyes are made up of thousands of separate lenses.

Insects do not focus their eyes in the same way that we do. They can, however, detect even the slightest movement. Some insects can see forwards, backwards and downwards all at the same time.

Some insects, such as Butterflies, Bees and Blowflies, can taste with their **feet**. When they land on something sweet, they immediately put out their proboscis and start feeding.

**Bluebottle
(or Blow-fly)**

How Grasshoppers and Crickets "Sing"

Male Grasshoppers and Crickets can 'sing' by rubbing together two parts of their body. Crickets rub together roughened parts on their wings. Grasshoppers rub their legs, which have a row of tiny "pegs" on them, against the hard vein on their forewings. Each type of Grasshopper makes a different sound. They sing to woo females or to compete against a rival.

They have ears on their first pair of legs or on the side of the abdomen.

Grasshoppers rub their legs against a hard vein on their wings

Legs move up and down

Roughened parts

Wings move towards each other and out again

Crickets rub together two roughened parts on their wings

144

Antennae

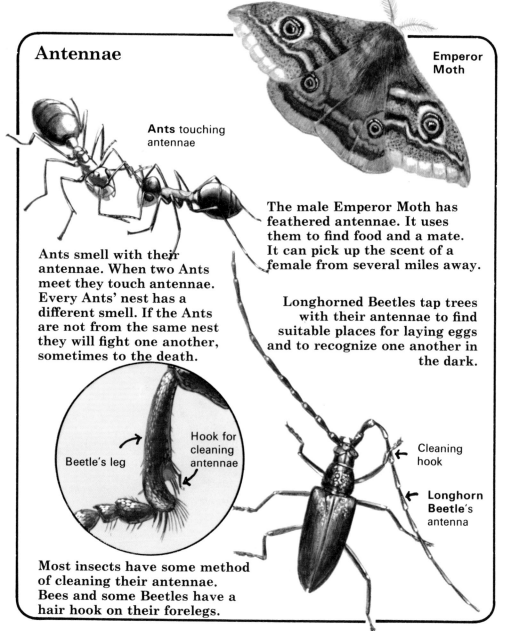

Ants touching antennae

Emperor Moth

Ants smell with their antennae. When two Ants meet they touch antennae. Every Ants' nest has a different smell. If the Ants are not from the same nest they will fight one another, sometimes to the death.

The male Emperor Moth has feathered antennae. It uses them to find food and a mate. It can pick up the scent of a female from several miles away.

Longhorned Beetles tap trees with their antennae to find suitable places for laying eggs and to recognize one another in the dark.

Beetle's leg

Hook for cleaning antennae

Cleaning hook

Longhorn Beetle's antenna

Most insects have some method of cleaning their antennae. Bees and some Beetles have a hair hook on their forelegs.

Hairs

Cerci

Crickets and Cockroaches have tail feelers at the end of their abdomen. These are called cerci and are sensitive to touch.

The stiff hairs on a caterpillar respond to sound waves in the air. If you clap or whistle near a caterpillar, watch how it curls up or suddenly "freezes".

Things to Do

1

ANTS CAN LEAVE A SCENT TRAIL. THEY PRESS THEIR BODIES ON THE GROUND, LEAVING A SMELL FOR OTHERS TO FOLLOW. IF YOU FIND A TRAIL, RUB PART OF IT OUT. WATCH WHAT THE ANTS DO

2

Ants' nest

Ant trail

Food

PUT A PIECE OF PAPER WITH FOOD ON IT NEAR AN ANTS' NEST. WATCH SEVERAL ANTS FIND THE FOOD. THEN MOVE THE FOOD TO ANOTHER PART OF THE PAPER.

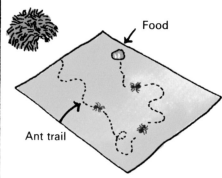

Food

Ant trail

WATCH WHAT THE ANTS COMING FROM THE NEST DO. DO THEY GO STRAIGHT TO THE FOOD? OR DO THEY GO FIRST TO WHERE THE FOOD WAS BEFORE YOU MOVED IT?

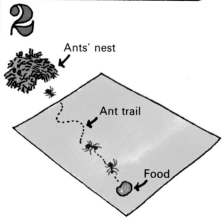
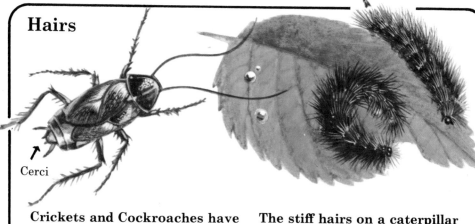

Watching Insects Move

Many insects have a particular way of moving. Once you can recognize their different movements you will be able to identify insects more easily. Insects that walk or run usually have long, thin legs. Insects that dig, such as Chafers or Dor Beetles, have forelegs that are shorter but stronger than the other two pairs. Insects that jump or swim often have specially developed hind-legs. Compare the way different insects fly. Wasps, Flies and Bees flap their wings faster than Butterflies.

Jumping

Grasshopper jumping

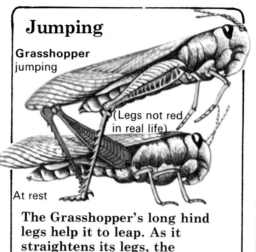

(Legs not red in real life)

At rest

The Grasshopper's long hind legs help it to leap. As it straightens its legs, the Grasshopper pushes itself high into the air.

Swimming

Water Boatman

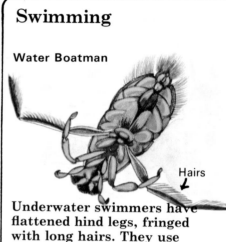

Hairs

Underwater swimmers have flattened hind legs, fringed with long hairs. They use these legs like oars, moving them both together.

Walking on Water

Pond Skater

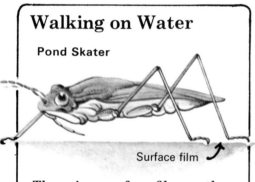

Surface film

There is a surface film on the top of water. Heavy objects break the film and sink. A Pond Skater is light and has long spread-out legs. It can walk on the surface without breaking the film.

Digging

Mole Cricket burrowing

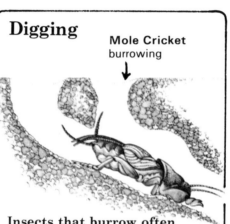

Insects that burrow often have short, wide front legs. These legs are flattened and sometimes toothed, which helps the insect dig into the soil.

How Caterpillars Move

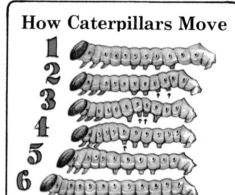

1 2 3 4 5 6

Caterpillars have three pairs of walking legs and up to five pairs of false legs. They move each pair of false legs in turn.

Flying

Look at the different shapes of insects' wings, and watch how fast or slowly they fly. Look to see if they have one pair of wings or two.

When a **Beetle** flies it holds up its stiff wing-cases, to let its wings move easily. When it lands it folds its wings back under the wing-cases.

Wing-case

Halteres

Many **Butterflies** have square-shaped wings, that flap quite slowly.

Cockchafer Beetle

Flies have only one pair of wings. Instead of hind wings they have two knobs, called halteres. These help the insect to balance.

Walking on Land

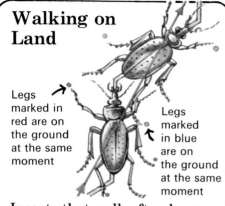

Legs marked in red are on the ground at the same moment

Legs marked in blue are on the ground at the same moment

Insects that walk often have long thin legs, which are all alike. They walk by moving three legs at a time and balancing on the other three.

Looper Caterpillars

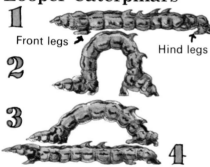

1

Front legs

Hind legs

2

3

4

A "looper" caterpillar moves forward by bringing forward its hind legs (1, 2) and then stretching out its front legs (3, 4).

Hawkmoths have pointed wings. They can fly fast and for a long time. In flight the two pairs of wings are joined and flap as one.

Catch on wing holds wings together

Hooks

Bees and Wasps have two pairs of wings. They are held together during flight by a tiny row of hooks.

How Flies Walk Upside Down

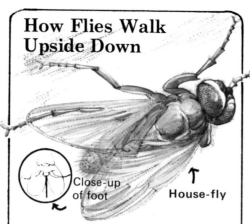

Close-up of foot

House-fly

House-flies have sticky, hairy pads on their feet. Because the fly is so light, the grip of the pads is strong enough to hold it on almost any surface.

How Click Beetles Click

Head

1

Peg

2

If a Click Beetle falls on its back (1), it arches its body until only its head and tail touch the ground. A peg on its thorax makes it double up (2). Its wing-cases hit the ground and the beetle is thrown into the air, with a "clicking" sound.

How Springtails Jump

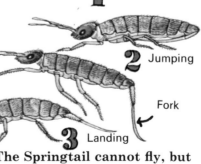

1 At rest

2 Jumping

Fork

3 Landing

The Springtail cannot fly, but it can jump. It has a forked tail which folds under its body. If the Springtail is disturbed, the tail flicks down on the ground and throws the insect forward.

FIND OUT WHAT HAPPENS WHEN DIFFERENT INSECTS MEET WATER, OTHER INSECTS OR THINGS IN THEIR WAY. PUT DOWN TWIGS, STONES OR SOME PAPER. NOTE DOWN WHAT YOU SEE

SEE WHETHER INSECTS MOVE AT THE SAME SPEED ON DIFFERENT KINDS OF SURFACE. COMPARE HOW THEY MOVE ON SOIL, GRASS AND WOOD

SMOKE A PLATE OVER A CANDLE. PUT THE PLATE ON THE GROUND AND WATCH INSECTS MOVE OVER IT. LOOK AT THE DIFFERENT TRACKS WITH A POCKET LENS AND SEE WHAT PATTERNS EACH INSECT MAKES

Watching Insects Feed

Insects feed on almost every kind of animal and plant. Some of them, such as Cockroaches, will eat almost anything, but most insects feed on one particular kind of food. There are insects that feed on cork, paper, clothes, ink, cigarettes, carpets, flour— even film or shoe-polish!

The diet of an insect may change at different stages in its life. Some insects eat only animals when they are larvae and plants when they are adult or vice versa. But most insects eat either plants or animals.

Insects that eat plants are called herbivores. More than half of all insects eat plants. Some feed on the leaves, flowers or seeds of plants, others bite the roots or suck the sap from inside plant stems. Some insects feed on nectar and pollen. You can find out more about them on the next page.

Some insects feed on animals smaller than themselves, or suck the blood from larger ones, sometimes after paralyzing or killing them. Female Mosquitoes and Horseflies usually need to have a meal of mammal's blood before they can produce eggs. Many insects feed inside the bodies of other animals, and live there all the time. They are called parasites.

Some insects are called scavengers. They eat any decaying material that they find in the soil, such as animals that are already dead. They also feed on the dung of animals. Flea larvae eat the droppings of adult Fleas, as well as dirt and skin fragments.

Plant Feeders

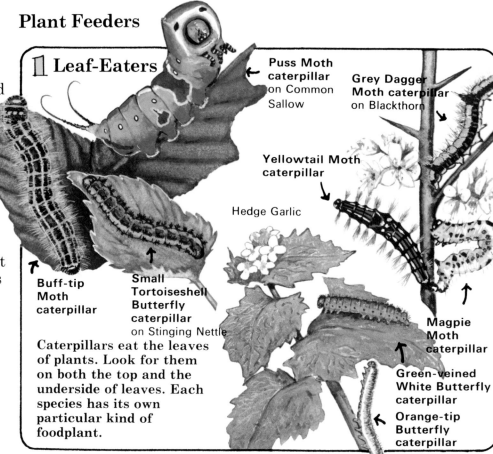

1 Leaf-Eaters

Puss Moth caterpillar on Common Sallow

Grey Dagger Moth caterpillar on Blackthorn

Yellowtail Moth caterpillar

Hedge Garlic

Buff-tip Moth caterpillar

Small Tortoiseshell Butterfly caterpillar on Stinging Nettle

Magpie Moth caterpillar

Green-veined White Butterfly caterpillar

Orange-tip Butterfly caterpillar

Caterpillars eat the leaves of plants. Look for them on both the top and the underside of leaves. Each species has its own particular kind of foodplant.

2 Wood-borers

Wood Wasps lay their eggs in pine trees. The larvae eat the soft wood.

Giant Wood Wasp

3 Sap-Feeders

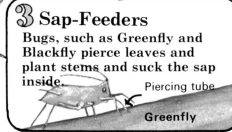

Bugs, such as Greenfly and Blackfly pierce leaves and plant stems and suck the sap inside.

Piercing tube

Greenfly

4 Leaf Miners

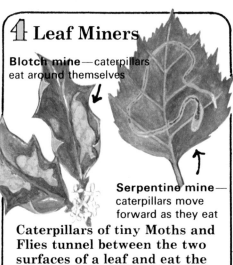

Blotch mine—caterpillars eat around themselves

Serpentine mine— caterpillars move forward as they eat

Caterpillars of tiny Moths and Flies tunnel between the two surfaces of a leaf and eat the tissues inside.

5 Seed-Eaters

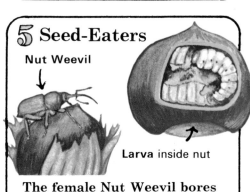

Nut Weevil

Larva inside nut

The female Nut Weevil bores a hole in newly formed hazel nuts and acorns and lays an egg. The grub hatches and feeds on the nut. The nut falls to the ground and the larva eats its way out and pupates in the soil.

Insects' Mouthparts

Insects either bite and chew solid food, or they suck liquids. Insects that suck have a hollow tube, called a proboscis. Bees, Butterflies and Moths suck nectar from inside flowers. Bugs can pierce plant stems and suck the sap inside. Mosquitoes pierce the skin of animals or humans and suck their blood. Insects that bite and chew have three pairs of jaws—a large pair called mandibles, a smaller pair called maxillae and a third pair which are joined together to form a kind of lower lip.

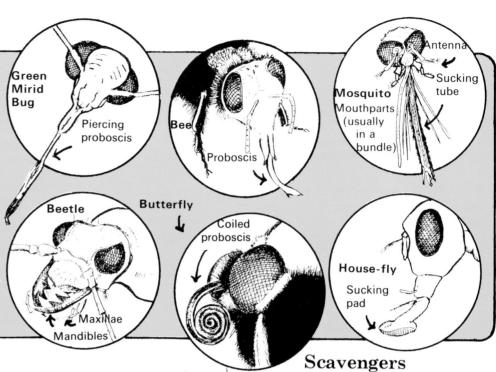

Green Mirid Bug — Piercing proboscis

Bee — Proboscis

Mosquito Mouthparts (usually in a bundle) — Antenna — Sucking tube

Beetle — Maxillae — Mandibles

Butterfly — Coiled proboscis

House-fly — Sucking pad

Animal Feeders

1 Aphid Eaters

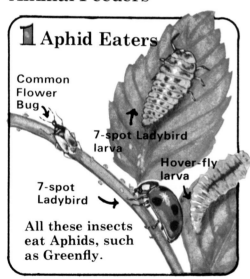

Common Flower Bug

7-spot Ladybird larva

Hover-fly larva

7-spot Ladybird

All these insects eat Aphids, such as Greenfly.

3 Wasps

Wasps sting caterpillars and take them to their nest to feed their larvae.

Red-Banded Sand Wasp

5 Dragonflies

Some Dragonflies are often called "Hawkers" because they fly so fast and overpower other insects.

2 Tiger Beetles

Tiger Beetles run fast and catch other insects with their strong mandibles. Their larva burrows a hole in the sand and waits for its prey.

Larva in burrow

4 Mosquitoes

Mosquitoes usually fly by night. The female sucks blood; the male sucks nectar from flowers.

Skin

6 Robber-flies

Robber-flies pounce on insects in the air and suck them dry.

Scavengers

1 Blow-flies

Blow-flies lay their eggs on meat. The maggots eat the meat when they hatch.

Bluebottle (Blow-fly)

Meat

2 Dor Beetles

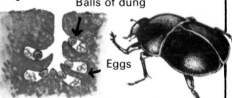

Balls of dung

Eggs

Dor Beetles dig tunnels under cow dung. The female lays her eggs in chambers. The larvae feed on balls of dung.

3 Burying Beetles

Burying Beetles dig a hole and pull dead animals underground. They lay their eggs near the corpse.

149

Insects and Flowers

Insects visit flowers for food. Moths and Butterflies feed on the nectar, a sweet liquid found inside most flowers. Honey Bees collect pollen, the yellow dust inside flowers, as well as nectar, for feeding their larvae.

Flowers do not need the nectar they produce, except to attract insects. The insects help the flowers to make new seeds. Most insects that visit flowers are hairy. When they feed on a flower they become dusted with pollen from the ripe stamens (the male parts inside a flower). Then they visit other flowers of the same species, and some of the sticky pollen may be accidentally brushed off onto the stigmas (the female parts of the flower).

This is called pollination. Only when a flower has been pollinated can new seeds start growing.

Flowers that attract insects usually have a strong scent. Insects do not see colours as we do. Flowers that look one colour to us, such as the yellow Tormentil, appear white with dark centres to an insect.

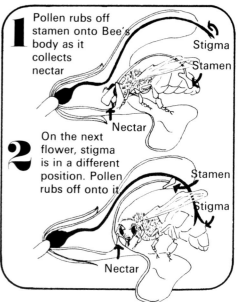

1. Pollen rubs off stamen onto Bee's body as it collects nectar

Stigma
Stamen
Nectar

2. On the next flower, stigma is in a different position. Pollen rubs off onto it

Stamen
Stigma
Nectar

Wasps, like Bees, collect nectar. This they eat themselves or store for their young. But, unlike Bees, they do not collect and store pollen.

Watch how a Butterfly extends its long proboscis into a flower as soon as it lands. Butterflies feed from bright-coloured flowers that have a strong scent. Most flowers that Butterflies like are red, orange or pink. These are colours that Butterflies can see well.

Nectar Guides

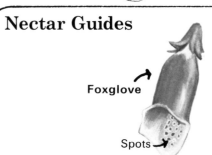

Foxglove

Spots

Some flowers that insects visit have lines or spots on their petals, pointing to where the nectar is. These patterns are called nectar guides. Flowers that have nectar guides are usually those where nectar is deeply hidden.

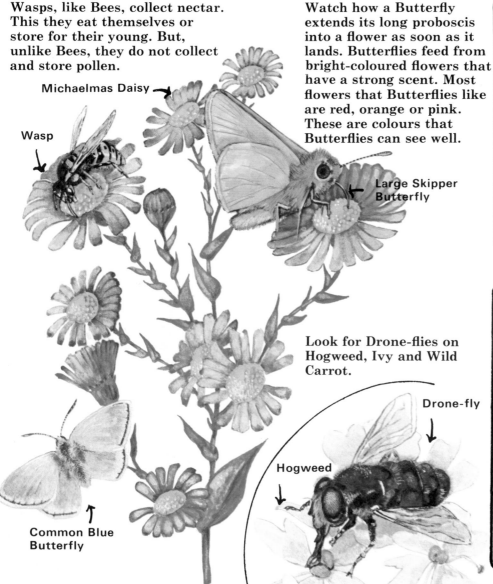

Michaelmas Daisy

Wasp

Large Skipper Butterfly

Look for Drone-flies on Hogweed, Ivy and Wild Carrot.

Drone-fly

Hogweed

Common Blue Butterfly

Make a Butterfly Garden

Try growing some of these plants to attract Butterflies. They feed on flowers like Buddleia and some of them lay eggs on weeds such as Ragwort, Nettles and Thistles.

THISTLE

BUDDLEIA

GOLDEN ROD

1 Feeding on Flowers

Garden Chafer Beetle

Beetles have mouthparts that bite and chew. They cannot suck nectar like Bees, so they can only feed on flowers where the nectar is easy to get at.

2

Hover-fly

Proboscis

Some Flies that suck nectar look like Bees. They have hairy bodies and their tongues are longer than those of other Flies. Look for them on wide-open flowers.

3

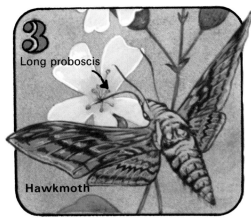

Long proboscis

Hawkmoth

Most Moths fly at dusk or at night. They are attracted to pale-coloured flowers that can be seen easily in the dark. The nectar is stored deep inside the flower.

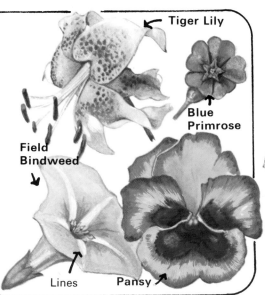

Tiger Lily

Blue Primrose

Field Bindweed

Lines   Pansy

4

Bumble Bee

Proboscis

Bees only gather nectar from one species of flower at a time. Watch this for yourself. Follow a single Bee and see what kind of flowers it visits.

5

Pollen on legs

Honey Bee

Honey Bees collect nectar and pollen. Nectar is sucked up through the tongue. Pollen is packed on the hind legs and held there by stiff bristles.

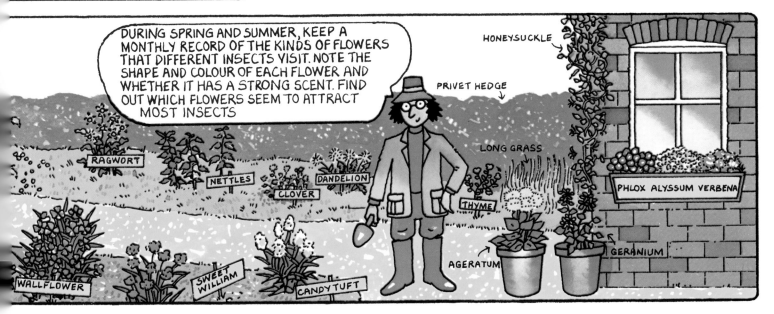

DURING SPRING AND SUMMER, KEEP A MONTHLY RECORD OF THE KINDS OF FLOWERS THAT DIFFERENT INSECTS VISIT. NOTE THE SHAPE AND COLOUR OF EACH FLOWER AND WHETHER IT HAS A STRONG SCENT. FIND OUT WHICH FLOWERS SEEM TO ATTRACT MOST INSECTS

HONEYSUCKLE

PRIVET HEDGE

LONG GRASS

RAGWORT

NETTLES

CLOVER

DANDELION

THYME

PHLOX ALYSSUM VERBENA

WALLFLOWER

SWEET WILLIAM

CANDYTUFT

AGERATUM

GERANIUM

Ants and Bees

Ants and Bees are "social insects." This means that they live in colonies, which may consist of thousands of insects, and share their food and work.

In any colony there are three kinds of insect: a queen, who is the only egg-laying female, males, called drones, whose only job is to mate with the queen, and undeveloped females, called workers, who do all the work in the colony. Each worker has a particular task; either to collect food, to care for the eggs and larvae or to repair or guard the nest.

An Ants' Nest

Queen in chamber
Workers and eggs
Worker and larvae
Young Ants hatch
Pupae
Rubbish

An Ants' nest is made up of a network of chambers and passages. The queen has a chamber of her own and there are separate chambers for eggs, larvae and pupae.

Other chambers are used for storing food or for rubbish. The Ants can change the temperature of the nest by opening or closing some of the passages.

1 How Ants are Born

In summer, when the weather is warm, the winged males and the queen Ants leave the nest on a mating flight. After mating the males die. The queens fly to the ground.

2

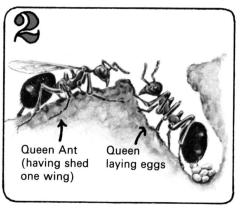

Queen Ant (having shed one wing)
Queen laying eggs

Each queen starts a new nest. She rubs or bites off her wings. Then she finds, or makes, a space in the soil where she can lay her first batch of eggs.

3

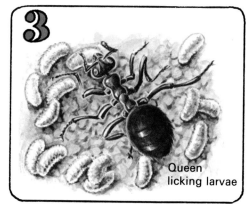

Queen licking larvae

When the larvae hatch, the queen feeds them with her own saliva. Later they emerge as worker Ants. They take over the job of looking after the nest and the eggs.

4

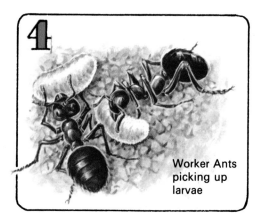

Worker Ants picking up larvae

Now the queen does nothing but lay more eggs. Workers feed the larvae and lick them clean. They even cut the pupae open to let the new Ants climb out.

Food

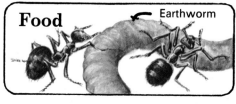

Earthworm

Aphid

Some Ants go out collecting small insects, worms and other food. Others lick the sweet honeydew that Aphids on nearby plants produce.

Defence Cleaning

Jaws
Worker moving rubbish

Some Ants guard the nest. They wait by the entrance, their jaws open. Ants keep their nest very clean. They remove rubbish to special chambers or take it outside.

Honey Bees

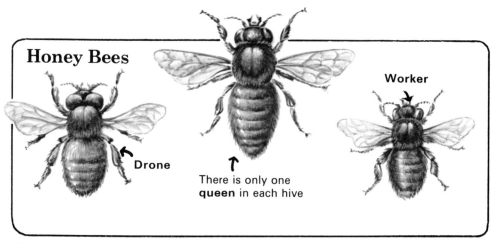

Drone

Worker

There is only one **queen** in each hive

These are three different kinds of Honey Bee that you will find in a hive. The only ones you will see flying around are the workers; the others stay in the hive.

The workers do all the jobs.

Young workers clean out cells, then, as they get older, they feed the larvae, build new cells and make honey. Later they collect nectar and pollen.

How a Bee Grows

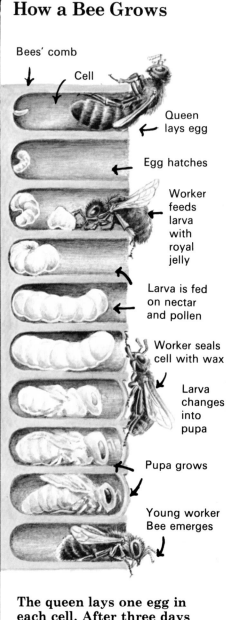

Bees' comb

Cell

Queen lays egg

Egg hatches

Worker feeds larva with royal jelly

Larva is fed on nectar and pollen

Worker seals cell with wax

Larva changes into pupa

Pupa grows

Young worker Bee emerges

The queen lays one egg in each cell. After three days the eggs hatch. At first, worker Bees feed the larvae with a special food called royal jelly. A few days later they are fed on nectar and pollen.

After six days the larvae are large and fat and fill their cells. Workers seal the cells with wax. Inside the cells the larvae pupate.

Two weeks later the young Bees bite through the wax and come out fully grown.

The Honeycomb

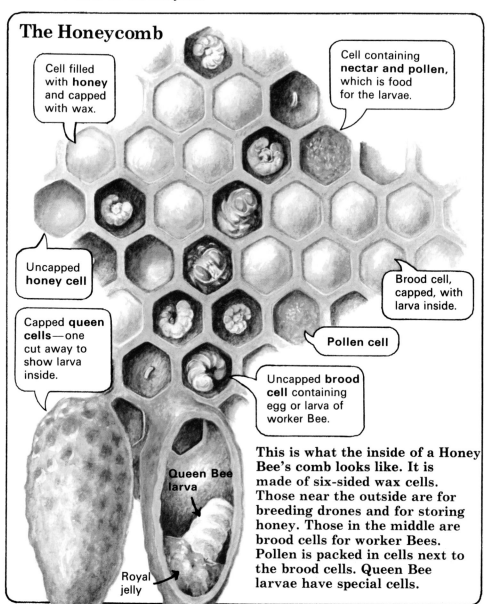

Cell filled with **honey** and capped with wax.

Cell containing **nectar and pollen**, which is food for the larvae.

Uncapped **honey cell**

Capped **queen cells**—one cut away to show larva inside.

Brood cell, capped, with larva inside.

Pollen cell

Uncapped **brood cell** containing egg or larva of worker Bee.

Queen Bee larva

Royal jelly

This is what the inside of a Honey Bee's comb looks like. It is made of six-sided wax cells. Those near the outside are for breeding drones and for storing honey. Those in the middle are brood cells for worker Bees. Pollen is packed in cells next to the brood cells. Queen Bee larvae have special cells.

153

Collecting and Keeping Insects

If you want to collect insects you must keep them in surroundings that are as near as possible like their natural homes. When you find an insect, put it in a small tin with a sample of the plant on which you found it. This will help you to identify it. Number each tin. Put down the numbers in your notebook and, against each one, write a description of the insect and where you found it. Was it in a dry or damp place, a sunny or a shady place?

When you get home, make a suitable home for your insects. You will need containers that are big enough to hold enough food and give the insects some room to move around. It is best to use glass or clear plastic containers, then you can see what is happening inside.

It is usually a good idea to put some sand or soil at the bottom, with a stone and some plants. Keep the containers in a cool place away from the sunlight, but not in a draught.

Make sure you have a good supply of fresh food and change it each day. Most caterpillars have their own particular food plant and will not eat anything else. There is no point in collecting them unless you can give them the right food supply.

Look at the insects in your "zoo" every day and record any changes that you see. You could keep a note of how much caterpillars eat and measure their length, or what happens to them when they pupate.

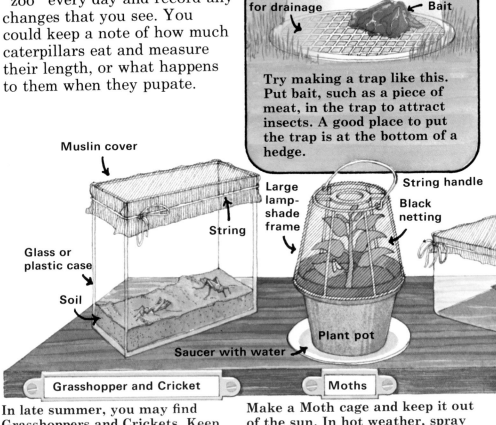

1 Collecting Crawling Insects

Cut hole in centre
Tin foil pie dish
Wire mesh for drainage
Bait

Try making a trap like this. Put bait, such as a piece of meat, in the trap to attract insects. A good place to put the trap is at the bottom of a hedge.

Muslin cover
String
Glass or plastic case
Soil
Large lamp-shade frame
String handle
Black netting
Plant pot
Saucer with water

Grasshopper and Cricket

In late summer, you may find Grasshoppers and Crickets. Keep them in a large glass case or jar and put sand in the bottom. Put in fresh grass every other day.

Moths

Make a Moth cage and keep it out of the sun. In hot weather, spray it with water. If you want the Moths to breed, put in the right plant for the larvae to feed on.

IT IS EASY TO COLLECT INSECTS BUT REMEMBER THAT THEY ARE VERY FRAGILE. HANDLE THEM AS LITTLE AS POSSIBLE AND DO NOT COLLECT MORE THAN YOU NEED TO STUDY. ONCE YOU HAVE FINISHED LOOKING AT THEM, TAKE THE INSECTS BACK TO THE PLACE WHERE YOU FOUND THEM. LET FLYING INSECTS GO AT DUSK SO THAT BIRDS OR CATS DO NOT ATTACK THEM

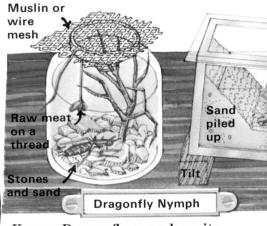

Muslin or wire mesh
Raw meat on a thread
Stones and sand
Sand piled up
Tilt

Dragonfly Nymph

Keep a Dragonfly nymph on its own in a large jam jar and feed it on raw meat. Put in an upright stick for the nymph to cling to when it sheds its skin.

②

Ground level · Stones

Glass jar · Bait

You could also make a pitfall trap. Try different baits, such as jam, raw meat, fruit or beer. Keep a record of the insects that are attracted by each bait.

Sugaring

Torch with red bulb

You can attract Moths by "sugaring". At dusk, paint tree trunks or posts with a mixture of black treacle and rum or beer. It is best to "sugar" on warm, still nights.

Lights

Many insect-watchers use special light-traps to catch insects, but insects are also attracted by lights in rooms, streets, or shop windows. See how many you can find in this way.

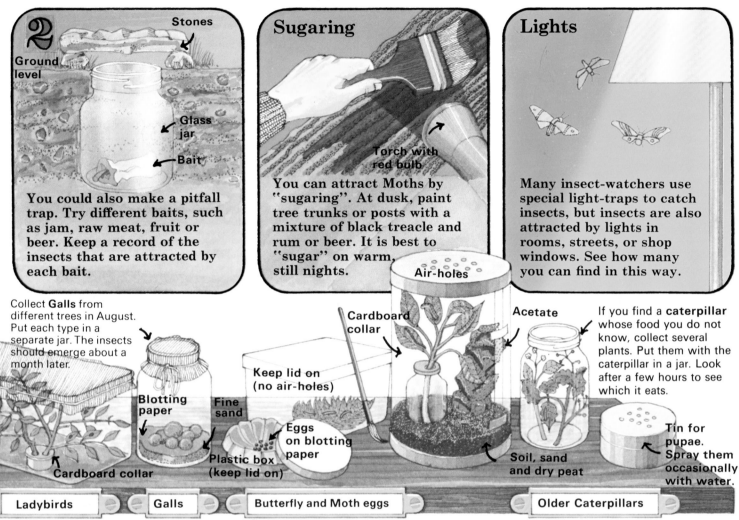

Collect **Galls** from different trees in August. Put each type in a separate jar. The insects should emerge about a month later.

Blotting paper · Fine sand

Cardboard collar

Keep lid on (no air-holes)

Eggs on blotting paper

Plastic box (keep lid on)

Air-holes

Cardboard collar

Soil, sand and dry peat

Acetate

If you find a **caterpillar** whose food you do not know, collect several plants. Put them with the caterpillar in a jar. Look after a few hours to see which it eats.

Tin for pupae. Spray them occasionally with water.

| Ladybirds | Galls | Butterfly and Moth eggs | Older Caterpillars |

Keep Ladybirds in a large case like this to give them room to fly. They feed on Greenfly, which are often found on rose shoots. Cut off the whole shoot and keep it in water.

Collect Butterfly or Moth eggs in small boxes, and wait for them to hatch. When the caterpillars are a few hours old, transfer them with a brush to a box with a young leaf of their food plant. Put them on a new leaf each day.

Make a case like the one above for older caterpillars. Roll up a length of acetate and fix it with sticky tape. Put one half of a small tin on one end of the roll, and its lid on the other end.

Dig up pupae in the soil when they are hard and keep them in a tin. Caterpillars you already have will pupate on either the food plant, or the lid of the case, or the soil. In spring, when the pupae are ready to emerge, put them in a Moth cage like the one on the opposite page, on some damp moss. Put in a few twigs so that the Moth or Butterfly has something to cling onto when it emerges.

(Glass cover)

Water weed held down by stones

Small pieces of plastic, wood shavings

Small stones, shells, sand

| Great Diving Beetle | Caddis Fly Larvae |

Great Diving Beetles and Water Boatmen are very fierce, so keep each one on its own. Feed them on maggots or raw meat attached to a thread, and changed daily.

See how Caddis Fly larvae make their protective cases. Collect several and carefully remove the larvae from their cases by prodding them with the blunt end

of a pin. Put them in separate aquariums with different materials in each, and watch what happens. Feed them on water weed.

Common Insects to Spot

Butterflies

Red Admiral. May to June and July to September.

Speckled Wood. April to June and August to September.

Orange-tip. May to June.

Small White. May to June and July to August.

Green-veined White. May to June and August to September.

Underside of wing

Common Blue. May to June and August to September.

Large White. May to August.

Wall. May to June and August to September.

Meadow Brown. Mid-June to September.

Moths

Buff-tip. July to August.

Eyed Hawkmoth. May to July.

Male **Puss Moth.** May to June.

Small Magpie. May to mid-July.

Brimstone. May to June and August to September.

Angle Shades. May to October.

Magpie. July to mid-August.

Vapourer. Late August to October.

Blood-vein. May to September.

Silver-Y. Migratory (June to October).

Burnished Brass. June to September.

Herald. Early Spring to Autumn.

Each caption tells you the time of year when you are most likely to see the insect. The Butterflies and Moths are drawn life size. The Beetles and Dragonflies are not.

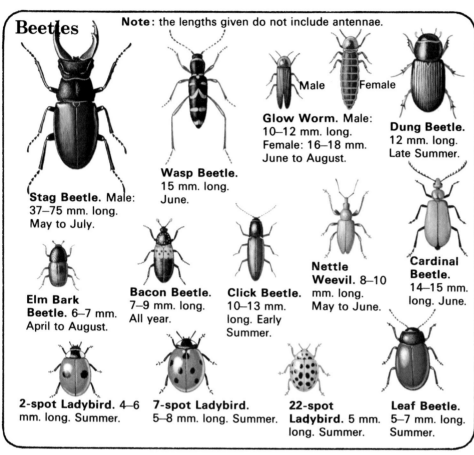

Beetles

Note: the lengths given do not include antennae.

Male Female

Glow Worm. Male: 10–12 mm. long. Female: 16–18 mm. June to August.

Dung Beetle. 12 mm. long. Late Summer.

Wasp Beetle. 15 mm. long. June.

Stag Beetle. Male: 37–75 mm. long. May to July.

Elm Bark Beetle. 6–7 mm. April to August.

Bacon Beetle. 7–9 mm. long. All year.

Click Beetle. 10–13 mm. long. Early Summer.

Nettle Weevil. 8–10 mm. long. May to June.

Cardinal Beetle. 14–15 mm. long. June.

2-spot Ladybird. 4–6 mm. long. Summer.

7-spot Ladybird. 5–8 mm. long. Summer.

22-spot Ladybird. 5 mm. long. Summer.

Leaf Beetle. 5–7 mm. long. Summer.

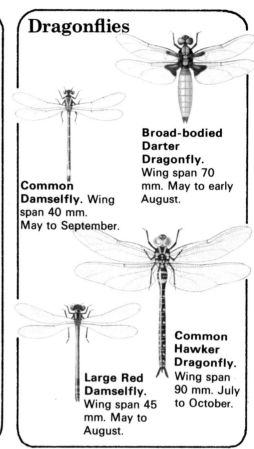

Dragonflies

Broad-bodied Darter Dragonfly. Wing span 70 mm. May to early August.

Common Damselfly. Wing span 40 mm. May to September.

Large Red Damselfly. Wing span 45 mm. May to August.

Common Hawker Dragonfly. Wing span 90 mm. July to October.

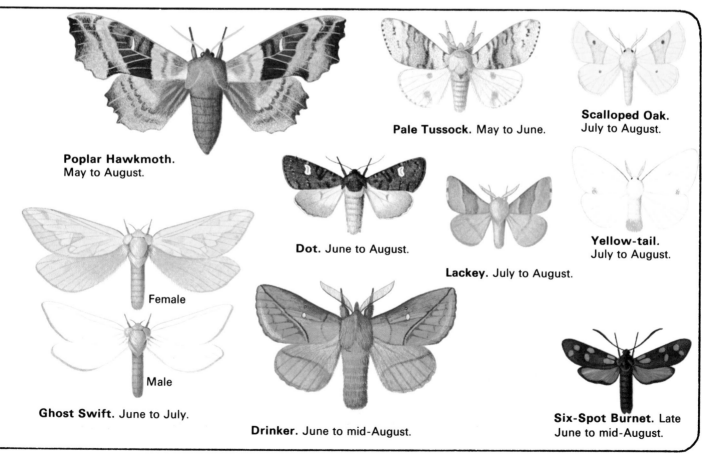

Pale Tussock. May to June.

Scalloped Oak. July to August.

Poplar Hawkmoth. May to August.

Dot. June to August.

Yellow-tail. July to August.

Lackey. July to August.

Female

Male

Ghost Swift. June to July.

Drinker. June to mid-August.

Six-Spot Burnet. Late June to mid-August.

Remember, if you cannot see the insect you want to identify on these pages, turn to the page earlier in the book which deals with the kind of place where you found the insect.

Each caption tells you at what time of year you are most likely to see the insect. The lengths given do not include antennae.

Bugs

Leaf Hopper. 5-7 mm. long. July to September.

Assassin Bug. About 10 mm. long. July to October.

Hawthorn Shieldbug. 13–15 mm. long. Spring to autumn.

Pied Shieldbug. 5.5–7.5 mm. Spring to autumn.

Whitefly. 3–4 mm. Summer.

Froghopper. 7–8 mm. long. June to November.

Blackfly. 3–4 mm. long. May to July.

Capsid Bug. 5–7 mm. long. June to October.

Water Boatman. 15 mm. long.

Saucer Bug. 12–16 mm. long. April to August.

Ants (All workers)

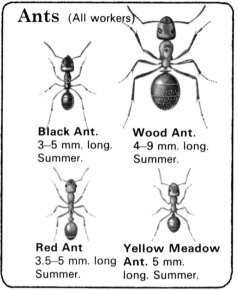

Black Ant. 3–5 mm. long. Summer.

Wood Ant. 4–9 mm. long. Summer.

Red Ant. 3.5–5 mm. long Summer.

Yellow Meadow Ant. 5 mm. long. Summer.

Grasshoppers and Crickets

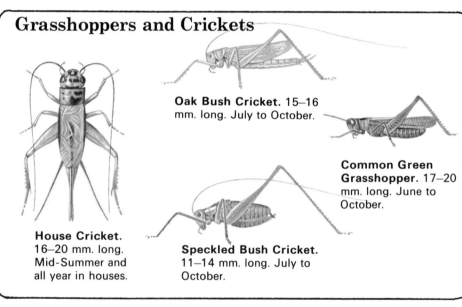

Oak Bush Cricket. 15–16 mm. long. July to October.

Common Green Grasshopper. 17–20 mm. long. June to October.

House Cricket. 16–20 mm. long. Mid-Summer and all year in houses.

Speckled Bush Cricket. 11–14 mm. long. July to October.

Wasps

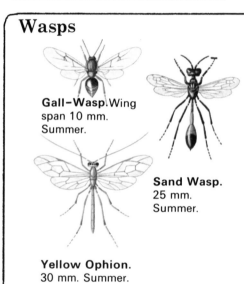

Gall-Wasp. Wing span 10 mm. Summer.

Sand Wasp. 25 mm. Summer.

Yellow Ophion. 30 mm. Summer.

Cockroach

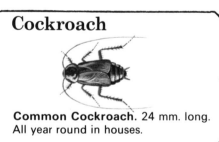

Common Cockroach. 24 mm. long. All year round in houses.

Lacewing

Green Lacewing. Wing span 30 mm. Summer.

Alder Fly

Alder Fly. Wing span 30 mm. May to June.

Earwig

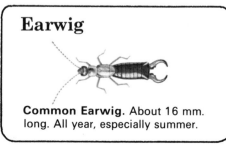

Common Earwig. About 16 mm. long. All year, especially summer.

Scorpion Fly

Common Scorpion Fly. Wing span 30 mm. May to July.

Snake Fly

Snake Fly. Wing span 28 mm. May to July.

Remember, if you cannot see the insect you want to identify on these pages, turn to the page earlier in the book which deals with the kind of place where you found the insect.

Flies

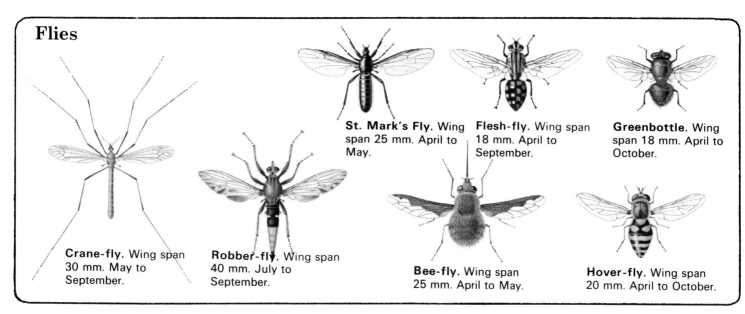

St. Mark's Fly. Wing span 25 mm. April to May.

Flesh-fly. Wing span 18 mm. April to September.

Greenbottle. Wing span 18 mm. April to October.

Crane-fly. Wing span 30 mm. May to September.

Robber-fly. Wing span 40 mm. July to September.

Bee-fly. Wing span 25 mm. April to May.

Hover-fly. Wing span 20 mm. April to October.

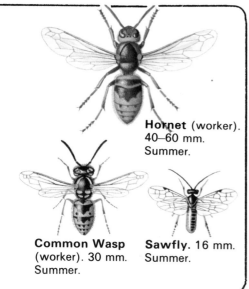

Hornet (worker). 40–60 mm. Summer.

Common Wasp (worker). 30 mm. Summer.

Sawfly. 16 mm. Summer.

Bees (All workers)

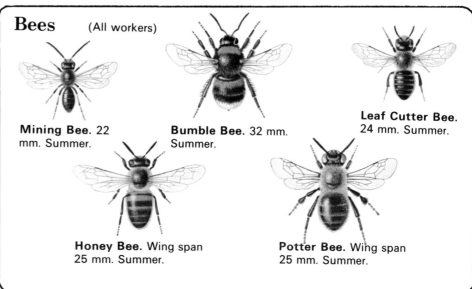

Mining Bee. 22 mm. Summer.

Bumble Bee. 32 mm. Summer.

Leaf Cutter Bee. 24 mm. Summer.

Honey Bee. Wing span 25 mm. Summer.

Potter Bee. Wing span 25 mm. Summer.

Caddis Fly

Caddis Fly. Wing span 35 mm. May to October.

Mayfly

Green Drake Mayfly. Wing span 25 mm. April to September.

Thrips

Onion Thrips. 2 mm. long. Summer.

Bristle-tails

Silverfish. 10 mm. long. All year round.

Stonefly

Stonefly. Wing span 20 mm. Summer.

Flea

Cat Flea. 2–3 mm. long. All year round.

Springtail

Water Springtail. 2 mm. long

Louse

Book Louse. 2.5 mm. long.

Spiders and their webs

This page shows you some of the interesting things you may see if you go spider-watching. Remember, a spider is not an insect (see p. 133). Spiders in bushes can be caught like insects (see p. 132-3), but in a wood or field, drag a strong bag through the plants and tip the contents out onto a white sheet.

If you want to study spiders closely, have a jam-jar ready to keep them in. Put them back where you found them afterwards.

Look for spiders' webs in early morning when they are covered with frost or dew.

Hammock web

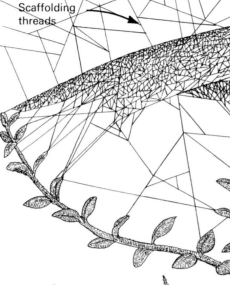

Scaffolding threads

The sizes given are body lengths.

Spider rests upside-down under hammock

A hammock spider
8-9 mm.

Hammock webs are quite common in hedges and bushes. Above the web are lots of tangled "scaffolding" threads. As well as holding the web in position, these threads act as trip wires. A flying insect bumping into them is tripped into the web below. The spider is waiting upside down under the web. When it feels the vibrations of an insect which has fallen on to the web, it will rush up and catch it.

Sheet web

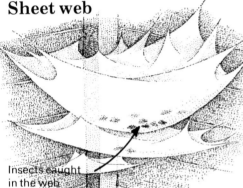

Insects caught in the web

This is a sheet web made by a house spider. You will find them behind pictures and in the corners of rooms and sheds. The spider will be hiding in a silken tube at the corner of the sheet web.

Catching prey without a web

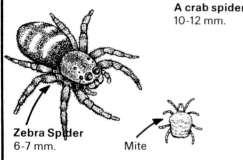

Zebra Spider
6-7 mm.

Mite

This spider has very good eye-sight. It stalks its insect prey and may jump several centimetres to capture it. Notice its large eyes.

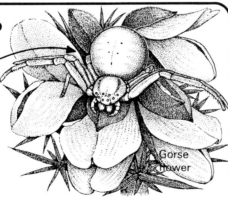

A crab spider
10-12 mm.

Gorse flower

Crab spiders can run sideways like crabs. They lie in wait for prey, often hiding in flowers to catch any insect that may come to collect nectar.

1 Spiders and their young

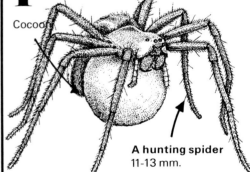

Cocoon

A hunting spider
11-13 mm.

Spiders lay eggs which they cover with a cocoon of threads. This hunting spider carries her cocoon with her.

160

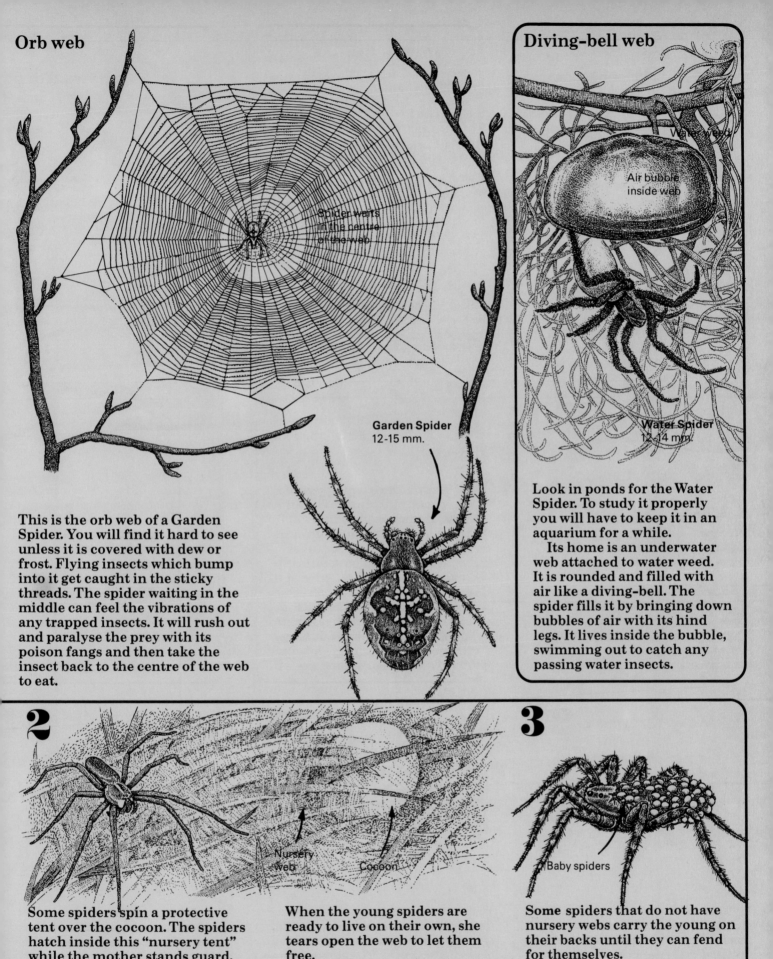

Orb web

This is the orb web of a Garden Spider. You will find it hard to see unless it is covered with dew or frost. Flying insects which bump into it get caught in the sticky threads. The spider waiting in the middle can feel the vibrations of any trapped insects. It will rush out and paralyse the prey with its poison fangs and then take the insect back to the centre of the web to eat.

Spider waits in the centre of the web

Garden Spider
12-15 mm.

Diving-bell web

Air bubble inside web

Water Spider
12-14 mm.

Look in ponds for the Water Spider. To study it properly you will have to keep it in an aquarium for a while.

Its home is an underwater web attached to water weed. It is rounded and filled with air like a diving-bell. The spider fills it by bringing down bubbles of air with its hind legs. It lives inside the bubble, swimming out to catch any passing water insects.

2

Nursery Web

Cocoon

Some spiders spin a protective tent over the cocoon. The spiders hatch inside this "nursery tent" while the mother stands guard.

When the young spiders are ready to live on their own, she tears open the web to let them free.

3

Baby spiders

Some spiders that do not have nursery webs carry the young on their backs until they can fend for themselves.

Part 6 written by
Su Swallow

Consultant Editor
Alfred Leutscher, B.Sc., F.Z.S.

Part 6
PONDS & STREAMS

Many different kinds of animals and plants are attracted to fresh water. This section of the book shows the common species of birds, fishes, insects, mammals, plants and amphibians that live in and around fresh water in Europe. It tells you how to find them, and how they have adapted themselves to life near the water.

This section also explains how to make a collection of things like frogs, toads, and insects, so that you can study them at home. Remember to always put animals back when you have finished looking at them.

If you feel you would like to go further with your study of freshwater life, you could try contacting your local natural history society. You may find members who have a special interest in a local pond or stretch of river and who would be keen to explore with you.

How to Start

The best time to study streams and ponds is in the spring and summer, when the plants are flowering and the animals are most active. But winter is a very good time to spot birds.

Move slowly and quietly and be careful your shadow does not alarm the fishes. You will find more life near the bank, where there is more plant cover.

Look for freshwater life in lakes, rivers, ditches and canals. You may even find plants or insects in drinking troughs and rainwater tubs.

What to Take

Empty margarine pot for watching animals

Fishing net

Jars

Binoculars

Magnifying glass

DO'S AND DON'TS

DO TEST WATER DEPTH WITH A LONG POLE BEFORE WADING IN.

DON'T USE LOGS OR STONES AS STEPPING-STONES WITHOUT TESTING THEM FIRST.

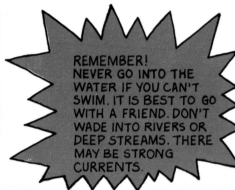

DO REPLACE STONES AND LOGS EXACTLY AS YOU FOUND THEM.

DO KEEP JARS WITH SPECIMENS IN THE SHADE TO KEEP THE WATER COOL.

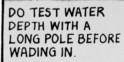

DON'T HANDLE ANYTHING YOU CATCH. PUT IT STRAIGHT INTO A DISH OR JAR.

DON'T SMASH ICE ON PONDS IN WINTER. THIS WILL DISTURB ANIMALS LIVING THERE.

DON'T STAMP YOUR FEET OR MOVE QUICKLY. THIS WILL FRIGHTEN ANIMALS.

DON'T TAKE TOO MANY ANIMALS OR WHOLE PLANTS. PART OF A PLANT WILL BE ENOUGH TO IDENTIFY IT.

DO PUT ANIMALS AND PLANTS BACK INTO THE POND AS SOON AS POSSIBLE.

A Pond Survey

Ask some friends to help make a map of your pond, showing the plants and animals you find. If you look carefully, you might find something rare. Repeat the survey to see how pond life changes with the seasons. Check for signs of pollution. You can survey part of a stream in exactly the same way.

What to Look for

Even a small pond can support a surprising variety of life if it is not too shaded or polluted. Here are some of the animals to look for and their hiding places.

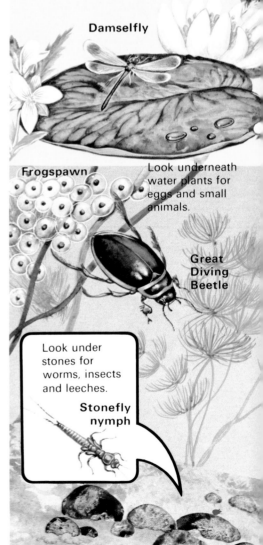

Damselfly

Frogspawn

Look underneath water plants for eggs and small animals.

Great Diving Beetle

Look under stones for worms, insects and leeches.

Stonefly nymph

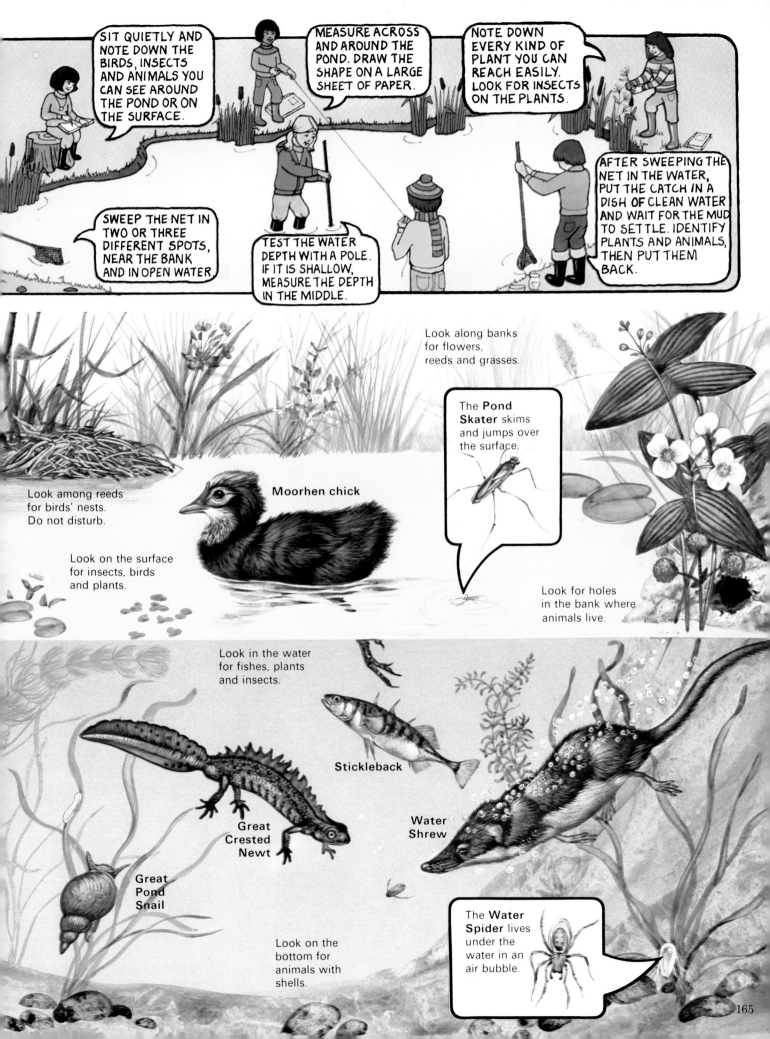

SIT QUIETLY AND NOTE DOWN THE BIRDS, INSECTS AND ANIMALS YOU CAN SEE AROUND THE POND OR ON THE SURFACE.

MEASURE ACROSS AND AROUND THE POND. DRAW THE SHAPE ON A LARGE SHEET OF PAPER.

NOTE DOWN EVERY KIND OF PLANT YOU CAN REACH EASILY. LOOK FOR INSECTS ON THE PLANTS.

SWEEP THE NET IN TWO OR THREE DIFFERENT SPOTS, NEAR THE BANK AND IN OPEN WATER.

TEST THE WATER DEPTH WITH A POLE. IF IT IS SHALLOW, MEASURE THE DEPTH IN THE MIDDLE.

AFTER SWEEPING THE NET IN THE WATER, PUT THE CATCH IN A DISH OF CLEAN WATER AND WAIT FOR THE MUD TO SETTLE. IDENTIFY PLANTS AND ANIMALS, THEN PUT THEM BACK.

Look along banks for flowers, reeds and grasses.

Look among reeds for birds' nests. Do not disturb.

Look on the surface for insects, birds and plants.

Moorhen chick

The **Pond Skater** skims and jumps over the surface.

Look for holes in the bank where animals live.

Look in the water for fishes, plants and insects.

Stickleback

Water Shrew

Great Crested Newt

Great Pond Snail

Look on the bottom for animals with shells.

The **Water Spider** lives under the water in an air bubble.

165

Living Together

In a thriving pond there is a balance of different kinds of animals and plants, so that there is enough food for them all to survive. It is important not to disturb this balance.

How Plants Help

Animals living in water need a gas called oxygen to breathe. They get some from the surface, but water plants also give off oxygen when they make their food. Plants need sunlight to make food and produce oxygen.

Canadian Pondweed

Try this experiment: put some Canadian Pondweed in water in the sun. Oxygen bubbles will soon appear.

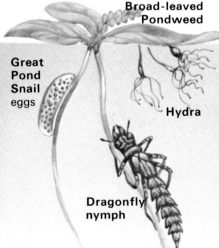

Broad-leaved Pondweed

Great Pond Snail eggs

Hydra

Dragonfly nymph

Plants not only produce oxygen for animals to breathe, but also help in other ways. They provide shade and shelter from enemies. They act as supports for eggs and tiny animals. Some insects use plant stems to climb out of the water when they are changing into winged adults.

Pond Food Chain

The process of one animal eating another and then being eaten by a larger animal is called a food chain. In the chain shown here, there are six links joined by arrows. At the top is the Heron which eats everything in the second link including Perch. Perch eat animals in the third link and so on down to the Algae at the bottom. Because each animal eats many things, a pond has many different food chains.

There are more animals at the bottom of the chain than at the top. This is because these animals are small, and a larger animal needs to eat many of them to survive.

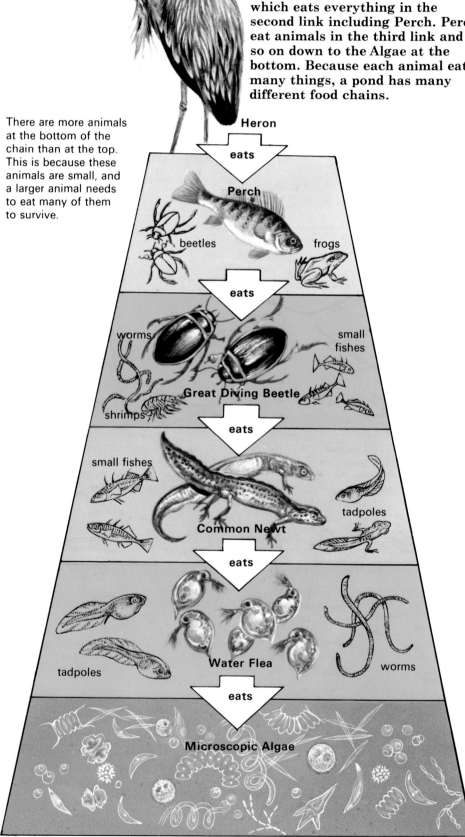

Heron

eats

Perch

beetles   frogs

eats

worms   small fishes

Great Diving Beetle

shrimps

eats

small fishes   tadpoles

Common Newt

eats

tadpoles   **Water Flea**   worms

eats

Microscopic Algae

Pollution

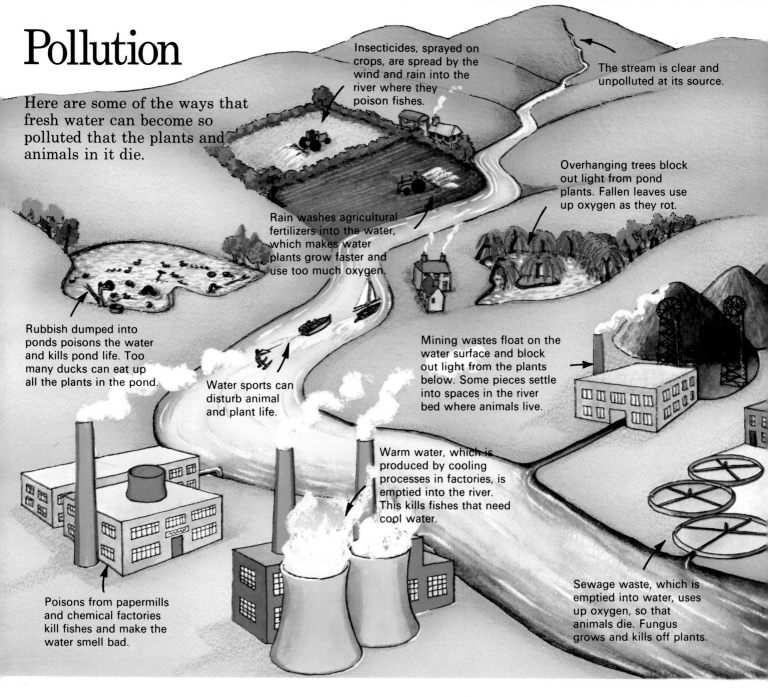

Here are some of the ways that fresh water can become so polluted that the plants and animals in it die.

Insecticides, sprayed on crops, are spread by the wind and rain into the river where they poison fishes.

The stream is clear and unpolluted at its source.

Overhanging trees block out light from pond plants. Fallen leaves use up oxygen as they rot.

Rain washes agricultural fertilizers into the water, which makes water plants grow faster and use too much oxygen.

Rubbish dumped into ponds poisons the water and kills pond life. Too many ducks can eat up all the plants in the pond.

Mining wastes float on the water surface and block out light from the plants below. Some pieces settle into spaces in the river bed where animals live.

Water sports can disturb animal and plant life.

Warm water, which is produced by cooling processes in factories, is emptied into the river. This kills fishes that need cool water.

Poisons from papermills and chemical factories kill fishes and make the water smell bad.

Sewage waste, which is emptied into water, uses up oxygen, so that animals die. Fungus grows and kills off plants.

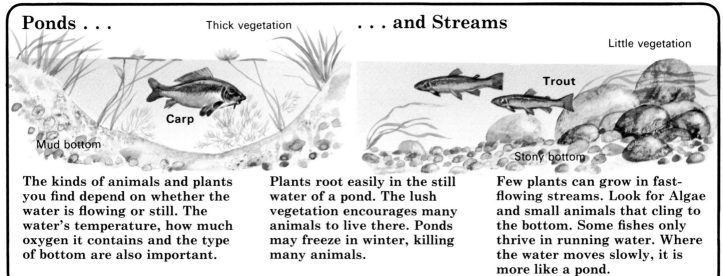

Ponds . . .   . . . and Streams

Thick vegetation

Carp

Mud bottom

Little vegetation

Trout

Stony bottom

The kinds of animals and plants you find depend on whether the water is flowing or still. The water's temperature, how much oxygen it contains and the type of bottom are also important.

Plants root easily in the still water of a pond. The lush vegetation encourages many animals to live there. Ponds may freeze in winter, killing many animals.

Few plants can grow in fast-flowing streams. Look for Algae and small animals that cling to the bottom. Some fishes only thrive in running water. Where the water moves slowly, it is more like a pond.

167

Plants of Ponds and Streams

Pond plants can be divided into groups depending on the zones, or areas, where they grow. Remember that the zones often overlap, and that you may not find all of the zones in one pond. Many of these common freshwater plants also grow in streams and rivers.

Notice how delicate many of the plants in deep water are. They do not need thick stems to support them, because the water holds them up. Their leaves are rather fine and thin because they do not need to hold water as land plants do.

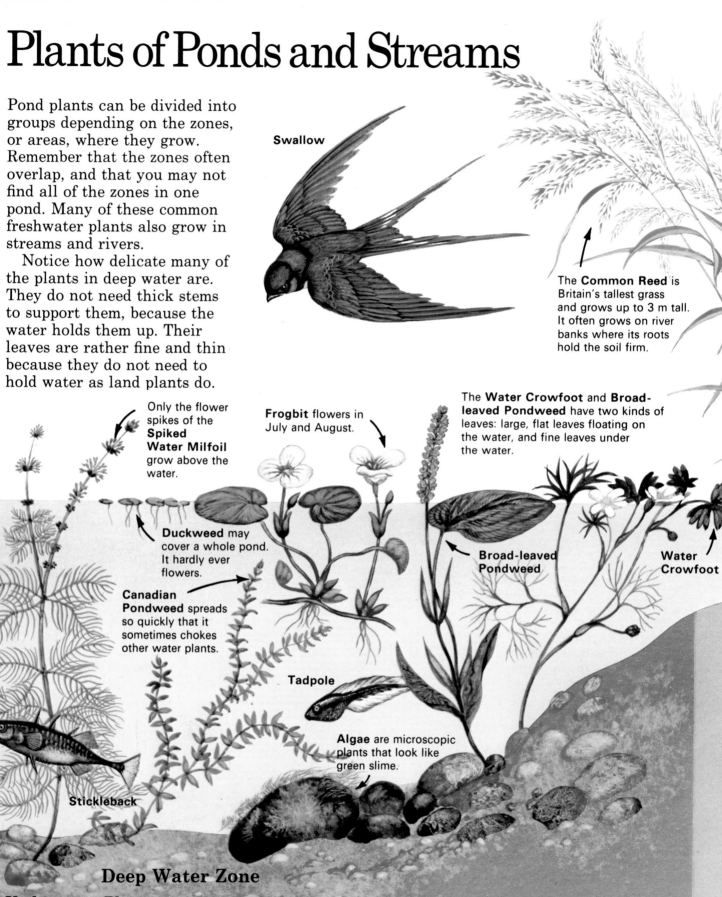

Swallow

The **Common Reed** is Britain's tallest grass and grows up to 3 m tall. It often grows on river banks where its roots hold the soil firm.

Only the flower spikes of the **Spiked Water Milfoil** grow above the water.

Frogbit flowers in July and August.

The **Water Crowfoot** and **Broad-leaved Pondweed** have two kinds of leaves: large, flat leaves floating on the water, and fine leaves under the water.

Duckweed may cover a whole pond. It hardly ever flowers.

Canadian Pondweed spreads so quickly that it sometimes chokes other water plants.

Broad-leaved Pondweed

Water Crowfoot

Tadpole

Algae are microscopic plants that look like green slime.

Stickleback

Deep Water Zone

Underwater Plants

In the middle of the pond, plants grow under the water, apart from some of the flower heads which rise above the surface. Their roots are in the mud.

Floating Plants

Some plants that grow near the centre of the pond float with their roots hanging free in the water.

Rooted Plants

Plants growing in fairly shallow water around the edge of this zone have their roots in the mud. Their leaves either float or stand out of the water.

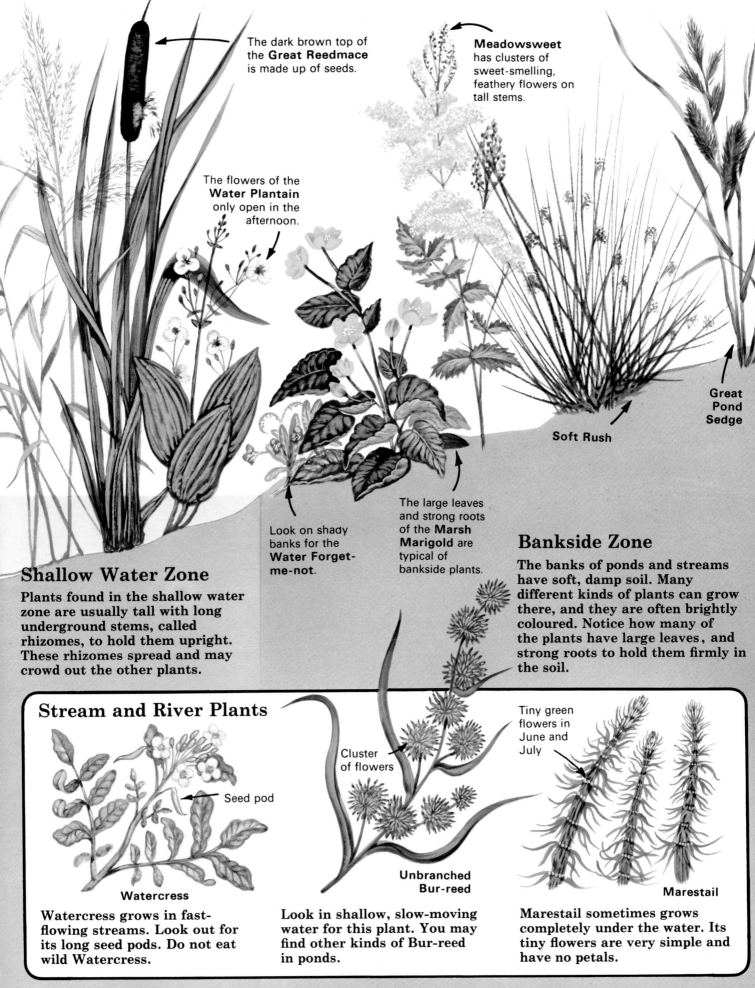

The dark brown top of the **Great Reedmace** is made up of seeds.

Meadowsweet has clusters of sweet-smelling, feathery flowers on tall stems.

The flowers of the **Water Plantain** only open in the afternoon.

Great Pond Sedge

Soft Rush

Look on shady banks for the **Water Forget-me-not**.

The large leaves and strong roots of the **Marsh Marigold** are typical of bankside plants.

Bankside Zone

The banks of ponds and streams have soft, damp soil. Many different kinds of plants can grow there, and they are often brightly coloured. Notice how many of the plants have large leaves, and strong roots to hold them firmly in the soil.

Shallow Water Zone

Plants found in the shallow water zone are usually tall with long underground stems, called rhizomes, to hold them upright. These rhizomes spread and may crowd out the other plants.

Stream and River Plants

Seed pod

Tiny green flowers in June and July

Cluster of flowers

Watercress

Watercress grows in fast-flowing streams. Look out for its long seed pods. Do not eat wild Watercress.

Unbranched Bur-reed

Look in shallow, slow-moving water for this plant. You may find other kinds of Bur-reed in ponds.

Marestail

Marestail sometimes grows completely under the water. Its tiny flowers are very simple and have no petals.

169

How Water Plants Grow

Many water plants grow from seeds. The seeds are formed after pollen from the male part of the flower (the stamen) reaches the female part (the style) of the same kind of flower. When the seeds are ripe, they are scattered and some of them grow. Some water plants can also spread by growing new plants from their rhizomes, or underground stems.

Some underwater plants do not spread by seed. Instead, new plants may grow from winter buds or from pieces that break off the old plant.

1 How Pollen Spreads

Purple Loosestrife

Water Mint

Pollen from some plants is spread by insects. The bright colours and scent attract insects, and the pollen rubs off on to their bodies. Then they carry it to other plants.

2

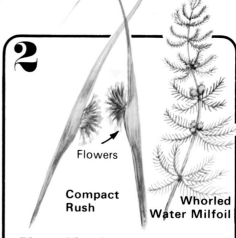

Flowers

Compact Rush

Whorled Water Milfoil

Plants like these are pollinated by the wind. Their flowers are often small and dull, because they do not need to attract insects.

How Seeds are Scattered

By Wind

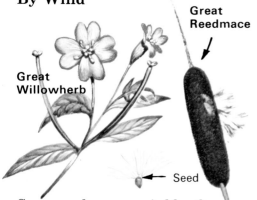

Great Reedmace

Great Willowherb

Seed

Some seeds are carried by the wind on a hairy parachute. Willowherb seeds may travel as far away as 150 kilometres.

By Water

Yellow Iris

Seed pods

Some plant seeds, like these pods from a Yellow Iris, are carried by water. They open when softened by water.

By Animals

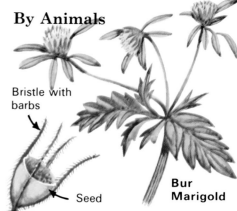

Bristle with barbs

Seed

Bur Marigold

Seeds with barbs, or hooks, catch on to animals' fur or people's clothing and later drop off.

How Water Lilies Grow

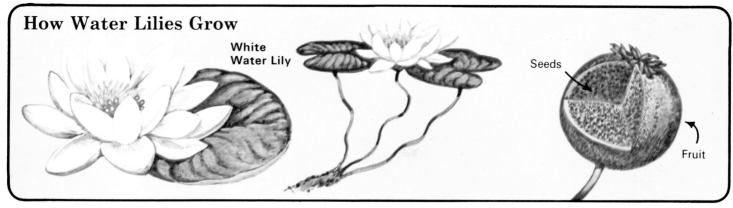

White Water Lily

Seeds

Fruit

Look in ponds for the White Water Lily. Its leaves and flowers float on the surface, but at night the flowers close, and sometimes sink just below the surface until morning.

The Water Lily is anchored to the bottom by stout rhizomes. The leaf stalks grow up from these stems at an angle. If the water level rises, they straighten up so that the leaves can still float.

The flowers are pollinated by insects. When the fruits are ripe, they sink to the bottom and release up to 2,000 seeds. The seeds float away, and some sink and start to grow into new plants.

3

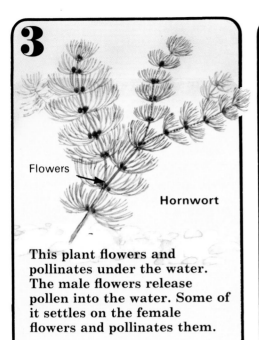

Flowers

Hornwort

This plant flowers and pollinates under the water. The male flowers release pollen into the water. Some of it settles on the female flowers and pollinates them.

How Other Water Plants Spread

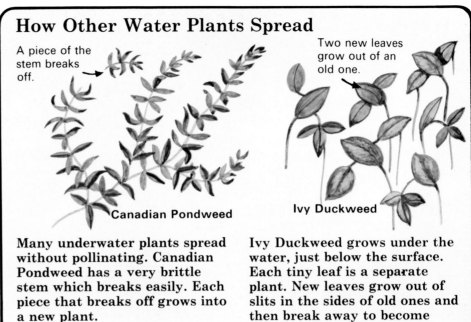

A piece of the stem breaks off.

Canadian Pondweed

Two new leaves grow out of an old one.

Ivy Duckweed

Many underwater plants spread without pollinating. Canadian Pondweed has a very brittle stem which breaks easily. Each piece that breaks off grows into a new plant.

Ivy Duckweed grows under the water, just below the surface. Each tiny leaf is a separate plant. New leaves grow out of slits in the sides of old ones and then break away to become new plants.

By Explosion

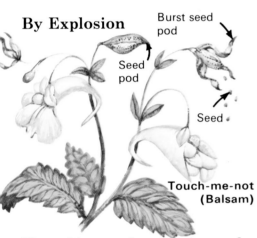

Burst seed pod

Seed pod

Seed

Touch-me-not (Balsam)

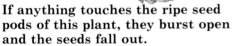

If anything touches the ripe seed pods of this plant, they burst open and the seeds fall out.

Watching a Plant Grow

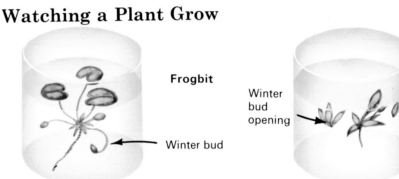

Frogbit

Winter bud

Winter bud opening

Frogbit grows winter buds on underwater roots. Each bud contains a new plant and a store of food. When the buds are ripe, they break off and sink. In spring, when the stored food is

used up, the buds float to the surface and grow into new plants. Collect some Frogbit in the autumn, and watch how it grows. Keep it cool in a jar of pond water.

In Winter

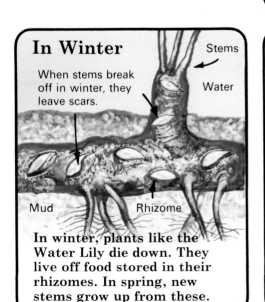

Stems

When stems break off in winter, they leave scars.

Water

Mud

Rhizome

In winter, plants like the Water Lily die down. They live off food stored in their rhizomes. In spring, new stems grow up from these.

Insect-Eating Plants

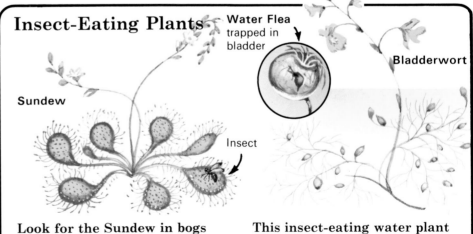

Water Flea trapped in bladder

Bladderwort

Sundew

Insect

Look for the Sundew in bogs and marshes. It traps insects on its hairs and digests them with special juices.

This insect-eating water plant catches tiny animals in its air-filled, underwater bladders. Then it feeds on them.

Watching Water Birds

Birdwatching by ponds and streams is exciting because of the variety of birds you may find there. Some birds spend most of their lives by water. Others may come to drink and bathe. In winter, sea birds fly inland for food and shelter.

The best place to look for birds is by water surrounded by thick vegetation. Early morning is a good time to see them.

In parks, some water birds are tame enough to be fed. Others are shy, so you must hide and wait quietly to see them. Keep a record of the birds you spot and their habits. If you find a nest, be sure not to disturb it.

Feeding

Watch the birds on and around a pond closely. See how many ways of feeding you can spot, the different bill shapes and how they are suited to these feeding methods. Time how long diving ducks stay under the water.

Mallards are dabbling ducks. They feed near the surface and eat mostly plants. They also up-end to get food from deep water.

Tufted Ducks dive down one or two metres for water plants, insects and small fishes.

Female   Male

Wigeon feed mainly on grasses and grain, cropped from fields. They also dabble in water.

The **Swift** feeds and even sleeps on the wing. It eats flies and beetles.

The **Shoveler** uses its wide bill to sieve food from water and mud.

The **Bittern** nests in reed beds where it is camouflaged well. It eats frogs, small fishes and insects.

The **Teal** is Britain's smallest duck. It is a surface-feeder and eats mainly water plants and their seeds.

The **Moorhen** eats plants and small animals in the water as well as seeds and grain on land.

The **Kingfisher** dives for small fishes and insects. It sometimes beats a fish against a branch to kill it. Then it swallows the fish head first, so that the fins and scales do not open and choke the bird.

Flocks in Flight

1 Taking a Count

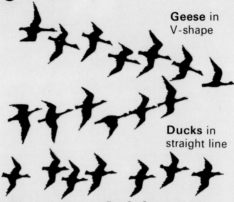

To work out the number of birds in a flock, count the first ten birds. Then guess what part that is of the whole flock. Multiply to get the total number of birds.

2 Flight Patterns

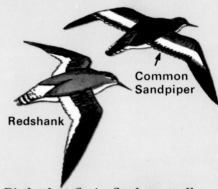

Geese in V-shape

Ducks in straight line

The pattern a flock forms can help you to identify the birds. Many birds fly in a line or a V-shape.

3 Keeping Together

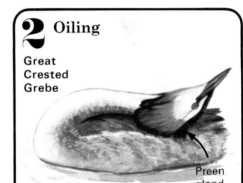

Common Sandpiper

Redshank

Birds that fly in flocks usually have distinctive markings for others to follow. They also call to each other to keep together, especially after dark.

The **Greylag Goose** spends a lot of time on land. It crops the grass with its bill.

Looking after Feathers

1 Bathing

Goosander

Water birds often bathe to keep clean. They flap their wings on the water and roll over to wet their bodies thoroughly. Then they shake themselves dry.

2 Oiling

Great Crested Grebe

Preen gland

Next, water birds spread oil from the preen glands near their tails, by rubbing their bills and heads over their feathers. The oil is good for the condition of the feathers.

3 Preening

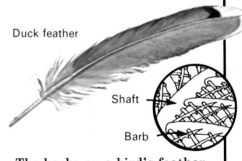

Pintail

Finally, they fluff up their feathers, nibble each one and draw them through their bills. This cleans and oils them still more, and settles them back into place.

How Feathers Work

Duck feather

Shaft

Barb

The barbs on a bird's feather grow out of the shaft. They fit together very closely, rather like the teeth of a zip. This helps keep the bird's body dry and warm.

Birds: Mating and Nesting

Birds become very active in the spring when most of them breed. The male birds attract females by showing off their bright feathers. Some develop crests and ruffs of feathers at this time. They make special mating calls and perform acrobatics in the air or on the water. Sometimes both male and female birds take part in these courtship displays.

When the female has accepted the male, a nest is built. Notice what materials each kind of bird collects for its nest.

Courtship

Great Crested Grebes start their courtship early in the year. Head-shaking (above) is a common display. The birds swim towards each other, calling and shaking their heads from side to side.

After head-shaking, the Grebes may "dance" together. First they dive to collect weed. Then they swim towards one another and rise out of the water, swaying their bills and paddling hard.

Fighting

This Swan is puffing out its feathers to frighten away an enemy. Sometimes birds fight to defend their nest or territory.

This Greylag Goose is standing in a threat position to chase away other adult geese that might come too close to its nest or territory.

Coots fight with their claws, holding themselves up with their wings. Fights do not last very long, and usually only the males take part.

Nesting

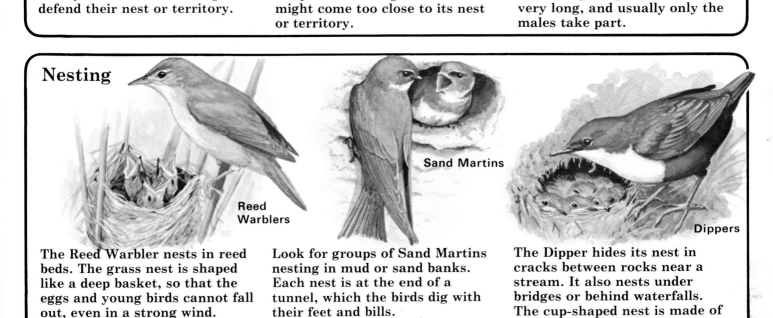

The Reed Warbler nests in reed beds. The grass nest is shaped like a deep basket, so that the eggs and young birds cannot fall out, even in a strong wind.

Look for groups of Sand Martins nesting in mud or sand banks. Each nest is at the end of a tunnel, which the birds dig with their feet and bills.

The Dipper hides its nest in cracks between rocks near a stream. It also nests under bridges or behind waterfalls. The cup-shaped nest is made of moss and grasses.

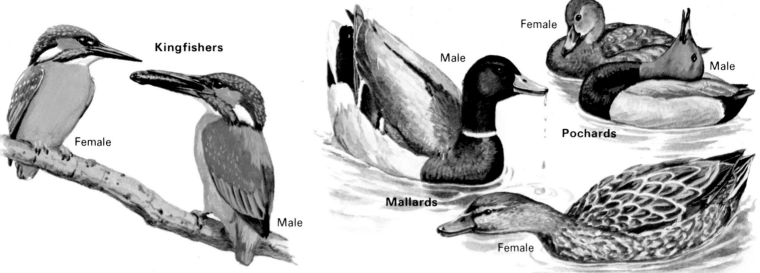

Kingfishers

Female

Male

Male

Mallards

Female

Female

Pochards

Male

Some male birds, like the Kingfisher, make a present of food to the female during courtship. When she has accepted it, they are ready to mate.

The Mallard is a common duck, and you are quite likely to see the male's striking courtship display. He dives, flaps his wings, sprays water with his bill, whistles and grunts. The female draws his

attention by jerking her head to and fro.

To impress a female, the male Pochard swims around her, jerking his head backwards and forwards.

Looking after the Young

Grey Herons

Some birds, like the Heron, are born helpless. They are blind, featherless, and cannot leave the nest for over a month. Young Herons beg for food by pecking at their parents' bills. Other young

birds beg with loud cries or gaping beaks. However, some chicks, like Ducks and Grebes, can swim a few hours after hatching. Ducklings can also feed themselves.

Keeping the Young Safe

Little Grebes (or **Dabchicks**)

Little Grebes can swim soon after they hatch, but sometimes they climb on to their parents' backs to keep safe from danger.

Little Ringed Plover

Like many other birds that nest on the ground, the Little Ringed Plover may pretend to be hurt to draw an enemy away from its nest.

How Insects Grow

You can find some strange and exciting insects in ponds and streams, even in polluted water. Most insects go through several stages of development between the egg and the adult. (Follow the steps in the development of the Caddis Fly.) The early stages may last for years, but the adult may live only for a few hours or days.

Some water insects, like water beetles, spend all their lives in the water, while others, like the Alder Fly, leave the water when fully grown.

The Caddis Fly

1 Egg

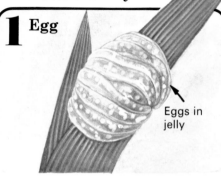

Caddis Flies develop in fresh water. The eggs are laid in jelly on plants or stones, either above or in the water.

2 Larva

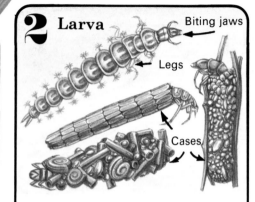

When the larva hatches from the egg, it makes itself a protective case of shells, stones or leaves. It eats plants on the pond bottom.

Where Insects Lay Eggs

1 On the Water

The Great Silver Beetle lays its eggs in a silky cocoon on the water's surface. The hollow "mast" is to allow air to reach the eggs.

2 Above the Water

Look for insect eggs on water plants and stones above the water. When the larvae hatch, they fall or crawl down into the water.

3 Below the Water

Some insects lay their eggs under the water, on plants or stones, or on the mud bottom. The Water Scorpion lays its eggs on plant stems.

Larvae and Nymphs

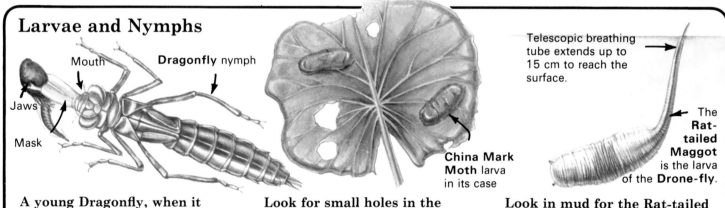

A young Dragonfly, when it hatches from the egg, is called a nymph. It has a strong pair of jaws fixed to a hinge, called a mask. The mask shoots out to catch prey.

Look for small holes in the leaves of Water Lilies and Pondweed. Underneath, you may see this moth larva, which makes a case out of the leaves and also feeds on them.

Look in mud for the Rat-tailed Maggot. Scoop up some mud and a little water in a dish, and wait for it to settle. Look for the Maggot's breathing tube.

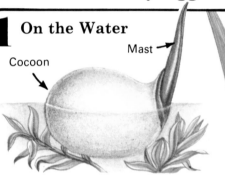

3 Pupa

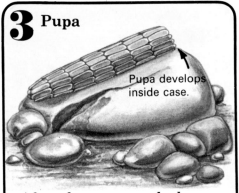

Pupa develops inside case.

After about a year, the larva stops eating and changes into a pupa inside the case. During the winter, the pupa slowly develops into an adult Caddis Fly inside the case.

4 Adult

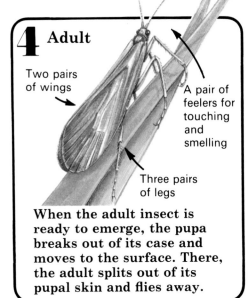

Two pairs of wings

A pair of feelers for touching and smelling

Three pairs of legs

When the adult insect is ready to emerge, the pupa breaks out of its case and moves to the surface. There, the adult splits out of its pupal skin and flies away.

An Underwater Viewer

Place sealed end in water.

Use a large tin to make this underwater viewer. Remove the top and bottom with a tin opener. Cover one end with clear plastic wrap and attach it tightly with a rubber band. Look through the open end.

A Dragonfly Emerges

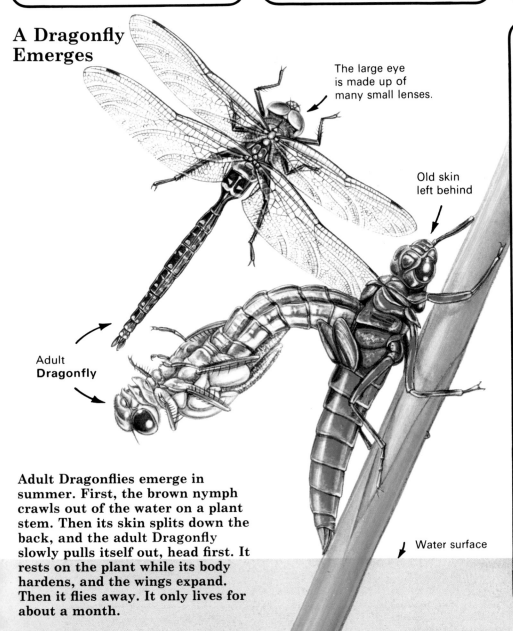

The large eye is made up of many small lenses.

Old skin left behind

Adult **Dragonfly**

Water surface

Adult Dragonflies emerge in summer. First, the brown nymph crawls out of the water on a plant stem. Then its skin splits down the back, and the adult Dragonfly slowly pulls itself out, head first. It rests on the plant while its body hardens, and the wings expand. Then it flies away. It only lives for about a month.

Watching Gnats Grow

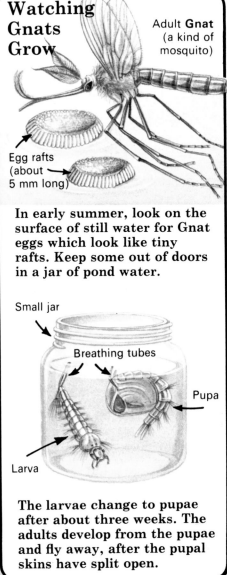

Adult **Gnat** (a kind of mosquito)

Egg rafts (about 5 mm long)

In early summer, look on the surface of still water for Gnat eggs which look like tiny rafts. Keep some out of doors in a jar of pond water.

Small jar

Breathing tubes

Pupa

Larva

The larvae change to pupae after about three weeks. The adults develop from the pupae and fly away, after the pupal skins have split open.

177

Watching Insects

If you sit by a pond or stream, you will soon spot several kinds of insects. Look in the air, on the water's surface and in the water. To help you to identify an insect, make a note of its colour, the shape and number of its wings, where you saw it and other details.

Remember that all adult insects have bodies with three parts, three pairs of legs, and usually a pair of antennae or feelers. Many have wings at some time in their lives.

Above the Water

A **Damselfly** at rest holds its wings together.

Swarms of **Mayflies** rise and fall over the water.

Dragonflies fly in pairs when mating.

A **Mayfly** has two or three long threads at the end of its body.

Look for these flying insects in spring and early summer, when they emerge from the pupa or nymph. Most stay close to the water, and they all breed there.

How Insects Stay on the Surface

Use blotting paper to place the needle on the water.

The paper will sink, but the needle will stay afloat.

A thin film on the surface of the water holds insects up. See how this works by floating a needle on water.

On the Surface

The **Water Measurer** moves slowly. The hairs on its body stop it from getting wet.

Tiny **Springtails** can jump 30 cm using their hinged tails.

The **Pond Skater** slides rapidly over the surface. It can also jump.

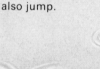

Whirligig Beetles whirl and spin, without colliding, while looking for food.

Notice the different ways that these insects move on the water surface. They feed mostly on dead insects that fall on the water.

Under the Water

Breathing tube

Its antenna breaks the surface film while it collects air.

The **Water Boatman** swims and takes in air at the surface, upside down.

It has strong legs for swimming.

Most insects breathe by taking in air through holes in their bodies. Many underwater insects carry a bubble of air on their bodies, which they collect at the surface and replace when it is used up.

The **Water Scorpion** takes in air at the surface through a breathing tube. It stores air under its wing cases.

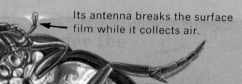

Air bubble

The **Great Silver Beetle** carries a bubble of air trapped by the hairs on its underside.

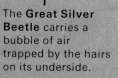

How Insects Feed

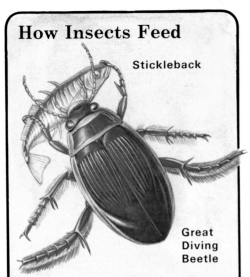

Stickleback

Great Diving Beetle

Many water beetles eat other animals. The Great Diving Beetle feeds on tadpoles and fishes. Its prey is often larger than itself.

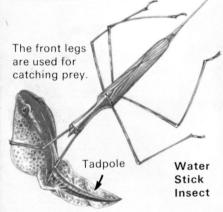

The front legs are used for catching prey.

Tadpole

Water Stick Insect

This insect hides among reed stems, waiting for its prey. It shoots out its front legs to catch any passing animal and then sucks out the juices.

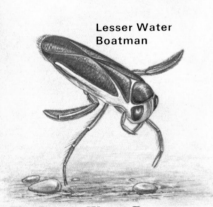

Lesser Water Boatman

The Lesser Water Boatman feeds on algae and rotting plants on the bottom. Unlike the Water Boatman, it swims right side up.

Making an Insect Aquarium

This picture shows the things you will need to make an aquarium. You can buy some of them at pet shops. Keep the aquarium near a window, but not in direct sunlight. If you use tap water, add some pond water and leave it for a few days before adding the animals.

Nymphs and Larvae

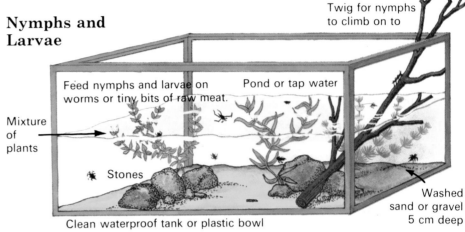

Twig for nymphs to climb on to

Feed nymphs and larvae on worms or tiny bits of raw meat.

Pond or tap water

Mixture of plants

Stones

Clean waterproof tank or plastic bowl

Washed sand or gravel 5 cm deep

Flying Insects

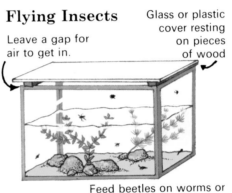

Leave a gap for air to get in.

Glass or plastic cover resting on pieces of wood

Feed beetles on worms or tiny bits of raw meat.

To keep water insects that can fly, like beetles, put a lid or netting on the aquarium to stop them from escaping.

Tiny Insects

Lid with air holes

Margarine pot

Magnifying glass

You can make a collection of tiny insects very easily. Put them in a jar or pot, with some pond water, a little mud and a few plants.

Fierce Insects

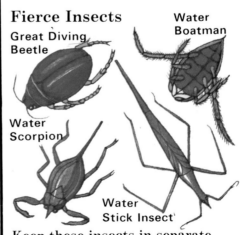

Great Diving Beetle

Water Boatman

Water Scorpion

Water Stick Insect

Keep these insects in separate containers, or they will eat each other. Feed them on pieces of meat or worms.

REMEMBER! ONLY TAKE A FEW INSECTS FROM THE WATER. MAKE SURE THEY HAVE THE RIGHT FOOD AND ENOUGH ROOM. ALWAYS RETURN THEM TO THE POND OR STREAM WHEN YOU HAVE FINISHED STUDYING THEM.

Mammals

Most mammals that live near fresh water are very shy and are not often seen. Some are nocturnal, which means that they are only active at night. Often all you will hear is a "plop" as the animal leaps into the water to get away. Mammals can hear well and have a good sense of smell. So if you go animal tracking, approach the water quietly, facing the wind. You may find animal tracks or feeding signs. Try to identify them, so that you know which animal you are looking for!

Spot the Difference

Water Vole — Tiny ears — Blunt snout — Short, furry tail

Brown Rat — Large ears — Pointed snout — Long, naked tail

The Water Vole is often confused with the Brown Rat. They look rather alike and both are often seen swimming. Look at the differences carefully, so that you can tell them apart if you spot them. The Water Vole often swims under the water, but the Brown Rat keeps more to the surface of the water.

The **Harvest Mouse**, driven out of the cornfields by farm machinery, now often nests in reed beds. It is an expert climber and can hang by its tail. It comes out in the day.

This bat often flies over water in the daytime, hunting for insects. It can swim well too.

Daubenton's Bat

The **Brown Rat** prefers rivers and canals. Look for it at any time of day. It eats almost anything.

The **Water Shrew** sometimes leaps out of the water to catch insects. It also eats fishes and frogs. You may see it walking on the bottom of streams, looking for food.

Look on banks of large ponds and slow rivers for the Water Vole. You may see it dive into the water. After a swim, it grooms its fur.

Look for plant stems which have been bitten off. This could be the feeding spot of a Water Vole.

Holes in the bank, either above or below water, could be the entrance to a **Shrew's** or **Vole's** burrow.

Rare Mammals

Beaver

European Mink

Muskrat

The Muskrat is a large vole that lives in parts of Europe, but not in Britain. It swims fast and keeps near the surface of shallow, overgrown water.

A few Beavers survive in Europe, mostly in remote northern areas. They build their homes, called lodges, with branches or logs that they cut from trees.

Some Minks are wild, while others have escaped from fur farms. You might see one in a reed bed or by a river. They hunt and swim at night. They are very fierce.

The Otter

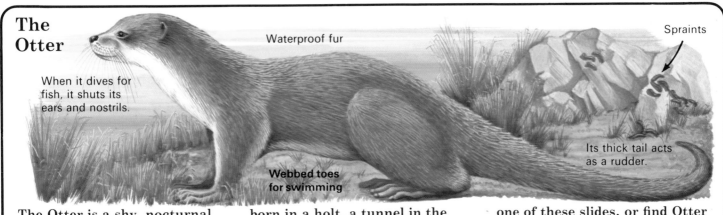

When it dives for fish, it shuts its ears and nostrils.

Waterproof fur

Spraints

Webbed toes for swimming

Its thick tail acts as a rudder.

The Otter is a shy, nocturnal animal. It lives in lonely places, and is well adapted for life in the water. It eats fishes, frogs and shellfish. Otter cubs are

born in a holt, a tunnel in the bank or among tree roots. Even the adults are playful and make slides down the river bank in the snow or mud. You might see

one of these slides, or find Otter droppings, called spraints, on a rock or clump of grass. Otters often leave behind remains of fish they have eaten.

Tracks

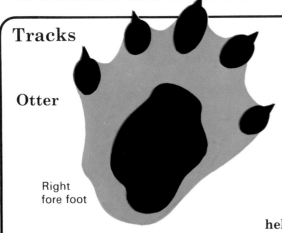

Otter

Right fore foot

Water Vole

Right fore foot

Right hind foot

Brown Rat

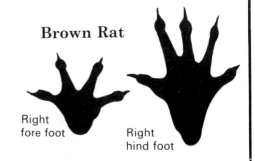

Right fore foot

Right hind foot

Look for animal tracks in firm mud and snow. Look especially in the morning, before the fresh tracks have been spoiled. To

help you identify them later, measure and draw the tracks, and the pattern, or trail, the tracks make together. Remember that you will not

often find a complete track showing all of the animal's foot. An Otter track, for instance, may not show the web, claw marks or even the fifth toe.

181

Fishes

There are nearly 40 kinds of freshwater fishes in Britain.

Notice which kinds prefer still or moving water, and make a check-list to help you to identify the fish: what colour and shape is it? Does it have whiskers, or barbels, near its mouth? Is it near the surface or on the bottom? How fast does it swim?

Most freshwater fishes spawn, or lay their eggs, in shallow water. Look for eggs among water plants and on the stones and sand of the bottom. Small fishes are called fry.

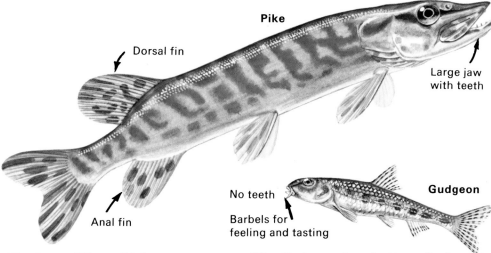

Pike

Dorsal fin

Large jaw with teeth

Anal fin

No teeth

Barbels for feeling and tasting

Gudgeon

The fierce Pike, which grows up to 1m long, hunts frogs, young birds, fishes, and even other Pike. It lurks in reeds, waiting for its prey, and then attacks with its sharp teeth.

The Gudgeon is a bottom-feeder. It sucks insect larvae, worms and shellfish into its mouth. Its mouth is toothless, but it has teeth in its throat which break up the food it swallows.

In a Pond

Most pond fishes are rounder and fatter than the slim, streamlined fishes of running water. They swim more slowly too.

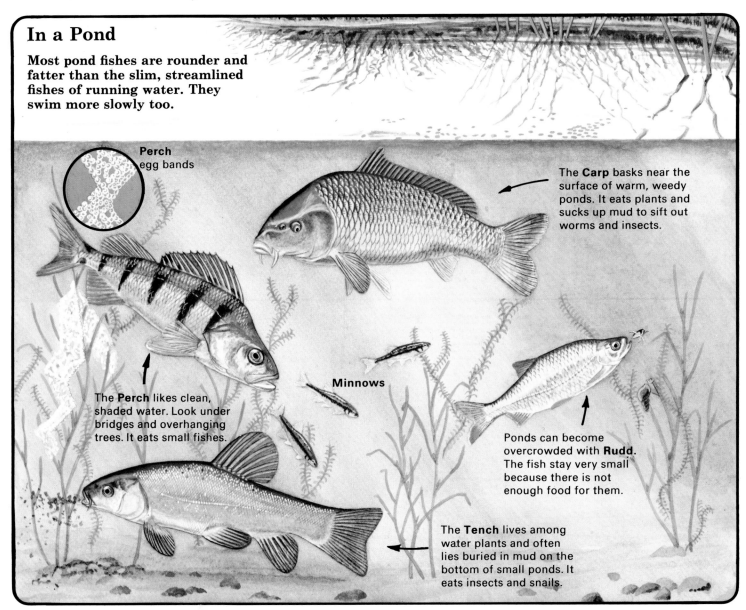

Perch egg bands

The **Carp** basks near the surface of warm, weedy ponds. It eats plants and sucks up mud to sift out worms and insects.

Minnows

The **Perch** likes clean, shaded water. Look under bridges and overhanging trees. It eats small fishes.

Ponds can become overcrowded with **Rudd**. The fish stay very small because there is not enough food for them.

The **Tench** lives among water plants and often lies buried in mud on the bottom of small ponds. It eats insects and snails.

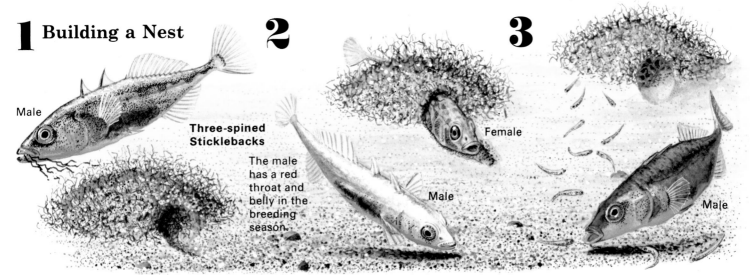

1 Building a Nest

2

3

Three-spined Sticklebacks

The male has a red throat and belly in the breeding season.

Male

Female

Male

Male

Look for this Stickleback in ponds and ditches. In May, a male builds a nest where the female will lay her eggs. He glues bits of plants together with sticky threads from

his body. The male "dances" to attract a female to the nest. The female leaves after laying eggs. The male then fans the eggs with his fins to keep fresh water

flowing over them. When the eggs hatch, the male guards the fry. He chases away enemies and catches stray fry in his mouth to bring them back to the nest.

In a Stream

The **Dace** is often found in large schools near the surface of the water.

The **Grayling** has a large dorsal fin. It eats insect larvae. It cannot live in polluted water.

The small **Minnow** often moves about in schools. It is eaten by other fishes and by water birds.

Trout live in fast-flowing streams. Their dark spots act as a camouflage on the stony bottom.

The **Bullhead** hides under stones in the day. It comes out at night to feed on insect larvae and small shellfish.

Eels

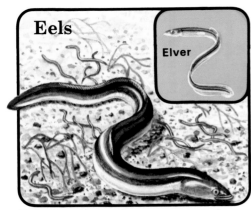

Elver

Eels live in fresh water until they are about ten years old. Then they move down rivers to the sea to breed and die. The young eels, called elvers, travel back to fresh water.

Salmon

Salmon spend some of their lives in the sea, but return to fresh water to breed. Most Salmon even reach the river where they were born. The female lays up to 15,000 eggs on the river bottom.

REMEMBER! IF YOU WANT TO SEE FISHES, APPROACH THE WATER SLOWLY AND QUIETLY. KEEP YOUR SHADOW OFF THE WATER. TRY FEEDING FISHES WITH BREAD OR MAGGOTS.

Frogs,Toads and Newts

Frogs, toads and newts are born in water, but spend most of their adult life on land. These animals are called amphibians. The young tadpoles develop from eggs, called spawn, laid in the water. They breathe by taking in oxygen from the water through their gills. As they grow, their gills and tails slowly disappear, and lungs and legs take their place (although newts keep their tails). Now the young amphibian leaves the water except when it returns to the pond to breed in spring.

Frogs

Common Frog

Long tongue joined to the front of the mouth

Dark patches around its ears and on its back legs

Smooth, moist skin

Long back legs for jumping

Webbed toes for swimming

The Common Frog lives in damp grass and undergrowth. Its basic colour can change to match its surroundings. This helps it to hide from snakes, hedgehogs, rats and other enemies. In winter, the frog hibernates in the mud bottom of a ditch or pond.

How Frogs Breed

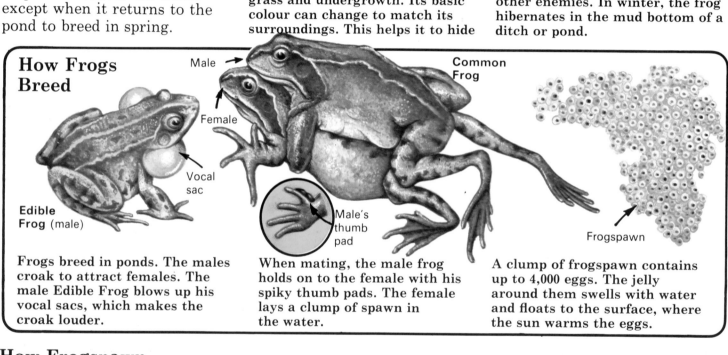

Male

Female

Vocal sac

Edible Frog (male)

Male's thumb pad

Common Frog

Frogspawn

Frogs breed in ponds. The males croak to attract females. The male Edible Frog blows up his vocal sacs, which makes the croak louder.

When mating, the male frog holds on to the female with his spiky thumb pads. The female lays a clump of spawn in the water.

A clump of frogspawn contains up to 4,000 eggs. The jelly around them swells with water and floats to the surface, where the sun warms the eggs.

How Frogspawn Develops

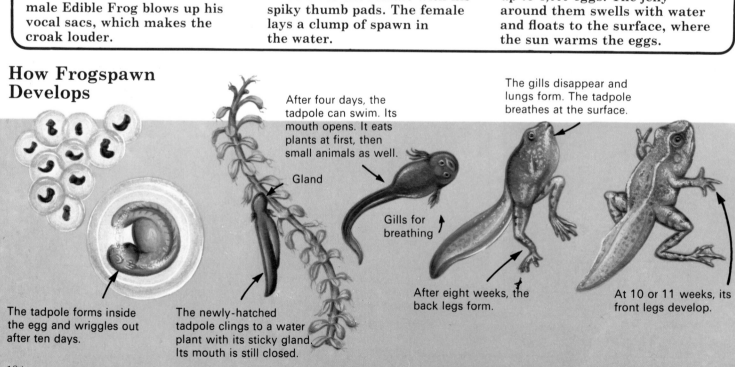

After four days, the tadpole can swim. Its mouth opens. It eats plants at first, then small animals as well.

The gills disappear and lungs form. The tadpole breathes at the surface.

Gland

Gills for breathing

The tadpole forms inside the egg and wriggles out after ten days.

The newly-hatched tadpole clings to a water plant with its sticky gland. Its mouth is still closed.

After eight weeks, the back legs form.

At 10 or 11 weeks, its front legs develop.

184

Toads

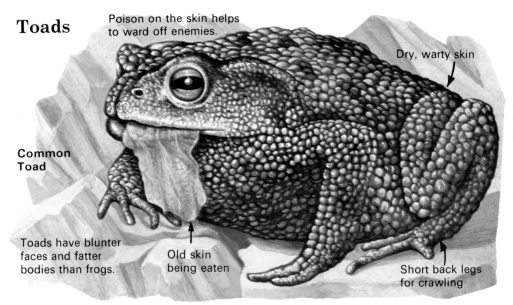

Poison on the skin helps to ward off enemies.

Dry, warty skin

Common Toad

Toads have blunter faces and fatter bodies than frogs.

Old skin being eaten

Short back legs for crawling

In the day, the Common Toad hides in holes in the ground. It hunts for food at night. A toad grows a new skin several times in the summer. It scrapes off the old one and eats it. In winter, it hibernates in an old animal burrow.

Danger

Toad

Grass Snake

If a toad is threatened by a Grass Snake, it may blow itself up so that the snake cannot swallow it.

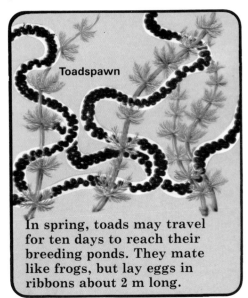

Toadspawn

In spring, toads may travel for ten days to reach their breeding ponds. They mate like frogs, but lay eggs in ribbons about 2 m long.

At 12 or 13 weeks, the tail disappears and the tiny frog, 1 cm long, is ready to leave the water. It will be fully grown in three years. Few tadpoles survive to this stage. Most are eaten by other pond creatures.

Newts

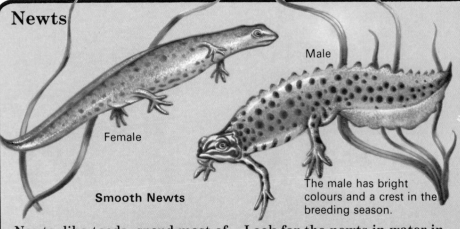

Male

Female

Smooth Newts

The male has bright colours and a crest in the breeding season.

Newts, like toads, spend most of their life on land, hiding by day and feeding at night. They look rather like lizards, but are not scaly.

Look for the newts in water in spring. You might see the male Smooth Newt's courtship dance. He arches his back and flicks his tail.

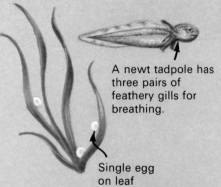

A newt tadpole has three pairs of feathery gills for breathing.

Single egg on leaf

Its front legs grow first. The tadpole eats water fleas and tiny worms.

Its gills disappear and its lungs and back legs develop.

Newts lay their eggs singly, on water plants. The leaves are often bent over to protect the eggs. The tadpoles hatch after about two weeks. The young newts, or efts, are ready to leave the water in August, but some stay in the water until the next year.

Keeping Amphibians

Frogspawn

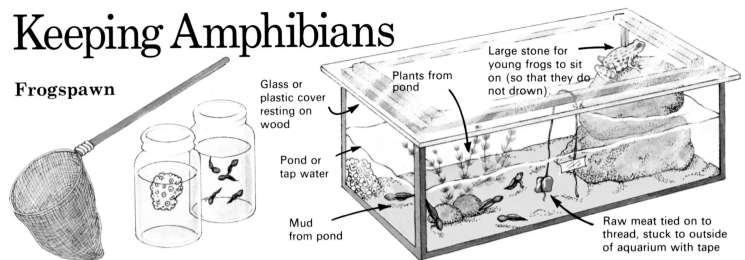

Glass or plastic cover resting on wood

Plants from pond

Large stone for young frogs to sit on (so that they do not drown).

Pond or tap water

Mud from pond

Raw meat tied on to thread, stuck to outside of aquarium with tape

How to collect: Look in ponds in March and April. Use a net to collect frogspawn. Put a little in a jar and return the rest to the water. If the eggs have already hatched, collect some tadpoles to study instead.

Where to keep: Put the aquarium in a light place, but out of direct sunlight. Change the water as soon as it smells bad. When the frogs have grown, return them to the edge of the pond where you found the spawn.

Feeding: Newly-hatched tadpoles will eat plants in the aquarium. After about a week, they will need raw meat too. Hang small pieces in the water, tied with thread, and replace them every two days.

Toads

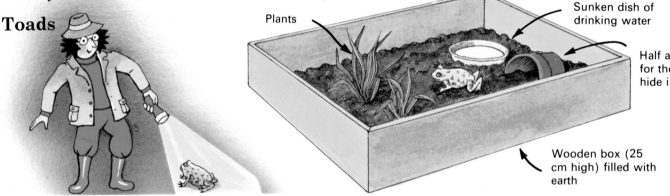

Plants

Sunken dish of drinking water

Half a flowerpot for the toad to hide in

Wooden box (25 cm high) filled with earth

How to collect: Visit ponds in the breeding season (March, April) at night. If you hear a male toad croaking, shine a torch at him. When the light hits his eyes, he will not move. Take the toad home in a wet plastic box with air holes.

Where to keep: Make a box like this. Put netting on top to keep the toad in. Put it in the shade, either in the garden or indoors. Handle it with wet hands. In the autumn, return it to the pond's edge, so that it can hibernate.

Feeding: Feed the toad twice a week with live earthworms, slugs and insects. Offer it small pieces of meat held in tweezers and moved about to look alive. Keep the dish filled with fresh water.

Newts

Stick for fishing rod

Cotton line

Matchstick float

Worm

Netting

Floating platform of wood or polystyrene for newts to sit on

Eggs

Pond plants

How to collect: In early spring, fish for newts or catch them in a net. When the newt bites the worm bait, pull the line in. Take it home in a jar with some pond water.

Where to keep: Keep newts in an aquarium in a light place. Take them back to the edge of the same pond in August, so that they can find a place to hibernate.

Feeding: If the newts mate and tadpoles hatch, feed them on Water Fleas from the pond. Feed adult newts on earthworms and small bits of raw meat dropped into the water.

Other Water Animals

Worms and Leeches

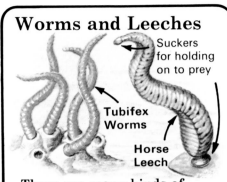

Suckers for holding on to prey

Tubifex Worms

Horse Leech

There are many kinds of worms and leeches in fresh water. The Tubifex Worm lives head down in a tube of mud. Leeches swim about hunting for fishes, frogs, larvae and snails.

Hydras

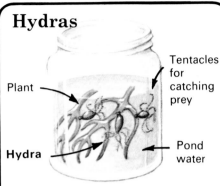

Plant

Tentacles for catching prey

Hydra

Pond water

These tiny plant-like animals contract into blobs if disturbed. Leave some water plants in water for an hour to see if there are any Hydras attached to them.

Spiders and Mites

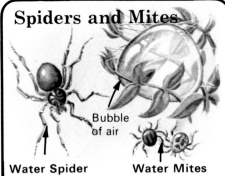

Bubble of air

Water Spider   **Water Mites**

Only one spider lives under water. It spins a web between plants, then fills it with air collected on its body from the surface. The spider can stay in this "diving bell" for a long time, without surfacing for air. Look, too, for the tiny Water Mites which are related to spiders.

Animals with Shells

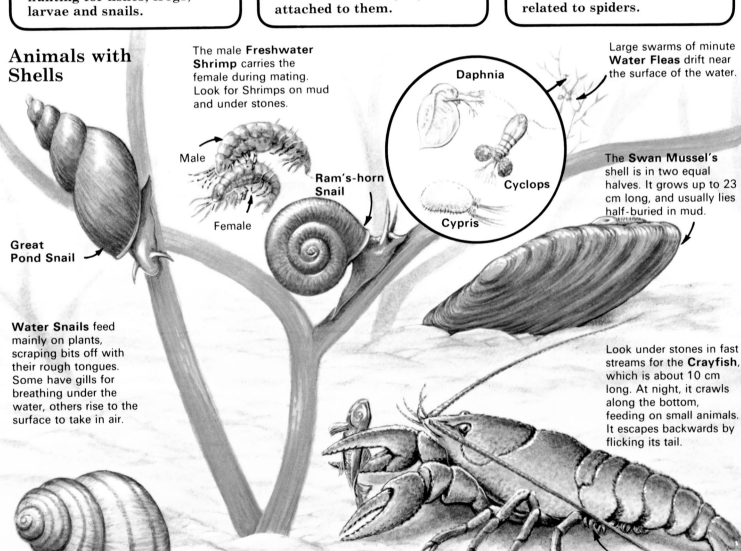

The male **Freshwater Shrimp** carries the female during mating. Look for Shrimps on mud and under stones.

Male

Female

Ram's-horn Snail

Daphnia

Cyclops

Cypris

Large swarms of minute **Water Fleas** drift near the surface of the water.

The **Swan Mussel's** shell is in two equal halves. It grows up to 23 cm long, and usually lies half-buried in mud.

Great Pond Snail

Water Snails feed mainly on plants, scraping bits off with their rough tongues. Some have gills for breathing under the water, others rise to the surface to take in air.

Look under stones in fast streams for the **Crayfish**, which is about 10 cm long. At night, it crawls along the bottom, feeding on small animals. It escapes backwards by flicking its tail.

Swimmerets

The female **Crayfish** carries her eggs on her underside all winter. In spring, the young hatch and cling to her tiny swimming legs, called swimmerets.

Freshwater Winkle

More Freshwater Life to Spot

Fishes

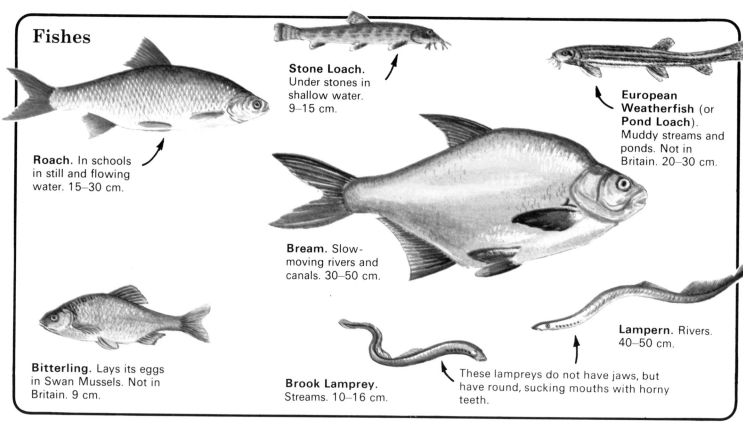

Roach. In schools in still and flowing water. 15–30 cm.

Stone Loach. Under stones in shallow water. 9–15 cm.

European Weatherfish (or **Pond Loach**). Muddy streams and ponds. Not in Britain. 20–30 cm.

Bream. Slow-moving rivers and canals. 30–50 cm.

Bitterling. Lays its eggs in Swan Mussels. Not in Britain. 9 cm.

Brook Lamprey. Streams. 10–16 cm.

These lampreys do not have jaws, but have round, sucking mouths with horny teeth.

Lampern. Rivers. 40–50 cm.

Plants

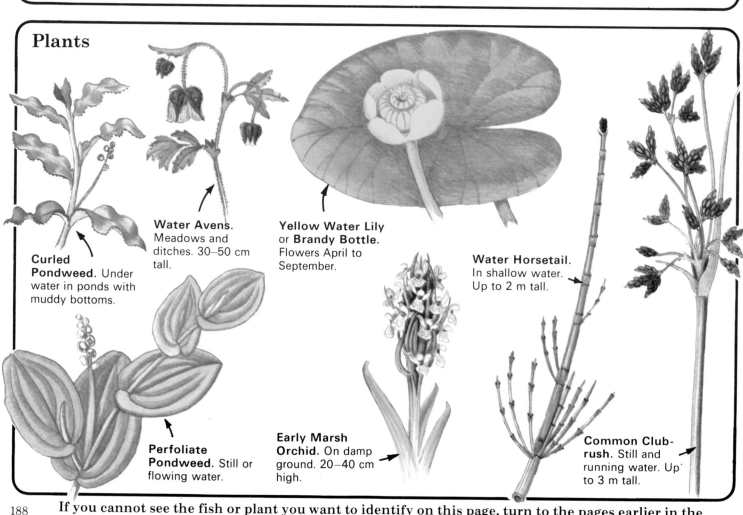

Curled Pondweed. Under water in ponds with muddy bottoms.

Water Avens. Meadows and ditches. 30–50 cm tall.

Yellow Water Lily or **Brandy Bottle.** Flowers April to September.

Water Horsetail. In shallow water. Up to 2 m tall.

Perfoliate Pondweed. Still or flowing water.

Early Marsh Orchid. On damp ground. 20–40 cm high.

Common Club-rush. Still and running water. Up to 3 m tall.

188   If you cannot see the fish or plant you want to identify on this page, turn to the pages earlier in the book that deal with these things.

Toads

Common Toad.
Hides under stones
or tree roots in day.
Often in gardens.
Female to 12 cm.
Male 6 cm.

Natterjack Toad.
Sandy and stony
places. Digs holes
to shelter in. Rare.
6–8 cm.

Green Toad.
Green shade
changes to match
background. Not in
Britain. 6–9 cm.

**Yellow-bellied
Toad**

Underside

The **Fire-bellied
Toad** and the
**Yellow-bellied
Toad** live in
water. Show off
bright warning
colours when
alarmed. Not in
Britain. 4–5 cm.

Spadefoot Toad.
Burrows with
spade-like growths
on feet. Smells like
garlic. Not in
Britain. 6–8 cm.

Fire-bellied Toad

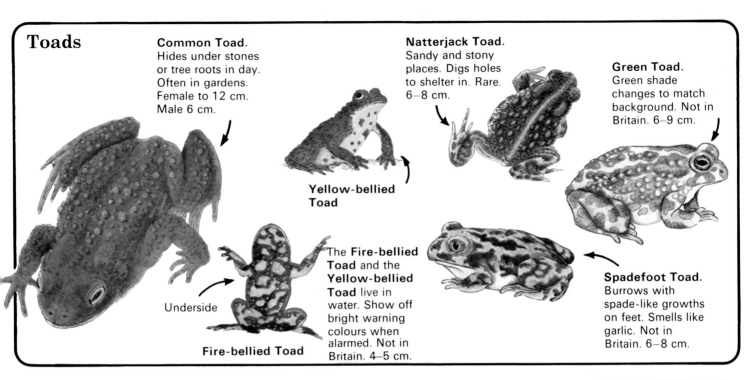

Frogs

Common Frog.
Damp shady places.
Size and colour
vary. 7–10 cm.

Painted Frog.
Lives in water.
France and Spain.
6–7 cm.

Parsley Frog. Near
ponds in France,
Italy and Spain.
4.5 cm.

**European Tree
Frog.** In trees.
Breeds in water.
Not in Britain.
3–5 cm.

Edible Frog.
Female larger than
male. Near water.
7–10 cm.

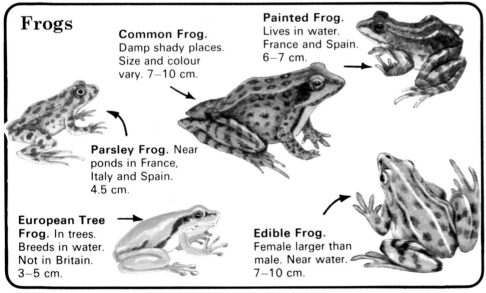

Tortoise

European Pond Tortoise.
Muddy ponds and marshes.
Central and southern Europe.
Up to 36 cm.

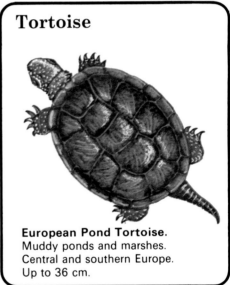

Newts

Male

Female

Palmate Newt.
8–9 cm.

Female

Male

Great Crested Newt.
12–18 cm.

Alpine Newt. Not
in Britain. 7–12 cm.

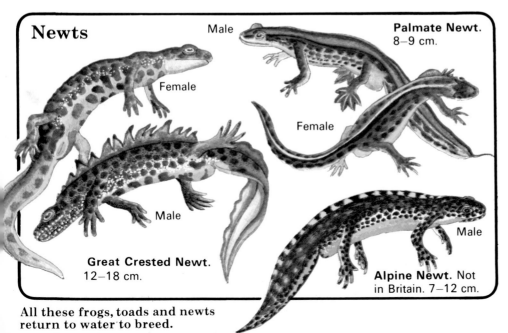

Snakes

Viperine Snake.
Often in water.
Zigzag markings
like Adder, but
harmless.
Southern
Europe.
1 m.

**Tesselated
Snake.**
Very good
swimmer.
Central and
southern
Europe.
1.5 m.

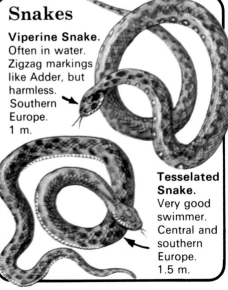

All these frogs, toads and newts
return to water to breed.

Water Insects and their Young

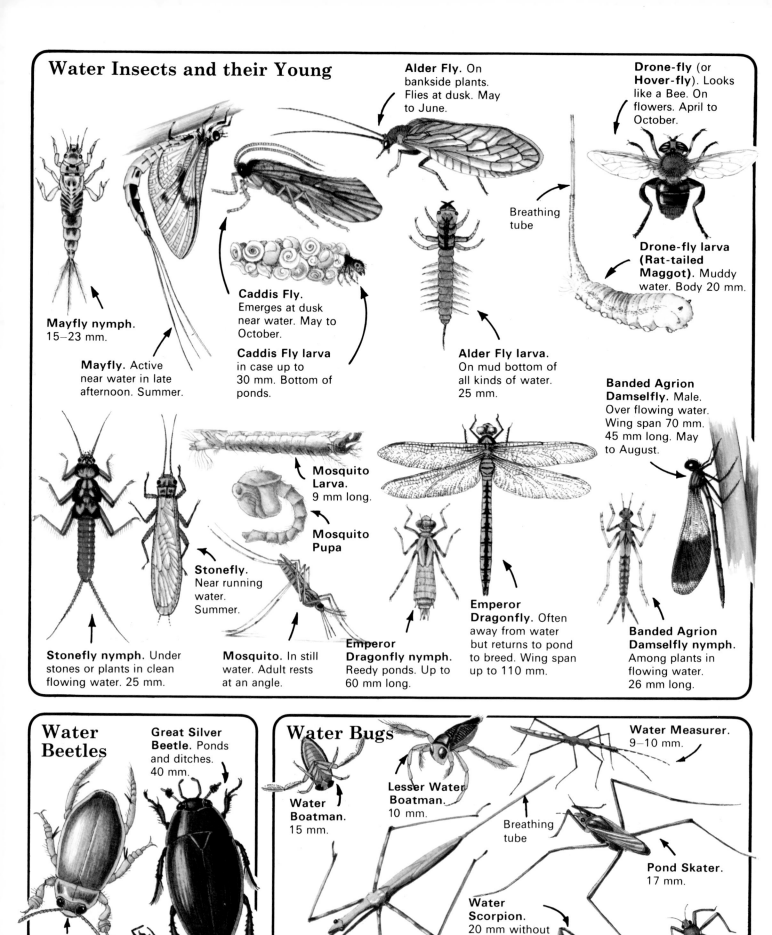

Alder Fly. On bankside plants. Flies at dusk. May to June.

Drone-fly (or Hover-fly). Looks like a Bee. On flowers. April to October.

Breathing tube

Drone-fly larva (Rat-tailed Maggot). Muddy water. Body 20 mm.

Mayfly nymph. 15–23 mm.

Mayfly. Active near water in late afternoon. Summer.

Caddis Fly. Emerges at dusk near water. May to October.

Caddis Fly larva in case up to 30 mm. Bottom of ponds.

Alder Fly larva. On mud bottom of all kinds of water. 25 mm.

Banded Agrion Damselfly. Male. Over flowing water. Wing span 70 mm. 45 mm long. May to August.

Mosquito Larva. 9 mm long.

Mosquito Pupa

Stonefly. Near running water. Summer.

Stonefly nymph. Under stones or plants in clean flowing water. 25 mm.

Mosquito. In still water. Adult rests at an angle.

Emperor Dragonfly nymph. Reedy ponds. Up to 60 mm long.

Emperor Dragonfly. Often away from water but returns to pond to breed. Wing span up to 110 mm.

Banded Agrion Damselfly nymph. Among plants in flowing water. 26 mm long.

Water Beetles

Great Silver Beetle. Ponds and ditches. 40 mm.

Great Diving Beetle. Ponds. 30–35 mm.

Whirligig Beetle. 5 mm.

Water Bugs

Water Boatman. 15 mm.

Lesser Water Boatman. 10 mm.

Water Measurer. 9–10 mm.

Breathing tube

Pond Skater. 17 mm.

Water Stick Insect. 35 mm without breathing tube.

Water Scorpion. 20 mm without breathing tube.

Breathing tube

Water Cricket. 7 mm.

If you cannot see the insect you want to identify on this page, turn to the pages earlier in the book on insects, where you may be able to see a picture of it.